The Myth of God Incarnate

EDITED BY

JOHN HICK

SCM PRESS LTD

CONTENTS

CONTRIBUTORS

DON CUPITT is a University Lecturer in Divinity and Dean of Emmanuel College, Cambridge.

MICHAEL GOULDER is Staff Tutor in Theology in the Department of Extramural Studies at Birmingham University.

JOHN HICK is H. G. Wood Professor of Theology at Birmingham University.

LESLIE HOULDEN is Principal of Ripon College, Cuddesdon.

DENNIS NINEHAM is Warden of Keble College, Oxford.

MAURICE WILES is Regius Professor of Divinity and Canon of Christ Church, Oxford, and Chairman of the Church of England's Doctrine Commission.

FRANCES YOUNG is Lecturer in New Testament Studies at Birmingham University.

Nor only Christianity. You believe or disbelieve anything according to the way it fits your frame of reference.

It must be credible, or it will die.

What is truth? – P.P.
Important to enable the preachers to stay in business

PREFACE

It is clear to the writers of this book – as to a great many other
Christians today – that Christianity has throughout its history been
a continuously growing and changing movement. As a result its
theology has developed an immense range of variation as the
church has passed through successive historical periods and
responded to widely different cultural circumstances. Indeed, as
T. S. Eliot said, 'Christianity is always adapting itself into something which can be believed'.

In the nineteenth century, Western Christianity made two major
new adjustments in response to important enlargements of human
knowledge: it accepted that man is part of nature and has emerged
within the evolution of the forms of life on this earth; and it accepted that the books of the Bible were written by a variety of
human beings in a variety of circumstances, and cannot be accorded a verbal divine authority. These two adjustments were not
made without much 'kicking against the pricks' of the facts, which
caused wounds that have even now not completely healed. Nevertheless, human knowledge continues to grow at an increasing rate,
and the pressure upon Christianity is as strong as ever to go on
adapting itself into something which can be believed – believed by
honest and thoughtful people who are deeply attracted by the figure
of Jesus and by the light which his teaching throws upon the meaning of human life.

The writers of this book are convinced that another major
theological development is called for in this last part of the twentieth century. The need arises from growing knowledge of Christian
origins, and involves a recognition that Jesus was (as he is presented
in Acts 2.21) 'a man approved by God' for a special role within the
divine purpose, and that the later conception of him as God incarnate, the Second Person of the Holy Trinity living a human life, is a
mythological or poetic way of expressing his significance for us.
This recognition is called for in the interests' of truth; but it also has
increasingly important practical implications for our relationship to
the peoples of the other great world religions.

Many people, including both conservative believers and perhaps a still larger group of conservative unbelievers, will take exception to the thinking that is going on in this book. They will hold that Christianity consists and always has consisted in a certain definite set of beliefs, and that theologians who seek to modify or 'reinterpret' those beliefs are being disingenuous: it would be more honest of them frankly to abandon the faith as no longer tenable. To this it must be replied that modern scholarship has shown that the supposed unchanging set of beliefs is a mirage. Christianity was from the first very diverse, and has never ceased developing in its diversity. Today's conservatives, for example, are themselves diverse, and their positions are in most cases of quite recent origin. 'Orthodoxy' is a myth, which can and often does inhibit the creative thinking which Christianity sorely needs today. We therefore ask that the ideas and arguments in this book be judged on their merits rather than by their conformity to some previous stage of Christian development.

Writing of the kind represented in this book is liable to strike many as disquietingly negative and destructive. Even those who sympathize with the questions to which it responds sometimes feel that Christianity suffers a setback in the process of criticism and restatement. It is partly that the task of clearing the ground for rebuilding is formidable, and partly that the critical temperament does not always engage equally readily in the task of construction. To that degree it is easy for the ground-clearers to seem to neglect the religious issues and needs. Let it then be said that our hope is to release talk about God and about Jesus from confusions, thereby freeing people to serve God in the Christian path with greater integrity.

The adjustments whereby in the past Christianity has changed in order to be believable were at the time traumatic; but they have made it possible for many inhabitants of our modern science-oriented culture to be Christians today. The adjustments that are now called for – and that have indeed been in process for several decades – are not likely to become generally accepted without further ecclesiastical trauma. But we believe that they will help to make Christian discipleship possible for our children's children. For Christianity can only remain honestly believable by being continuously open to the truth.

There is nothing new in the main theme of this book and we make no pretence to originality. A growing number of Christians, both professional theologians and lay people, have been thinking along these lines. But we have written this book in order to place its topic firmly on the agenda of discussion – not least in England, where the traditional doctrine of the incarnation has long been something of a shibboleth, exempt from reasoned scrutiny and treated with unquestioning literalness.

It should perhaps be said that the division of the chapters into two sections, dealing respectively with Christian sources and with the development of doctrine, is far from absolute. For the discussion of the sources is sometimes directly related to contemporary issues, and the discussion of recent and contemporary issues sometimes involves reference back to the sources. Indeed this book illustrates the way in which historical study continually affects the work of contemporary reconstruction.

In the course of writing the book we have met together for discussion five times during the last three years, and we now offer the results in the hope that they will stimulate a wider discussion both inside and outside the churches.

We would like to express our gratitude to Dr A. S. Worrall for making the index.

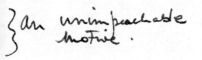

Before I read further, I should say at this point that the intermingling of the traditional 'sacrificed king' and the teacher of wisdom seems entirely plausible. If there were no X'tian documents until 50AD, by that time the resurrection myth could be well & truly established.

1

Christianity without Incarnation?

MAURICE WILES

Christianity is often described as an incarnational faith. The phrase may be understood in a looser or a stricter sense. The looser meaning characterizes Christianity as a religion in which man's approach to God is through the physical world rather than by escape from it. In its narrower sense it constitutes a description of Christianity as a faith whose central tenet affirms the incarnation of God in the particular individual Jesus of Nazareth. Incarnational faith in this sense need not be tied to the specific categories of the Chalcedonian Definition, but it does affirm that Jesus of Nazareth is unique in the precise sense that, while being fully man, it is true of him, and of him alone, that he is also fully God, the Second Person of the co-equal Trinity. The question that I shall be asking in this chapter is whether incarnational faith in this second, more precise sense is in fact essential to Christianity. Could there be a Christianity without (in this sense) incarnation? I propose to approach the issue by considering in turn whether the question I am asking is (1) a proper, (2) a necessary and (3) a constructive one to ask.

1. A Proper Question?

The phrase 'death of God theology' had considerable currency a few years ago. Etymologically the phrase is self-contradictory, and it had to be given a carefully qualified meaning before it could lay claim to be an intelligible concept deserving consideration. The words 'Christianity' and 'incarnation' are to many ears so nearly synonymous that the suggestion of a possible 'Christianity without incarnation' will sound to them equally paradoxical and unintelligible.

But the parallel is not exact. Incarnation (in the more precise sense in which I am using the term) is *an* interpretation of the significance of Jesus. In the course of Christian history it has become so dominant an interpretation that 'incarnation' and 'Christianity' have often functioned as virtually interchangeable terms. But they are not synonymous. There is nothing intellectually perverse in drawing a distinction between the two concepts and asking whether it might be possible to have one without the other.

The point I am trying to make can be illustrated by three analogies from Christian history. In the Middle Ages the eucharist, the central act of Christian worship, was understood to involve the transformation of the consecrated bread and wine into the actual body and blood of Christ. Philosophically this conviction was expressed in the doctrine of transubstantiation but the underlying belief in a conversion of the elements was fundamental to the faith of many who were entirely unversed in the niceties of transubstantiation doctrine. When at the time of the Reformation some Christians began to affirm eucharist without transubstantiation, without, in some cases, any conversion of the elements at all, it seemed to others that such a concept was an impossibility. A eucharist without a real conversion of the elements was for them no eucharist at all. A second example is the relation between the authority and the inerrancy of scripture. For much of Christian history the authority of scripture was understood to reside in its conveying to us otherwise inaccessible knowledge about the nature and the saving purposes of God. Such knowledge was to be believed solely because it came to us from God with the seal of God's authority. How could such a divinely authoritative source be other than wholly true? If its inerrancy were to be disproved, it would cease to be authoritative. For people who thought in these terms an authoritative but fallible scripture seemed an absurd and impossible concept. A third example is the relation between the doctrine of the incarnation and the virgin birth. When, around the beginning of this century, doubts were expressed about the literal truth of the virginal conception of Jesus, these were frequently treated as direct attacks upon the doctrine of the incarnation. The virgin birth was so firmly regarded as the means by which the incarnation was effected that the two were widely regarded as standing or falling together.

Yet today the distinctions which our forefathers felt it impossible to make would be held by very many Christians to be proper in all three cases. There are widely accepted doctrines of the eucharist which dispense with any conception of a conversion of the elements such as the doctrine of transubstantiation was designed to explicate. The authority of scripture is strongly maintained by many who would dissociate themselves from any suggestion of its inerrancy. The 1938 Doctrine Report of the Church of England, in acknowledging the divergence of views about belief in the virgin birth on the part of members of the commission, insisted that 'both the views outlined above are held by members of the Church, as of the Commission, who fully accept the reality of our Lord's incarnation'.[1] Of course, these are only analogies, not exact parallels. They do not of themselves prove that the concept of a 'Christianity without incarnation' is a viable concept. But they take us, I believe, far enough along the road to suggest that the question being raised is a proper question. It cannot be dismissed in advance as an absurdity. The case needs to be heard before judgment is given.

[handwritten marginal notes: "On years to come, this way seem as absurd as the discussion of angels sitting on the head of a pin. 1938! (Seems fairly absurd in 1977)"]

2. A Necessary Question?

There are many questions which are not self-contradictory or patently absurd but which there is no particular point in asking. One only raises a question if there is something puzzling or unsatisfactory about the accepted position in which one finds oneself. Are there grounds for claiming that the possibility of separating 'Christianity' and 'incarnation' is not merely an admissible question to raise but an inescapable one? I propose to indicate briefly the reasons which seem to me to point firmly to that conclusion. They derive in turn from the origins, the long history and the contemporary expression of incarnational doctrine.

(a) The origins of incarnational doctrine

This issue is dealt with much more fully in chapters 2 to 5. My aim here will be to give a brief, impressionistic account of the story that Frances Young spells out in far greater detail.

Incarnation, in its full and proper sense, is not something directly presented in scripture. It is a construction built on the variegated evidence to be found there. Increased historical knowledge has enabled our generation to see this truth about the way in which incarnational doctrine emerged more clearly than some earlier generations. The New Testament writers were not simply reporters of the teaching of Jesus or of agreed church doctrine. They were interpreters and describe the specialness of Jesus to which they all bear witness in a wide variety of ways. They speak of him as the eschatological prophet, the Son of Man, the Messiah. Some envisage him as the embodiment of that pre-existent wisdom of

God, of which the Old Testament wisdom literature speaks, or of
the Logos (word or reason) of God. At times this line of thought is
developed in a more personal way and they talk of him as God's
pre-existent Son come down to earth. All (even the Fourth Gospel,
which comes nearest) stop short of the assertions that have come to
characterize the later doctrine of the incarnation. At the outset,
then, incarnation was one of a number of ways in which Christians
thought and spoke of Jesus, but it was the one which (in developed
form) was to establish itself as the pattern for all thought about
Jesus in the later faith of the church.

Two reflections about this process need to be borne in mind. In
the first place the setting in which the process took place was one in
which the idea of supernatural divine intervention was a natural
category of thought and faith, in a way that is no longer true of the
main body even of convinced believers today. It was within the
context of such a general belief in divine intervention that belief in
the specific form of divine intervention which we know as the incarnation grew up. Secondly, the later stages of that development were
greatly influenced by the evidence of the Fourth Gospel understood
in a straightforwardly historical way. How else could one interpret
a Jesus who said 'Before Abraham was I am' and 'I and my Father
are one'? As I was still being taught in my confirmation class, such
a Jesus must be either 'mad, bad or God'. But if the Fourth Gospel
is understood in a less straightforwardly historical way (as on
general critical grounds I believe it has to be) then its implications
for doctrine may prove to be somewhat different from what they
appeared to earlier ages to be.

Such considerations do not, of course, disprove the doctrine of
the incarnation. What I believe they do, is to make it more reasonable for us to see the doctrine as an interpretation of Jesus appropriate to the age in which it arose than to treat it as an unalterable
truth binding upon all subsequent generations.

(b) The history of incarnational doctrine

Negative generalizations are notoriously dangerous claims to make.
Nevertheless, it seems to me that throughout the long history of
attempts to present a reasoned account of Christ as both fully
human and fully divine, the church has never succeeded in offering
a consistent or convincing picture. Most commonly it has been the
humanity of Christ that has suffered; the picture presented has been
of a figure who cannot by our standards of judgment (and what
others can we apply?) be regarded as recognizably human.

Don Cupitt provides some of the evidence for seeing the history of the doctrine in these terms in chapter 7. Here two examples must suffice. The seventh century saw the Monothelite controversy – a debate whether Christ had two wills or only one (divine) will. The outcome favoured the assertion of two wills, the position, that is to say, which gave greater weight to Christ's human nature. Yet even this dyothelite position insisted that since there was no ignorance or concupiscence in Christ, his human will never needed to weigh up the pros and cons of possible actions; it was always capable of recognizing and siding with the good immediately. How genuinely human is so qualified a human will?

Similar problems surround all attempts to give any account of Christ's human knowledge. Dr Mascall, who is a distinguished continuator of this ancient tradition into our own day, writes of Christ's human knowledge in these terms:

In Christ, however, the Person is really distinct from the human nature; the nature with which the Person is really identical is not the human but the divine, and in this it shares in the omniscience which is the inalienable possession of the Godhead. Is it therefore unreasonable to suppose that the content of Christ's human mind will include not only that experimental knowledge which is acquired by him in the course of his development from infancy to manhood in a way substantially the same as, though immeasurably more consistent and unimpeded than, the way in which we acquire ours, but also an infused knowledge which is directly communicated to his human nature from the divine Person who is its subject, and which is a participation in the divine omniscience and is limited only by the receptive capacity of human nature as such?[2]

That quotation ends with a rhetorical question expecting the answer 'No, it is not unreasonable'. But the only answer that I can give is 'Yes, it is unreasonable'. The argument seems to me to have reached a conclusion far beyond anything that the evidence could conceivably justify.

In entering such a demurrer I am not claiming that one ought to be able perfectly to fathom the mystery of Christ's being before one is prepared to believe. We do not after all fully understand the mystery of our own or one another's beings. But when one is asked to believe something which one cannot even spell out at all in intelligible terms, it is right to stop and push the questioning one stage further back. Are we sure that the concept of an incarnate being, one who is both fully God and fully man, is after all an intelligible concept?

(c) Contemporary affirmation of incarnational doctrine

Some modern exponents of the doctrine of the incarnation react in much the same way that I have done to statements like that which I have quoted from Dr Mascall. They stress that Jesus had no privileged knowledge, no access to knowledge of a kind different from that which is available to us. They insist that he had no idea that he was Son of God incarnate; to have done so, they declare, would indeed have made him less than fully human. And yet they insist with equal firmness that he was in fact precisely that, the Son of God incarnate. Thus John Baker writes that 'Jesus did not see himself just as Everyman, nor as the Saviour of the World, even less as a divine pre-existent being from heaven'.[3] He admits that Jesus 'was mistaken about the programme which God planned to follow' and goes on to argue that 'to be in error about the details of the future' is a 'feature of the human condition' that 'could be overcome only by investing Jesus with superhuman powers which might indeed have satisfied the tired old dreams of paganism but would utterly exclude any true incarnation of God'.[4]

Here the difficulties that arise are of a different order. Many of the problems that have bedevilled christological debate down the ages disappear, because the empirical content of what is understood to be involved in incarnation is changed almost out of recognition. Indeed what has to be asked of such a position is whether the idea of incarnation has not so changed that, though the same word is being used, it is not genuinely the same idea that is being expressed. It may be that a radically revised interpretation of 'incarnation' along such lines is possible, but it is at least worth asking as an alternative possibility whether some concept other than incarnation might better express the divine significance of Jesus that is intended.

3. A Constructive Question?

Some people may agree that the difficulties I have raised are real ones, but feel that if they were to lead to the abandonment of traditional incarnation doctrine, that could only be regarded as an entirely negative and destructive outcome. So we have to ask: is the alternative a return to an old-fashioned unitarianism which the main body of the church in the past has rejected as something lacking the dynamic of a living faith? Or can the suggestion of a 'Christianity without incarnation' be seen as a positive and constructive one?

The question is not easy to answer. Religion is much more than a set of intellectual ideas. It is an evolving, living tradition and within Christianity much of the greatest religious significance is intimately linked with images and ideas of the incarnation. The same was true in the case of some of the analogies to which I referred earlier. The consecrated elements, understood as the very body and blood of Christ, were a focus of eucharistic devotion, and veneration of the Virgin was (amongst other things) a deeply felt form of response to the mystery of the incarnation. So the question I am now raising cannot be dealt with simply at the intellectual level. If the suggestion that is being made is to prove a constructive one, there would have to be shifts in religious understanding and response of a kind that are not intrinsically impossible but which can only develop gradually. Nevertheless, though they are not the whole story, there are intellectual issues involved and it will be best to start there.

I propose to consider three ideas that in Christian faith as it has developed are very closely linked with the incarnation. In each case I shall argue that despite that link the idea is not necessarily bound to the incarnation and would not therefore be eliminated from a 'Christianity without incarnation'.

(*a*) I began this chapter with reference to a looser sense of the phrase 'incarnational faith' by which it expresses the conviction that the physical world can be the carrier of spiritual value. This anti-dualist emphasis in Christianity has very naturally and properly been seen in close inter-relation with the more specific affirmation of the incarnation itself. Yet the underlying conviction is one that Christianity shares with Judaism. It is implied not exclusively by the doctrine of the incarnation but equally by the doctrine of creation and the whole idea of a positive purpose in history as seen in God's dealings with Israel and with the church. A 'Christianity without incarnation' in the more precise sense of the word 'incarnation' would not be a non-incarnational faith in the much broader sense in which those words are so often used.

(*b*) The doctrine of the incarnation has usually been understood to imply the absolute significance of Jesus as a human ideal. If in his life we have human life as it was lived by the Son of God, that must surely give it an absolute authority over us as the true pattern of human living. In practice we have to acknowledge that the types of life that men have with full sincerity thought to be derived from the model of Jesus' life are immensely diverse. The point has been forcefully made by Don Cupitt in his article 'One Jesus, many Christs?'

An immense variety of ideals of character have been ostensibly based upon the example of Jesus: an historical man who lived only one life has been made the exemplar of a great range of different forms of life. Jesus has been declared to be a model for hermits, peasants, gentlemen, revolutionaries, pacifists, feudal lords, soldiers and others. Even if we restricted attention to the religious life of men in the Latin West alone, the diversity is great among the ideals of Benedict, Francis, Bruno and Ignatius Loyola.[5]

And this is not just a result of human sin and blindness. In a famous phrase R. H. Lightfoot declared that 'the form of the earthly no less than of the heavenly Christ is for the most part hidden from us'.[6] That may be a somewhat extreme statement of the position, but it expresses vividly a truth that seems inescapable in the light of scholarly work on the gospels. Even if Jesus be the Son of God incarnate and his life was a humanly perfect one, that perfect manhood is not directly available to us as an absolutely authoritative model for our own lives. So the significance of Jesus as a model for human life is not directly affected by the way in which his relationship to God is understood. On no showing can the records of his life have absolute significance for us; on any showing to which the name of Christian could conceivably be given his life would remain of substantial importance for us.

(c) But the primary importance of Jesus for Christians has never been as a model for human living; it has resided rather in the conviction that he is the one in whom we meet God, the one through whom God has acted decisively for the salvation of the world. How, apart from a full doctrine of the incarnation, could Jesus be the saviour of the world? Would not any change of the kind suggested imply that the worship of Christ, traditional throughout the whole of Christian history, was idolatrous in character? It is at this point that the greatest difficulties are likely to be felt. Can they be met? It is important to remember that in the strictest sense it is never simply Jesus who saves nor is Christ by himself the object of man's worship. Jesus as Second Person of the Trinity incarnate is the one through whom we come to the trinitarian God, the one through whom the whole Trinity acts towards us. And, as the liturgy so carefully expresses it, the norm of Christian worship is an offering to God through Jesus Christ as Lord. The absence of incarnational belief would not simply destroy this mediatorial function altogether. It would still be possible to see Jesus not only as one who embodies a full response of man to God but also as one who expresses and embodies the way of God towards men. For it is always through the lives of men that God comes to us and we are enabled to meet him and respond to him. It was through the personality and leadership of Moses in their escape from Egypt that the Israelites experienced the redemptive power of Yahweh. It was through the experience and prophetic ministry of Hosea that they grasped the inexhaustible depth of his demanding but forgiving love. So, it may be claimed, it is supremely through Jesus that the self-giving love of God is most fully expressed and men can be caught up into the fullest response to him. For Jesus was not merely a teacher about God; the power of God was set at work in the world in a new way through his life, ministry, death and resurrection. On such a basis it is reasonable to suggest that the stories about Jesus and the figure of Jesus himself could remain a personal focus of the transforming power of God in the world. They could still properly fulfil that role, even without the concept of 'incarnation', though they would not impinge upon us in precisely the same way. But as we have seen already the precise way in which Jesus is understood and impinges upon the life of the church has been a constantly changing phenomenon in the history of the church and has undergone particularly great change in recent years, even where the concept of incarnation has been strenuously preserved. The particular direction of change which would result from the abandonment of the incarnation model cannot easily be predicted in advance, for religious development is not simply a matter of logical deduction but of an evolving life. The most likely change would be towards a less exclusive insistence on Jesus as *the* way for all peoples and all cultures. This theme is developed in John Hick's essay in this volume. It does not involve the judgment that all religions are of equal truth and worth. It does rule out the judgment of the superiority of one religion over another in advance of an informed knowledge of both faiths. Such a change can only be regarded as a gain.

So we come back at the end to the point with which I began – the complex interweaving of ideas that are associated with 'incarnation'. I have been arguing that its abandonment as a metaphysical claim about the person of Jesus (for which there seems to me to be a strong case) would not involve the abandonment of all the religious claims normally associated with it. Of course it would make a difference. But the truth of God's self-giving love and the role of Jesus in bringing that vision to life in the world would remain. For myself much even of the traditional incarnational language and imagery would still seem appropriate as a pictorial way of expressing these truths. I have attempted in my other contribution to this volume to justify such a claim by an examination of the role of 'myth' in Christian theology. How far that attempt is successful is for others to judge. It is at least evidence that our general intention in this book includes the full range of prophetic activity demanded of Jeremiah in his inaugural vision, not only 'to pluck up and to break down, to destroy and to overthrow' but also 'to build and to plant' (Jer. 1.10). In the case of Jeremiah it was the first set of activities that was the more evident to his contemporaries. From the larger perspective of history, we can see more clearly the constructive character of his ministry. It is in the conviction that the approach represented by these essays has similarly a constructive potential that we have brought them together for publication in this volume.

NOTES

1. *Doctrine in the Church of England*, SPCK 1938, p. 83.
2. E. L. Mascall, *Christ, the Christian and the Church*, Longman 1946, pp. 56–7.
3. J. A. Baker, *The Foolishness of God*, Darton, Longman & Todd 1970, p. 242. Fontana edition 1975, p. 250.
4. Ibid., p. 312. Fontana edition p. 321.
5. In *Christ, Faith and History*, ed., S. Sykes and J. P. Clayton, Cambridge University Press 1972, p. 137.
6. R. H. Lightfoot, *History and Interpretation of the Gospels*, Hodder & Stoughton 1935, p. 225.

PART I

Testing the Sources

2

A Cloud of Witnesses

FRANCES YOUNG

'In Jesus Christ I perceive something of God': a confession of that
kind lies at the heart of Christian belief; it sums up the common
mind of the faithful. Yet, as a matter of fact, Christian believers
have experienced and understood this confession in more than one
way. Since Jesus is confessed and has been confessed in many different cultural environments by many different types of people with
many different hopes and expectations, there must be potentially a
multiplicity of christological affirmations analogous to and dependent upon the multifarious ways in which atonement and salvation
have been experienced and expressed. Indeed, one theme that runs
throughout this chapter is that christological expositions are parasitic upon definitions and concepts of salvation; but its main contention is that christological statements should be regarded as
belonging not to the language of philosophy, science or dogmatics,
but rather to the language of confession and testimony.

Exclusive claims that there can be only one way of understanding
salvation in Christ have never been 'canonized' in creed or definition, though they have often caused intolerance between Christians.
By contrast, an exclusive claim that the only way of understanding
the nature of Jesus is in terms of a unique divine incarnation has
been enshrined in authoritative statements traditionally used as
tests of orthodoxy. This has caused living witness and faith to
appear as improbable scientific fact, and has encouraged arrogant
and intolerant attitudes among the faithful. It has also obscured the
potential richness and variety of christological images and insights
by tending to subordinate everything to the confession of Jesus as
incarnate Son of God. To recognize the possibility that diverse

responses to Jesus Christ have equal validity may well be the only
constructive way forward in a world which is beginning to value the
enriching aspects of its variety and pluralism.

In order to open the way to exploring this possibility, it is necessary to show that the traditional formulations of christology, so far
from enshrining revealed truth, are themselves the product of
witness and confession in a particular historical environment. To
this end, the first two sections of the paper consider the witness of
the New Testament and the development of patristic theology. If
we avoid reading the New Testament with spectacles coloured by
later dogma, we find emerging a christological picture – or rather
pictures – quite different from later orthodoxy; if we look at the
contemporary environment, we discern not only the cultural factors
which led the fathers to the dogmatic position from which the New
Testament has traditionally been interpreted, but also the inherent
difficulties of their theological construction.

In the light of this historical study, the primacy of soteriology
becomes plain; and with this as background, it is possible to go on
to consider in the third section, a personal approach to soteriology
and the sort of christological affirmations it necessitates within the
cultural context of the Western world. The conclusion then returns
to the question of pluralism, some problems and some advantages.

1. The New Testament Witness

The New Testament is the first and greatest 'testimony-meeting', in
the sense that here are gathered together a group of documents
which testify to the saving effects of the life, death and resurrection
of Jesus. The documents have a variety of purposes, they come
from differing backgrounds, and their dates of origin span approximately three-quarters of a century; they are of various literary
genres and written in several different styles, both of language and
theology. Yet virtually every page is affected by the fact that for
each author Jesus Christ has become the central focus of his life
and of his faith in God.

Such a statement, though a broad generalization, would on the
whole be endorsed by the majority of New Testament scholars
today. Whether or not the particular conclusions of form-critical
and redactional-critical studies are accepted, their common presupposition is that the faith of the church in a given historical setting
affected the preservation and handing on of traditions about Jesus;
and the faith of the gospel-writers in another given situation affected their selection of material, its arrangement and preservation.

Before such conclusions had been reached about the synoptic gospels, the Gospel of John had for generations been treated as a profound reflection on the life of Jesus, rather than a biographical account, and the most fruitful approach of more recent studies has been to see this gospel as built out of homilies based on synoptic-type traditions.[1] To turn to the epistles, the interpretation of Paul, it is generally agreed, depends upon seeing his theology as the set of presuppositions in the light of which he wrestled with contemporary problems in the Christian communities. Likewise, the Johannine Epistles can only be understood if they are set against a background of division in the church which forced further thinking about the nature of Christian witness to faith in Jesus Christ.[2] The catalogue could go on, but the point of it is to stress the fact that it is the witness of communities and individuals to the effects of faith in Jesus Christ in their own particular situation which gives the New Testament writings their prime and distinctive characteristics – in other words, to stress the historical particularity of the documents and the cultural particularity of the images and concepts used to express faith in Jesus Christ.

To turn to the more particular area of New Testament christology, discussion here has tended to revolve around the various 'titles' of Jesus; the possible connotations, both in the contemporary background and in their New Testament context, of Messiah, Son of Man, Son of God, Lord, Logos, etc., have been repeatedly explored and exhaustively discussed.[3] A number of conclusions seem to emerge: (*a*) that the titles and concepts were there to be used before the early Christians adopted them – that is, they can be found in non-Christian documents and with non-Christian interpretations; (*b*) that by their application to Jesus they were filled with new content, and new interpretations became inevitable as a new combination of once distinct concepts was made; (*c*) the combination was probably the result of believers searching for categories in which to express their response to Jesus, rather than Jesus claiming to be these particular figures; and (*d*) each block of writings in the New Testament has its own emphases and combinations, that is, its own christological picture, and since a total christology is not merely a combination of titles, these different christological schemes have to be explored in their own right and on their own terms, not simply by means of the titles-method. Some comments on each of these four points follows.

(*a*) *The titles were pre-Christian.* It is clearly impossible either to review here all the evidence for this statement or to embark now on questions which are still in debate. Amongst other things, it is still

by no means clear whether Son of Man is to be regarded as a title at
all in the original Aramaic,[4] and current Messianic expectations
seem to have been of an extremely diverse kind. Nevertheless, it is
agreed that the Old Testament and near contemporary literature
must be used to establish possible connotations in the first place,
and this applies not merely to the Palestinian background and the
possible Aramaic originals, but also to the background of
Hellenistic Judaism and the actual Greek words of the New
Testament. While it is becoming increasingly apparent that to
envisage a sharp cultural division is perhaps unrealistic, and all re-
translation projects are bound to be grossly hypothetical, yet it
cannot be denied that there are signs of a developing understanding
of terms like Lord and Son of God according to differing linguistic
and cultural environments. For further discussion readers are
referred to the relevant literature.[5] The point here is: New
Testament christology is built out of material which was part of the
cultural heritage of the period, a point further illustrated elsewhere.[6]

(*b*) *The titles were changed and developed by their application to
Jesus.* It seems likely that there were around at the time within the
Jewish community, political, social, nationalistic, prophetic,
religious, apocalyptic and supernatural hopes of various kinds,
sometimes overlapping, sometimes distinct, sometimes incompatible, all associated with particular kinds of title and particular ways
of interpreting scriptural promises. The remarkable thing is that the
New Testament reflects a kind of compulsion to see all possible
expectations as fulfilled in Jesus. Jesus was not a particularly good
political Messiah, but they claimed he was Son of David. He was
not obviously a supernatural visitant, yet they claimed he was Son
of Man.[7] If he was Son of David, he could not be a priest according
to the regulations of the Torah, but the Epistle to the Hebrews finds
a way round that difficulty in order to assert that he is High Priest
par excellence. Probably he came nearest to being a charismatic
prophet heralding the coming of God's kingdom, yet that role was
attributed to John the Baptist, because they found a greater significance in Jesus. But to return to the main point, what was the effect
of applying many different roles and titles to Jesus in this way?
Because he did not fulfil current nationalist hopes but died as a
martyr, the idea of Messiahship regained the role of the suffering
king;[8] because he was not obviously a supernatural visitant, his
glory veiled in a mystery on earth, was to be revealed on his return;
because he appeared as a prophet, he could be seen as a new Moses
establishing a new covenant and a new Torah[9] – and the combina-

tion of these ways of thinking that we find in various ways in the various gospels, produces a figure quite different from any of the possibilities which have contributed to the pattern. We could add the further implications of Son of God, Lord, Logos, particularly as they gain additional connotations in a Hellenistic environment, but let this suffice to illustrate the point that the new christological combination becomes more than and different from the concepts which have contributed to it. A similar thesis is presented elsewhere to account for the unusual characteristics of the Christian doctrine of incarnation – namely a unique combination of a variety of current motifs in relation to Jesus of Nazareth.[10]

(c) *The titles were attributed to Jesus by the early Christians and were not claimed by Jesus himself.* This was assumed in the last paragraph, and it is an assumption which has the backing of a good deal of recent work on the subject, though it must be admitted that not all have been convinced.[11] The extremely radical position that little or none of the synoptic material goes back to Jesus himself is clearly unreasonable, but the fact remains that it has obviously undergone modification and transformation as it was used in the preaching, teaching, worship and polemic of the church for the period of approximately one generation. What is the most likely kind of transformation? Surely a gradually increasing stress on its *christological* implications. The epistles of Paul – and indeed the speeches of Acts – reveal that the early Christian gospel was about *Jesus Christ.* This makes it the more likely that the gospels correctly report that the message of Jesus was different – it was about the *kingdom of God.* There was no doubt implicit in that message some pretty far-reaching claims: his exorcisms display the sovereignty of God confronting the powers of evil (Matt. 12.28//Luke 11.20); his healings display the forgiveness of God (Mark 2.10//Matt. 9.6 and Luke 5.24); his teaching is the word of God (Mark 1.22//Matt. 7.29 and Luke 4.32); the judgment of God can be seen in the way people reject or respond to him.[12] Yet there are difficulties in tracing explicit Messianic claims back to Jesus himself. Apart from John where interpretative material is clearly placed upon the lips of Jesus, the gospels invariably portray not Jesus but others as using phrases like the 'Holy One of God', or 'Son of David', or 'Son of God'. Alone of all the titles 'Son of Man' regularly appears as used by Jesus himself, and even here the evidence is puzzling, partly because of the continuing uncertainty as to the implications of the phrase, but also because in some texts Jesus seems to be referring to a figure other than himself (e.g. Mark 8.38). Furthermore, Mark's gospel conveys the impression that Jesus attempted to keep his identity as Messiah a secret divulged only to his inner circle. This 'Messianic secret' motif in Mark remains an unsolved problem, especially since it appears sometimes to be introduced rather artificially; yet it adds to the impression that Jesus may well have preferred to remain enigmatic, in the interests of directing his hearers away from false enthusiasm for himself, to the consequences of the coming of God's kingdom for their lives here and now. This is not to say that Jesus did not reflect upon his role himself; rather it is to say that we do not have the evidence available now to speculate realistically about Jesus' so-called Messianic consciousness. (If we were to try and read between the lines we might even speculate that Jesus regarded personal claims as a Satanic temptation.)[13] Of course it remains true that the church's christological preaching must have some continuity with, and basis in, the mission of Jesus, but its content need not be, and probably was not, identical. The challenge and the judgment of Jesus' preaching recalls that of the prophets, who also spoke the 'Word of the Lord'. But in the context of first-century Judaism, it is not surprising that that word of authority which ignored religious conventions and traditions, and spoke of God's kingdom coming immediately, even *now*, was greeted as God's final fulfilment of his promises,[14] and current expectations were focused on the figure who brought this message. The implicit claims were not merely made explicit, but developed by the faith of the church.

So far we have argued that the common stock of christological titles found in the New Testament derive from the surrounding cultural background and were used by the early Christians to express their faith-response to Jesus of Nazareth. The early Christians were searching for categories which could adequately express their sense of salvation in him. It is significant that some saw him as a Rabbi, others as a prophet, others as a zealot, others as a miracle-worker and healer; that some called him Lord, some Messiah, some Son of God and so on. Both in his lifetime and in the context of the early church, groups and individuals responded to him in their own way as the one who fulfilled their needs and hopes.[15] It is impossible to overemphasize the fact that common to the many different ways of thinking is the sense that Jesus came on God's initiative. It is fundamental to New Testament theology that *God's* activity of redemption was at work in Jesus in fulfilment of his promises. Yet even so, different promises were valued by different people, and expectations revolved around different speculative figures constructed out of the promises. By the very fact that Jesus was identified as each of these figures, a new combination and mutual modification was inevitable, so that a different kind of figure emerged, whose essential characteristic was that he was the embodiment of all God's promises brought to fruition. Such a characterization, I suggest, represents New Testament christology better than the idea of incarnation, and it was in fact the germ of more and more christological ideas as the whole of the Old Testament was seen as fulfilled in Christ;[16] in the patristic writings we find the christological application of Old Testament texts firmly established. It was the sense that they had found what they were looking for in Jesus that started the whole christological ball rolling – in other words, christological formulations derive from a sense of having experienced God's promised salvation (however interpreted) in and through Jesus Christ.

This becomes all the clearer when we turn to the final point (*d*) made at the start, namely that to approach New Testament christology solely in terms of titles and their development is to fail to appreciate its real nature. New Testament christology is actually found in a number of different kinds of writing, stemming from different areas and 'thought-worlds', and each type of christology reflects particular difficulties and crises of faith as well as particular ways of reacting to Jesus as the fulfilment of man's hopes for salvation. The exposition of these differing christologies, so that they may be compared and contrasted with one another, as well as with later dogmatic developments, should be the next step in our argument. We could explore the peculiar characteristics of the christology of each of the gospels; we could show how the Johannine understanding of salvation in terms of revelation has given this christology its distinctive marks; and so on. However, space hardly allows so full a treatment, and instead an interpretation of the Pauline material is offered which illustrates (*i*) the fact that one of the most important New Testament christological schemes, although containing incarnational elements, is not a doctrine of God's incarnation; and (*ii*) the way in which a christology, built up out of various traditional and scriptural elements, was formed both in reaction to contemporary pressures and problems, and as an expression of a particular understanding of salvation. (These points are not treated in turn, but are intertwined in the course of the following exposition.)

In the Pauline epistles, the truly significant title for Jesus is not Messiah but 'Kyrios', Lord. Jesus is still 'Son of David' (Rom. 1.3), but the nationalist implications are irrelevant and 'Christos' appears to have become virtually a 'surname'.[17] Kyrios now expressed both the religious and the political significance that Paul and his converts saw in Jesus. For it was to him as Risen Lord that they owed total allegiance. They confessed him as Lord in their baptismal initiation (Rom. 10.9); they continued to confess him in the face of persecution (I Cor. 12.3). What that meant to them, was informed by their acquaintance with other contenders for the title. They contrasted their Lord with Lord Caesar [18] and with the Lords of contemporary mystery-cults. They could not have communion with their Lord's table and also that of some other Lord (I Cor. 10.21). Unlike their neighbours who confessed gods many and lords many, they affirmed one God and one Lord (I Cor. 8.5–6). The Lord Jesus Christ was exalted at God's right hand (Rom. 8.34); he had been given the name which is above every other name, Kyrios (Phil. 2.11). The Word of the Lord that came to the prophets in the past, was now the gospel of Christ (I Thess. 1.8); the Day of the Lord of which the prophets warned, was now the Day of Jesus' Parousia (I Thess. 5.2). Thus, their God was the God of the Old Testament and their Lord, Jesus, was 'God's Vicegerent'.

For Paul, Jesus held this position as a result of having acted on God's behalf to overcome the powers of sin, death and evil. He was 'made sin' (II Cor. 5.21), he 'became a curse', he annulled the law (Gal. 3.13), he humbled himself and became obedient unto death, even death on a cross (Phil. 2.8), in order that men might be redeemed, reconciled, justified and sanctified, that men might be in him a new creation (II Cor. 5.17). 'God made Christ Jesus our wisdom, our righteousness and sanctification and redemption' (II Cor. 1.30). Therefore God highly exalted him and believers now lived in him. It is christologically significant that Paul could speak of us being the body of Christ (Rom. 12; I Cor. 12), of us being in him and of Christ living in us (Gal. 2.20). Although the historical fact of his death and resurrection was the basis of Paul's faith, his conviction that Christ was presently alive and that in him a new humanity was created, constituted his experience of 'faith-living'. Christ's dying and rising became our dying and rising (Rom. 6), so that our life became the life of Christ himself, and we became the righteousness of God (II Cor. 5.21).

So far what we have said in interpretation of Paul could be given the anachronistic tag 'adoptionist', and indeed, it implies not just the adoption of Jesus but of all men in him. It certainly does not imply the incarnation of an essentially divine being. However, there is also in the Pauline writings a developing conviction of the pre-existence of this figure who is now Lord of the Christians. This is clearest, of course, in Colossians (whether Paul himself wrote it or a close disciple makes no difference here). This epistle is directed at a situation in which the Lordship of Christ was threatened by belief in other mediators and spiritual beings who contributed to man's salvation. Utilizing ideas which had been used of the divine Wisdom,[19] the author claims that the church's Lord had always been God's 'right-hand man' from the moment of creation. In him all the fullness of God was pleased to dwell, and it was not sub-divided among a number of spiritual descendants or minions. Though the full development of this idea may well owe its existence [20] to 'Gnostic' christologies which were clearly inadequate from Paul's point of view, hints of this kind of claim are to be found in some earlier, undoubtedly Pauline writings. I Corinthians 8.6 is unintelligible except against a 'wisdom' background, and the sense of renunciation of a former superior status is undoubtedly to be found in II Corinthians 8.9 as well as Philippians 2.5 ff. Further-more, Romans 8.3 speaks of God *sending* him in the likeness of sinful flesh, which seems to imply the incarnation of a previously existing 'Son of God'. Is this then a 'divine incarnation christology' in germ?

Two points suggest that this is not the case; (*i*) Paul neither calls this figure God, nor identifies him anywhere with God.[21] It is true he does God's work; he is certainly God's special supernatural agent, who acts because of God's initiative. But ultimately he is to give up his delegated authority so that God will be all in all. (*ii*) This figure is pre-existent not simply as a kind of divine being (though hypostatized Wisdom comes near to that), but as the 'man from heaven';[22] and his Sonship to God is not expressed in terms of 'divine nature', but as the result of divine creation and election on the one hand, and on the other hand, his own perfect obedience in doing God's work and obeying God's will. Indeed, he is the archetypal man and the archetypal Son of God in whom we become sons of God, fellow-heirs with Christ, who will bear the image of the man of heaven.[23] In other words, we are back at the point stressed earlier – that for Paul, it is our incorporation into Christ and his 'incarnation' in us that is the centre of his living faith. It is this alone which can enable us to fulfil the law, to resolve our moral dilemma and enter into a perfect covenant-relationship with God. When Paul wrote: 'God was in Christ reconciling the world to himself,' he is unlikely to have envisaged a Nicene con-clusion. He was expressing graphically that it was God's saving initiative which had provided this means of salvation: 'All this is from God, who through Christ reconciled us to himself (II Cor. 5.18–19).'

When Paul wrestles with problems of conduct in his churches, when he faces Judaizers and 'Gnostics', his replies are always informed by a far-reaching 'Christocentricity', for Christ alone has always been the true 'image of God' as man was created to be, and in him alone, he believes, men find their true selves and learn the way of true obedience to God. To preach this gospel is his burning passion, and his expression of it develops according to the opposition or difficulties with which he is presented. In order to give expression to it, he draws upon the Jewish religious literature he has inherited as scripture, and upon the traditional titles used by Christians to express faith in Jesus. He evolves a scheme which has incarnational elements, and probably owes a good deal to the syncretistic and potentially Gnostic religious atmosphere of the time. But fundamentally it is the expression of the fact that Paul's moral impotence has found its resolution in Jesus Christ, who now becomes the unique focus of his perception of and response to God.

From this inevitably sketchy survey of New Testament christology, both negative and positive conclusions may be drawn. On the negative side, we are bound to admit (*i*) that the New Testament provides us with evidence about how the earliest Christians reacted to Jesus, and how they utilized current concepts, especially eschatological speculations, to express their reaction; it does not provide directly revealed information about his divinity; and (*ii*) the notion of God being incarnate in the traditionally accepted sense is read into, not out of, the Pauline epistles, and I suggest that, space permitting, the same could be argued for the other New Testament documents. On the positive side, we may stress (*i*) that it is more than remarkable that Jesus should have stimulated such a far-reaching response from so many different quarters. Galilean fishermen and learned rabbis, Zealots and 'Gnostics', Pharisees and sinners, Jews and Gentiles – somehow he was all things to all men and broke down social, political and religious barriers. All manner of men found their salvation in him, and were driven to search for categories to explain him, never finding any single one adequate, always seeking higher ways of honouring, worshipping and understanding him; and (*ii*) that even though Jesus is always distinguished from God the Father, in his risen as well as his earthly state, even though he is not directly confessed as *God*, yet the confessions used do show that he 'stands for' God, and is the focus through which God is revealed to those who respond. On the whole the New Testament is totally Christocentric. Maybe the content and form of the confessions are not all that distinctive, yet their combined application as interpretative categories for the person of Jesus of Nazareth is unparalleled; and the force of this is to make Jesus the one intermediary through whom God is revealed and can be approached with confidence.

2. *The Development of Patristic Christology*

There may be some who although admitting the cultural particularity of the New Testament, want to argue that the New Testament writers were groping towards a full understanding of who Jesus was, and this was provided by the patristic development of incarnational belief. There was a gradual dawning of the full truth about the person of Jesus Christ, a development steered by the providence of God and inspired by the Holy Spirit.

But this view surely demands radical questioning, just as much as the idea that it is all already there in the New Testament. It was inevitable that further 'intellectualizing' should take place, that philosophical questions should be asked about Christian claims, which certainly contained highly paradoxical elements. But this does not mean that the questions were asked in the right way, or the right solutions found. As in the case of the New Testament writings, the development of doctrine in the early church was both culturally conditioned and determined by the course of controversy and debate, not to mention factors such as politics, personalities and the chances of history. Different christological positions were intimately related to different ways of understanding salvation; they were upheld by inadequate arguments and distorting exegesis of scripture; and compromise formulae were devised which did nothing more than restate the impossible paradox and leave it unresolved.

Oversimplification is bound to be the main fault of an essay covering so much ground, but broadly speaking, it can be said that the Christian theologian of the first few centuries was faced with two key questions: (*i*) how is the exalted Jesus whom we worship as Lord, related to the one and only God? and (*ii*) how is God related to the world? The first of these questions inevitably pressed upon a group whose theology derived from the monotheism of the Old Testament. Within Judaism, the 'hypostatization' of Wisdom or Torah did not seem to undermine monotheism, since ultimately it was a kind of periphrasis used to circumvent the implication of direct contact between the transcendent God and the creation; true it had a positive function in this respect, but a faith so theocentric could never allow it really to challenge God's 'monarchy', his ultimate originality and sovereignty. By identifying an actual person, Jesus, with such a mediating figure, by worshipping him and proclaiming so Christocentric a faith, the Christians both utilized current ideas and raised questions about their status. It was not only in apologetic to Jews and philosophers that they had to explain how they worshipped one God and one Lord but not two gods;[24] they had to justify their contradictory claims to themselves. The so-called Monarchian heresies were internal controversies which made explicit the problem of the relationship between the Lord Jesus and God his Father. The most influential way of solving that problem had already been provided by the translation of the Jewish 'Wisdom'-language into the Logos-concept of contemporary philosophy.[25]

While it is true that to the average onlooker at the time, philosophy in this period appeared fragmented into schools with varying presuppositions and apparently opposing claims,[26] nevertheless, the predominant framework of thought was a sort of popularized Platonism, with influences from Stoicism and Pythagoreanism. Educated men believed in a Supreme Being, and were attracted by a life of virtue and contemplation of spiritual realities.[27] Not only was this Platonism popular, but it seemed congenial rather than alien to the ethical monotheism of Judaism.[28] So naturally enough, it became the prevailing philosophical environment which dictated the presuppositions within which Christian theology was to develop.

This philosophical tradition both posed and purported to answer the second question mentioned earlier: how is God related to the world. The ultimate One was conceived as the 'ground of Being' which provided the stability and eternity underlying the changes and chances of this life and the multiplicity of the world. In so far as God was identified with the One, he was perfect in form and substance; change from perfection could only mean degradation; therefore he was undifferentiated and indivisible within himself, and he was impassive and unaffected by anything external. He could have no history or development, no involvement.[29] The consequences of such a concept was that it was hard to relate God, or the One, with the multiplicity of things, the world of which he was supposed to be the source and ground of Being. His utter transcendence meant his substantial irrelevance to the problem of which he had originally been the solution. Middle Platonism and its successor, Neoplatonism, wrestled therefore with the problem of God's relationship with the world; it was a problem endemic in their whole approach to reality. Inevitably the solutions involved some kind of system of mediators or a 'hierarchy of Being' linking the ultimate transcendent One, who was even 'beyond Being', with the known world.[30] Thus we find schemes of emanation and mediation in both philosophical and Gnostic systems,[31] a fact which shows how widespread were these presuppositions in the thinking of this period.

Educated Christians shared the same fundamental outlook. So Christian theology found itself obliged to wrestle with the same inherent problems and contradictions, but with the solution apparently offered by their christological traditions. For the Christian philosopher, the quasi-divine Logos filled the role of the one and only mediator who was both One and Many, sharing in some sense the nature of both and bridging the gulf between them.[32] Logically there was no room in this scheme for the Holy Spirit, but he found his place as another sort of mediating link in the chain of Being, forming a triad or Trinity not unlike that of the Neoplatonists. It is true that in their own contemporary context, the rival schools, including the Christians, were chiefly aware of the radical differences between their various solutions, but from our vantage point, they all look much the same in principle if not in detail.

To this picture, the doctrine of incarnation provided the fitting culmination. It is well known that that was how Augustine viewed the situation: in the Neoplatonists he read all about the Logos, except for the most important thing of all, that the Word was made flesh and dwelt among us.[33] In this connection, it is interesting that the Greek word '*oikonomia*' was used both for the incarnation and for the trinitarian nature of God, since both doctrines were concerned with the accommodation of God's essential nature to the world. The ultimate mediation, then, was the coming of the Logos into the conditions of this world in order to bring men salvation from its changes and chances, its suffering and evil, its 'non-Being'.[34] However, debate about the real nature and implications of this 'fitting culmination' ultimately drew attention to the illogicalities of the scheme as a whole. It was the Arian controversy which showed this up and made inevitable the consequent christological *impasse*.

While based upon a contrast between the transcendent God and the world, the Platonic scheme avoided drawing a line between the divine and the created in its hierarchy of existence; there was a succession of descent. But Arius raised the implicit question about where the line should be drawn. It was a question which also pressed upon the Christian because of the biblical insistence on God's otherness, the contrast between the Creator and his creation. Once the question was raised, it destroyed the logic of the total scheme and dogged all subsequent theological discussion. In a hierarchy of Being without firm ontological distinctions, the mediator could have some substantial relationship with what was above and what was below his own rung on the ladder, so providing an effective link. But an ontological distinction, a real line between the divine and the created, could not be drawn without insisting that the mediator fell on one side or the other, thus destroying his ability to mediate. The Nicene line was no better than the Arian; the mere fact that there was a line undermined what had seemed an admirable solution to the problem of God's relationship with the world.[35]

Arius defined God as '*agenetos*' – that is, the ultimate source of everything who himself derived from no source.[36] This is what distinguished God in his essential being from all other beings. Logically enough, Arius was forced to assert that the Logos derived his being from God and was therefore not God in the absolute sense. Arius destroyed the hierarchy and ruined the 'mediator christology' by severing the mediator from God. Yet in one sense he voiced the implicit assumptions of the scheme which he had destroyed. We should never forget that his language was so firmly in the mainstream tradition that solid churchmen like Eusebius of Caesarea felt more at home with his ideas than those of the opposition.[37] Arius could accept all traditional creeds, and like his opponents, he asserted that the Son of God was the first-born of all creation through whom God created the world and revealed himself; in the incarnation, he brought knowledge of God to men, and conquered the sin and evil which held men in bondage. Indeed, Arius could give a thoroughly realistic exposition of those New Testament texts which assume that in temptation, Jesus had the same moral experience as we have; because the Logos was a mutable creature, the possibility of his sinning was open. The fact that he did not sin was of profound soteriological significance, for it meant that by following him, other men were potentially capable of not sinning. It is unjust to Arius to describe his doctrine as utterly unbiblical, or to accuse him of being exclusively concerned with logic at the expense of soteriology.

Why then did the church react against his scheme? It is Athanasius who represents the 'nerve-centre' of anti-Arian reaction. Athanasius argued that the Logos 'became man in order that we might become "god" ';[38] and if this is so, he must have been God himself, or he could not have endowed men with divinity. Soteriology determined christology. Because of the argument's emotional appeal to those who lived by faith in Jesus, in the divine power received in the eucharist and the hope of divine life hereafter, the inherent difficulties and illogicalities of this position were largely disregarded. However, Athanasius' position is problematical for two reasons: (*i*) a real son is not needed to produce adopted sons.[39] Since we only receive an adopted sonship and a derivative divinity, the *essential* Godhead and Sonship of the one who passes it on to us is not logically required. (*ii*) Because of the definition of divinity generally assumed (and expounded above), once the Son is defined as '*homoousios tōi patri*' the incarnation becomes logically impossible, and the problem of 'Patripassianism' is simply raised in a new guise. For, if the Logos is inherently perfect and incapable of change, progress or suffering, he is no more able to mediate than the transcendent God himself. Consequently Athanasius' exegesis of those New Testament texts which assume that in temptation Jesus had the same moral experience as we have, that he was ignorant and weak, *etc.*, is inevitably docetic in tendency, though not in intent.[40] Where Arius severed the mediator from God, Athanasius severed him from the world.

The christological controversies which ensued were largely concerned with the now insoluble problem of how the '*atreptos Logos*', incapable of change or suffering, could be incarnate at all. The Antiochenes inherited a long-standing tradition of approaching christology from the angle that saw Jesus as a man uniquely endowed with the Logos;[41] the Alexandrians represented an equally long-standing direction of approach which concentrated on the incarnation of a supernatural figure. The basis of these different approaches is to be found in quite different understandings of salvation, similar to the differences already noted between Arius and Athanasius. In the post-Nicene situation, neither side could expound their approach in a completely consistent way; so that both were open to the criticisms of the other side. Like God, the Logos could not really be involved in the world. So the Antiochenes found themselves insisting on the difference between the two natures, each with its own inherent characteristics, to such an extent that they were unable to give a satisfactory account of the union between them, even when pressed. The Alexandrians, stressing the one nature of the Logos enfleshed, inevitably compromised the distinction between divine and human as currently defined. The paradox is summed up in the phrase '*apathōs epathen*', he suffered without suffering – the suggestion that while the 'body' or the 'man Jesus' suffered on the cross, the Logos somehow suffered in sympathy because it was 'his body' or 'his man', even though by his very nature he could not possibly suffer.

The problem was insoluble – hence the controversies, and hence the unsatisfactory character of the Chalcedonian compromise. This so-called definition defines only in a negative sense, by excluding the extremes of both christological approaches, without being able to offer any positive christological understanding. In that philosophical context, a positive christology had become a logical impossibility once the Nicene *homoousion* was firmly established. The insoluble problem of God's relationship with the world was crystallized into the likewise insoluble problem of the relation of Godhead and manhood in the Christ.

The above sketch is intended to show (*i*) that the patristic discussion of christology was conducted within the framework of contemporary philosophical presuppositions – in other words, like New Testament christology, it was culturally determined; (*ii*) that inevitably, by the use of contemporary categories of thought, Christian theology produced results which have a clear similarity to other philosophical schemes of the time, and therefore can hardly be regarded as any more 'timeless' than the rest; (*iii*) that even within that framework of thought, inherent illogicalities are apparent; and (*iv*) that as long as their intellectual presuppositions were determined by the surrounding philosophical cultures, they were logically incapable of making sense of the biblical message of God's involvement with his world, and in particular could not help being led into a docetic reading of the gospels. Platonism did not ultimately prove congenial to biblical faith, in spite of its superficial similarities. It is also clear (*v*) that 'faith-reactions' and soteriological assumptions had a profound effect upon christological expositions.

If space permitted, we could go on to document the fact that the course of doctrinal controversies was shaped not merely by the inherent quality of the arguments used, but by personalities and politics. Suffice it to give a simple reminder of how Cyril's attack on Nestorius is related to the political struggle between the ecclesiastical power-centres of Alexandria and Constantinople, already evidenced in Theophilus' scurrilous treatment of John Chrysostom; it is significant that Cyril compromised in the Formulary of Reunion once Nestorius was out of the way. The course of doctrinal development should never be studied in isolation from the historical context of the debates. Rightly or wrongly, deep emotions and profound intolerance stirred up councils, churches and armies of monks into horrific attacks upon one another, and to the excommunication and exile of upright and sincere church leaders. It is a distressingly human story.

There are strong reasons then for seeing the patristic development and interpretation of incarnational belief, not as a gradual dawning of the truth inspired by the Holy Spirit, but as a historically determined development which led to the blind alleys of paradox, illogicality and docetism. It is not satisfactory to assert that nevertheless it was in the providence of God that the philosophical system was available and made possible the resultant true formulations. Appeals to providence are too easily invalidated by subsequent history. Eusebius of Caesarea provides an instructive example: he saw the hand of providence at work when he heralded Constantine as almost a new manifestation of the Logos bringing the kingdom of God on earth;[42] yet from our historical vantagepoint, he surely appears as an abject flatterer subservient to imperial greatness, and his insight into the workings of providence seems less than convincing. Likewise, if we appeal to providence bringing good out of evil in spite of obvious political, sociological and other human factors, we are in danger of pursuing a route which later generations will judge to be false – especially in view of the problematical character of the christological formulations reached. For the philosophical apparatus with which the fathers worked, though an asset in some respects, in others was a grave disadvantage. Maybe it did facilitate the verbal and mathematical contortions to which they resorted in Trinitarian theology: three divine beings did not imply tritheism, because the divine substance they shared was in principle indivisible and undifferentiated.[43] Yet, while facilitating this sort of statement, it prevented a meaningful account of God's self-revelation in Jesus, one of the most important factors which had stimulated the development of Trinitarian theology in the first place. The presuppositions within which they formulated the questions made it impossible to produce answers. It is hardly surprising that the fathers themselves were driven to admit that the ultimate nature of the divine and his relationship with the world is a mystery inexplicable in terms of human philosophy.[44] It would be less than true to this insight to regard their theology, and the philosophy on which it was based, as timeless and unquestionable.

Should we then feel committed to the results of the development we have been discussing? Does Christian faith have to be tied to a christological position which was never very satisfactory and certainly determined by a particular cultural environment? There is no doubt that a good deal of modern radical theology fails to convince because insufficient attention has been paid to the powerful motivations behind the bitter struggles of the patristic period. Too often the so-called out-dated substance-categories have been spotlighted and criticized without any appreciation of what drove the churchmen of the past to elucidate their faith intellectually in the way that they did. The old heresies constantly reappear in modern dress, and are rejected for remarkably similar reasons. Before anyone casts aside past formulations, a sympathetic awareness of the *religious* compulsions that found expression in this form is vitally necessary. The formulation of Trinitarian and christological definitions was the result of a living *fides quaerens intellectum*, and within their contemporary context, they were a remarkable achievement.

So again I wish to draw not merely a negative conclusion from this survey. As we have seen, it is a remarkable fact that the earliest Christians felt compelled by their confrontation with Jesus of Nazareth or with his story to respond by using more and more supernatural and mythical categories to envisage his nature and origin; it is also important to recognize that the sense of salvation received through him was the driving force of the subsequent philosophical and doctrinal formulations. It was the dynamic reality of their experience which they sought to preach to and articulate for their contemporaries. It is not by accepting traditional formulations as God-given and unquestionable that we join the band of witnesses in the New Testament and the early church, but by wrestling with the problem of expressing intelligently in our own contemporary environment, our personal testimony to the redemptive effect of faith in Jesus of Nazareth.

3. A Personal Testimony

In any attempt to rethink christological belief, the primacy of soteriology must be recognized. This sense that the story of Jesus Christ provides the key to life, the answer to man's moral idealism, and above all, a revelation of divine involvement in the suffering and evil of the world, has been mediated to us through the faith of generations committed to the church, and through the witness of the New Testament. Our response has been conditioned by the traditional way of spelling this out in terms of incarnation. If we now suggest that this account is not entirely satisfactory, we nevertheless have to do justice to our own faith, our own identity as members of the church and our own sense of redemption in Christ. Some sort of christology is inevitable in so far as we come to terms with evil, suffering and sin by meditating on the story of the 'crucified God'. This response to the cross was very inadequately expressed by the patristic christology, precisely because it was tied to the philosophical presuppositions of that particular time; and if we re-open the question, it is in order to grasp more realistically how it is that we, like our predecessors, have met God disclosed in the man, Jesus.

The Christians of the early church lived in a world in which supernatural causation was accepted without question, and divine or spiritual visitants were not unexpected. Such assumptions, however, have become foreign to our situation. In the Western world, both popular culture and the culture of the intelligentsia has come to be dominated by the human and natural sciences to such an extent that supernatural causation or intervention in the affairs of this world has become, for the majority of people, simply incredible. The transformation in popular assumptions has been recent and far-reaching. It could be illustrated from many sources; let me simply refer to a striking instance which recently came to my notice. The great metal craftsman of the Renaissance, Benvenuto Cellini, wrote an autobiography which reveals him as a thoroughly 'worldly' man, concerned with his career and very little about religion; yet he always attributes his escapes from street brawls or his survival in battle to the providence of God or even to direct divine intervention. Such a reaction from such a man, so natural in his day, would be unthinkable now. This is not to say that nowadays the world is necessarily viewed in a crude mechanistic sort of way, but regular and predictable patterns of behaviour are presupposed, in all areas of life. There is no room for God as a causal factor in our international, industrial or personal lives, for statistical probabilities and natural patterns of cause and effect are presupposed in sociology and psychology, in medicine and genetics, as well as all the natural sciences. History is to be explained in terms of politics and personalities, or economics and power-structures. Heavenly powers have given way to earthly forces.

What is faith in Jesus Christ going to mean in this cultural environment? That is not, of course, a new question; but I want to offer a way of approaching the problem which I hope avoids the reductionism of radical 'humanist' theologies, while not simply being a conservative reassertion of the old view; for such a reassertion is not only blind to the seriousness of the question, but tends in an equally reductionist direction in that it is obliged to keep pushing God out of territory which he once occupied into ever-decreasing 'gaps'.

Christology is one among many areas where the difficulties arise. Jesus must have been part of world history and the inheritor of the normal genetic links in human descent.[45] We do not feel happy about appealing to a supranormal break in our understanding of humanity and human history. Jesus cannot be a *real* man and also unique in a sense different from that in which each one of us is a unique individual. A literal incarnation doctrine, expressed in however sophisticated a form, cannot avoid some element of docetism, and involves the believer in claims for uniqueness which seem straightforwardly incredible to the majority of our contemporaries. But it is not only christology which is affected by this problem. Like the fathers, we find that the problem of christology is intimately related with the more general problem of God's relationship with the world. Our acceptance of the biblical accounts of God's dealings with the people of Israel is equally problematical – not to mention the fact that belief in God's providence and caring involvement in our own time is so called into question that faith and prayer can seem irrelevant and meaningless. In other words, the present climate is alien to the whole Christian position as traditionally conceived.

Yet many of us remain Christian believers. Looking back over the years, we descry God's care for us in the remarkable coincidences and creative chances of our lives. When faced with difficulties or crises, we turn naturally to prayer. In moments of joy, we instinctively offer thanksgiving. Sunday by Sunday we take ourselves to a place where the presence of other believers will assist us in praising and worshipping God who, we claim, is the author and sustainer of the universe. We confess our sins and accept forgiveness in the name of Jesus Christ; we battle against evil and suffering in the power of the Lord. We offer intercessions for the sick and pray about situations of political conflict and war. None of these activities can be regarded as 'rational' in so far as they appear inconsistent with our fundamental assumptions about the world in which we live.

How is it then that we go on living in this way? Are we all schizophrenics? I suspect that many of us are – that most of the time we in fact make little real attempt to integrate two world-views which must be related in some way and yet appear so incompatible. Those theologies which try to relate the two invariably face criticism because they are reductionist. They narrow the areas of our life to which faith is relevant by mapping out which parts can be assigned to which view – whereas we instinctively feel that the *whole* of life belongs to *each*. Dividing life into compartments does not work. So we find ourselves living and understanding at two different levels at the same time. We expect the world to work in accordance with known patterns of cause and effect, but we believe that somewhere God is involved in the total process.

What we are doing is instinctive. When we spell it out like this it appears irrational. But it is surely not the only situation in which we find ourselves having to live with unresolved contradictions or provisional and unsatisfactory analyses. Even science has its apparent inconsistencies. When a scientist interprets the results of his experiments, he proceeds by using 'models'. For example, he says, 'Let an electron be a particle', and calculates its behaviour as if it were a minute tennis ball. This model will account for much of his data, but there comes a point where his mathematical predictions on this basis do not fit the evidence, and he is obliged to turn to another complementary model and calculate the electron's behaviour on the assumption that it is a wave. The wave model supersedes the particle model because it is a deeper understanding of how an electron behaves, though less convenient in most cases. This example has been introduced to indicate what is meant by a model. For our purposes, the interesting point is that there have been situations, for example in nuclear physics, where two models have been used at the same time although it is difficult to see how they fit together. Each model fails to predict accurately all that the physicist 'sees', and he is obliged to use two different definitions and two different mathematical languages, each adequate up to a point, but neither capable of describing the total complex picture produced by the experimental data. It may be that with advances in understanding, these two incompatible models can be superseded by a deeper and more adequate model which resolves more of the complexities; but meanwhile, the physicist works with two apparently inconsistent models alongside one another.

What I want to suggest is that when we move from the 'Trivial Plane' to the 'Tragic Plane', to use Arthur Koestler's phrases,[46] when we turn from day to day events to contemplate at a deep level the significance of human life, it is usual for us to proceed concurrently with different models, one of which is at any one moment perhaps temporarily suspended though not denied. In reflecting upon man's nature and destiny, especially as it is explored in literature and drama, we accept categories of 'truth' to which we would assign no literal, factual or scientific meaning. We accept that Tess has been the plaything of the president of the immortals, because we recognize that this metaphorical way of speaking says something profoundly truthful about the human situation.

So, the Christian believer lives in more than one dimension. In trying to understand the world in which he lives, he finds himself obliged to use different, apparently incompatible, models. Each is self-sufficient and adequate up to a point, but no single model represents on its own the total complex reality which we perceive, and in our present state of knowledge it is impossible to see how they ultimately fit together. As Paul said in a quite different context, 'Now I know in part; then I shall understand fully . . .'.

As Christian believers, then, we work with (*i*) the scientific model which finds explanations of phenomena, behaviour and events in terms of natural causes, and (*ii*) what we can only describe as 'mythological' or symbolic models, models which however inadequately represent the religious and spiritual dimension of our experience. To call them 'mythological' is not to denigrate their status, but to indicate that they refer to realities which are not only inaccessible to the normal methods of scientific investigation, but are also indefinable in terms of human language, and in their totality, inconceivable within the limited powers and experience of the finite human mind. Whereas the 'scientific' model is to a large extent known, predictable, coherent and in principle understood (though we may not all have equal knowledge, and different specialists know different bits of it), there is not one 'mythological' model but a number of different analogies, pictures, gropings, which may themselves seem incompatible; and different people may have different mythological models. This kind of truth is communicated – even conceived – in dramatic and poetic forms. Criteria are hard to formulate. This is bound to be the case since all language about God is analogical; it is the expression of the unknown and inexpressible in terms of the known. To take the simplest example: God is not literally 'our Father', or literally 'a person'. It is impossible to conceive of the transcendence, immanence and omnipresence of a person like the persons we know, and yet such characteristics are essential to our understanding of God in any but the crudest 'Daddy-in-the-sky' picture. God may have sufficient characteristics in common with a father or a person to make the analogy meaningful, but each model is bound to be 'poetic truth' or 'mythological truth' rather than 'literal fact'.

In the light of this discussion, how am I going to express in the contemporary environment my own testimony to the redemptive effect of faith in Jesus of Nazareth?

Salvation and atonement are the core of the Christian message. For me, experience of suffering, sin, decay and 'abnormality' as a constituent part of the world, would make belief in God impossible without a Calvary-centred religious myth. It is only because I can see God entering the darkness of human suffering and evil in his creation, recognizing it for what it really is, meeting it and conquering it, that I can accept a religious view of the world. Without the religious dimension, life would be senseless and endurance of its cruelty pointless; yet without the cross, it would be impossible to believe in God. Faith demands a doctrine of atonement, and atonement means a conviction that God has somehow dealt with evil, with sin, with rebellion; that on the cross, God in Christ entered into the suffering, the evil and the sin of his world – entered the darkness and transformed it into light, into blazing glory; that God himself took responsibility for the existence of evil in his creation; that he bore the pain of it and the guilt of it, accepting its consequences into himself; that he in his love reconciled his holiness to a sinful and corrupt humanity, justifying the ungodly, accepting man just as he is. Yet, to say this kind of thing is to use poetic, anthropomorphic or 'mythological' language; it is not to present a theological conclusion based on logical argument.

However, whatever the status of the language, if such a faith is to have any grounds whatever, it does appear at first sight to require the conclusion that Jesus on the cross *was God*; in other words, it seems to force me back to the sort of 'literal incarnation' doctrine which I dismissed as docetic earlier on. The question is: will my myth cease to be real if I find it intellectually impossible to make the ontological equation: Jesus = God? It is often argued, and more often assumed, that this is the case. But is it? There are, I think, good reasons for thinking that this is not so: (*i*) The simple equation Jesus = God not only fails to represent what Christian tradition has claimed, but is distinctly odd. To reduce *all of God* to a human incarnation is virtually inconceivable, a fact to which Trinitarian doctrine is the traditional response. The status of all language about God, as we have already noted, is peculiar. The simple equation cannot help confusing the two models with which, I have suggested, we are obliged to work; in other words, it turns 'myth' into 'science'. An exactly parallel confusion may help to illustrate the point. At the Reformation, controversy raged over the exact way in which the eucharistic bread and wine is the body and blood of Jesus Christ. One side wanted to treat it as symbolic, the other side as literal. An account of the literal meaning according to the 'science' of the time was offered: the underlying *substance* became the body and blood of Christ, while the *accidents* remained those of bread and wine. Such an explanation of the literal meaning ceases to have any value when we think in terms not of substance and accidents, but of molecules, atoms, electrons and nuclei. The cause of the whole debate lay in the confusion between 'myth' and 'science'. That in some real sense the bread and wine represent the body and blood is what Christian tradition has been concerned to affirm, but it does not help that concern to tie it to a literal or scientific way of expressing it. When the science becomes out-dated, the myth is endangered. (*ii*) I have used the word 'mythological'. This is because, amongst other things, it is a *story* which treats God in a thoroughly anthropomorphic way, psychologically if not physically. This may be a suitable analogy which expresses as well as possible what we want to say about God, but it is inevitably inadequate, and certainly not literally true. But if we no longer accept it as literal fact, does the story cease to be meaningful? Perhaps we shall find our answer if we consider some other examples. The story of Adam remains meaningful even though I accept that it is extremely improbable that Adam ever existed or that all men are descended from one ancestor; and Berlioz's *Grande Messe des Morts* convicts and terrifies, even though I no longer accept as literal the picture of a heavenly assize after death. In other words, there are many areas where Christians habitually use stories which were once believed to be fact but are no longer. The 'myth' remains evocative and conveys 'truth' at a level beyond the merely literal. (*iii*) The 'truth' of my myth can be summarized approximately by saying that God is to be understood as *a suffering God*, at least in the same sense as we can talk of him as loving. How might I find out that God shares my grief and suffering, my struggles with temptation, evil and sin – indeed, that his grief and suffering at the evil in his creation is far more profound than my self-centred tears at my own difficulties? Surely I am most likely to be convinced of this, not by a single, isolated and unique occurrence, but *by repeated experience* of the fact that innocent sufferers and martyrs who bear the abuse of their fellow-men with forgiveness, have a godlike quality of a transforming kind; by repeated experience of the fact that one who trusts entirely in God, in spite of the apparent stupidity and irrelevance of such an attitude, one who refuses to run away from evil or to meet it with more evil, can turn darkness into light; from repeated experience of the fact that real love involves a person in suffering whether he likes it or not. *It will then seem to be part of the make-up of the world, which in some sense reveals to the believer the God who created it and sustains it.*

The Book of Daniel speaks of the sufferings of persecuted Jews in the author's own time; but his words can be taken (as by Israelis) as prophecy of the sufferings of Jews under Hitler; or they can be taken (as traditionally by Christians) as prophecy of the sufferings of Jesus. But surely there is no need to limit the application to any one of these occasions or fulfilments. Potentially, if not actually, what is expressed here is universal insight into the suffering of

God's faithful, a suffering which tells of God's suffering. This insight is hinted at in many places in the biblical tradition, in the experiences of Jeremiah and the poetry of Isaiah 53. It is a suffering which Christian disciples are called to share. Jesus is not the only evidence for the suffering of God.[47]

But it is of course true that Christian tradition has seen this truth about God as supremely to be witnessed in the suffering of Jesus on the cross, and it is doubtful if the other examples would be seen in the same light without the story of Jesus. His associates responded to his death as the suffering of the martyr *par excellence*, the full, perfect and sufficient sacrifice for the sins of the whole world. Thus our attention has been focused upon one central story which for the Christian believer provides the revelation that God's redemptive activity, God's love for his creatures, involves him in the suffering and evil of the world, involves him in a way which is in some sense *real* though inconceivable apart from analogy, and inexpressible apart from myth.

So I find myself driven to tell *two stories*, to think in terms of two models, which cannot be fitted together in a literal way, or spelled out in relation to one another, but which in some sense reflect both the 'scientific' model of the world which my culture forces upon me and the 'mythological' model from which my religious faith cannot escape:

(*a*) The story of a *man* who lived as the 'archetypal believer', who lived and died trusting in God, and accepted the bitter consequences of the stupidity of such a career and his inevitable failure.

(*b*) The story of *God* being involved in the reality of human existence with its compromises, its temptations, its suffering, its pain, its injustice, its cruelty, its *death*;[48] not running away from it, not pretending that all this does not exist, but transforming its darkness into light, demonstrating that he takes responsibility for all that seems wrong with the world that he created.[49]

These two stories together provide me with the challenge to trust in God against all odds and to join in the costly work of turning darkness into light, and also with the assurance that God is worth trusting and shares with me in the battle and the victory. This is a christology which 'works', a christology which is not incredible in so far as Jesus is a real man in the human context, and a christology which transcends the limits of human understanding and allows for the mystery and the paradox of belief in God.

So I find myself able to say: 'I see God in Jesus', and 'God was in Christ reconciling the world to himself', and other such traditional statements, without necessarily having to spell it out in terms of a literal incarnation. I find salvation in Christ, because in him God is disclosed to me as a 'suffering God'. God is not *only* disclosed in him, nor is revelation confined to 'biblical times'; but Jesus is the supreme disclosure which opens my eyes to God in the present, and while remaining a man who lived in a particular historical situation, he will always be the unique focus of my perception of and response to God.

4. Conclusion

If we admit the primacy of soteriology, we inevitably open the gates to a multiplicity of christologies, rather than insisting upon one to which all are expected to conform. There is no suggestion that the approach of the last section will be meaningful or acceptable to everyone. Genuine faith in Jesus Christ does not take the same form in all believers. A little 'historical theology' soon reveals this, but it is also true in the church today. I do not simply refer to the phenomenon of 'Black Theology', or to the obvious differences between the expressions of Christian belief in different cultures, art-forms, etc. It is true of any average congregation. There are a fair number of residual Christians who go on believing what they were taught as children and adolescents, but increasingly individuals who have not 'made the faith their own' drift away under the pressures of this non-religious age. There are blocks of Christians who claim to have conversion-experiences of a remarkably similar type, and 'sects' which assert particular narrow beliefs as the only true Christianity, and in each case their members conform to the pattern both psychologically and intellectually. But apart from such exceptions, in the average congregation there are as many different responses to Jesus Christ as there are different fingerprints. The 'gut-centre' of each person's faith is different even where conformist language is used to describe it.

It is surely undeniable that an honest recognition of this fact could be a positive move in this ecumenical age. The slogan, 'unity but not uniformity', must apply not only to the so-called 'non-theological' factors. To reduce any living faith to a set of definitions and propositions is bound to distort it. Attempts to produce creeds are inevitably divisive or compromising: Eusebius of Caesarea signed the creed of Nicaea for the sake of church unity, but he was clearly embarrassed about it. What we need is not new creeds, but a new openness which will allow manifold ways of responding and elucidating that response. These ways may not seem consistent; they may have to co-exist in tension and paradox; but they need not pass judgment on each other. Even when in friction they may simply provide a valuable way of mutual criticism. No single one is to be regarded as 'the truth' or beyond critical discussion.

A number of objections to this position may be raised: (*a*) By what criteria can we define orthodoxy or heresy if we abandon credal definition? To this question, I ask the counter-question, how far ought we to discriminate between orthodoxy and heresy? Heresy hunts have always done more harm than good; the intolerance of the past still produces its sad harvest. Fanatical adherence to 'truth' is divisive. We need to break down barriers, not build them up. It is spiritual arrogance to be convinced that we have the truth and everyone else is misguided. We want today to be free to commend Jesus as Saviour without the harmful attitude to others which inevitably accompanies dogmatic and arrogant claims. The questions we ought to ask, surely, are which 'myths' or claims to truth are dangerous or harmful rather than healing and constructive. This criterion would exclude much that has passed for orthodoxy, but would welcome any positive insight, and any signs of reconciliation between people.

(*b*) If we all have our own christologies, how can there be any 'ontological' or *real* basis or justification for them? To this question some response has been indicated in the last section. To what was said there I would add two points:

(*i*) Response to Jesus as Saviour and Christ is not something we make in isolation from 'the tradition' – indeed, each individual's faith is parasitic upon the faith of others, and ultimately on the response of Jesus' immediate followers. There is therefore *a common ground* to our response, and that common ground must have some reasonable basis. The New Testament witness cannot be entirely out of character with the sort of person Jesus was: for example, Brandon's suggestion [50] that Jesus was really a nationalist, closely associated with the Zealot guerrilla movement will not do, because it totally fails to account for Christian faith with its stress upon self-giving love, love even of one's enemies. However complex historical reconstruction may be, there must have been something about Jesus which elicited the response whereby each follower saw him as the answer to his deepest needs, and claimed to see God disclosed in him.

(*ii*) 'What does Christ mean to me?' usually elicits from a Christian believer some sort of claim that 'God' is disclosed in him. What we want to say is: *He is 'as-if-God' for me.* The question is, how do we spell that meaning out? Does it really matter if we spell it out in lots of different ways? I am not sure that it does. This is not my first reference to the fact that when we bring in talk about 'God' we introduce an unknown, or only dimly known, quantity into the situation. Everything we say enters the realm of analogies which are only half-adequate. If we were 'flat-landers' living in a world of two-dimensions, we could only experience a three-dimensional object in two-dimensional terms. Suppose we found a circular ashtray: we would experience its base as a circle, or its side, if it were upturned, as a line. We might become aware of a number of different aspects of it if it were 'projected' on to our two-dimensional plane. All these different experiences might suggest to us that the three-dimensional ashtray was more complex and mysterious than our perception of it, but we could not realistically visualize it or even conceptualize it; we could only describe some of its properties, which to us would appear almost incompatible. The mathematician who tries to construct or perceive a four-dimensional object is not unlike the religious man in his perception of a complex reality which is not conceivable in its totality within the limits of our present experience. We are bound to attempt to describe the unknown in terms of the known, indeed to experience the 'beyond' in terms of the 'here and now'; but this leaves areas of 'mystery', where we think we may perceive something but cannot grasp it fully. Every statement about God is inevitably inadequate, expressing one among many possible 'projections' of his reality; and it may be that manifold ways of expression are the only way in which we can dimly perceive the depth of riches beyond. So, if we say that 'God is disclosed in the man Jesus', we may all perceive different facets, so that a multiplicity of christologies is inevitable by the very nature of our subject. To recognize this can only help to enrich and deepen our theology.

(c) Is it possible to safeguard the uniqueness and finality of Christ if we abandon a clear dogmatic stance? It should be clear from remarks made earlier that I doubt whether there is any necessity to safeguard this in an 'ontological' sense – indeed, it may be detrimental to do so. Truth about the world is found nowadays not in unique particular exceptions, but in statistical averages: many witnesses are more convincing than one. In a world context, the witness of differing prophets and differing faiths to the 'beyond' is more important to all religions than the exclusive claims of any one. Of course, for the New Testament writers, for the church, for all believers, Jesus Christ undoubtedly holds a unique position; no one else has the same role for faith. But in the case of outsiders, has it not become increasingly difficult to maintain that faith in Christ is indispensable for salvation? The idea of Christ's finality is surely linked with the eschatological presuppositions of the early church, presuppositions which were central and fundamental to them but which we can only make our own in some kind of 'de-mythologized' form. Within one cultural stream, namely the Judaeo-Christian European tradition, some case can be made for seeing Christ as a kind of 'coping-stone' to religious developments in the ancient world, the spiritual climax, as it were, of Hellenistic philosophy, which determined the subsequent religious culture of Europe; but to claim that Jesus as the cosmic Christ has the same ultimate significance for all mankind irrespective of time, place or culture is surely unrealistic.

(*d*) If our christology is allowed to become ill-defined, how can we uphold a Trinitarian doctrine of God? It must be admitted that the development of Trinitarian theology was intimately, though not exclusively, linked with patristic christology; so does this mean that re-thinking incarnational belief involves us in abandoning the characteristically Christian theology of God as 'Three-in-One'? While for some to do this would be a welcome release from an incomprehensible and cramping burden, for many others it would appear a serious break with Christian tradition. Would we have left anything which could be called a *Christian* doctrine of God?

It seems to me that a discussion of these issues is hampered as long as we insist on a one-to-one identification of Christian affirmations about God with factuality. To the comments made above we may add the observation that modern discussions have insisted on the impossibility of treating God as a thing like other things about which factual statements can be made. Besides this, it is notoriously difficult to elucidate Trinitarian doctrine without falling either into Sabellian or tritheistic statements. The only thing that enabled the Cappadocians to avoid these pitfalls was their understanding of the divine substance, an understanding intimately linked with the philosophical heritage within which they worked. It would not be surprising if the Trinitarian concept of God is found unintelligible in a different philosophical environment.

Perhaps then we shall get further by raising the question what *function* the Trinitarian concept of God has had in Christian theology and devotion, and whether our concept of God needs in one way or another to perform the same functions. It seems to me that the doctrine has had two important roles:

(*i*) Logos-theology and Trinitarian doctrine made it possible for God to be *involved*. The impassible, transcendent *One*, beyond Being, was intellectually adequate and mystically inspiring, but could not elicit the faith and devotion of most ordinary mortals. The doctrines of the Logos and the Spirit made it possible to believe in a God who was both transcendent and immanent, however paradoxical that might seem to be. We cannot afford to lose this element in our understanding of God, and it is interesting that prior to reaction against Christianity, Judaism was itself developing a theology of divine hypostases to preserve this aspect of belief in God. For Christianity, it has been Trinitarianism which has made possible a concept of richness, variety and adaptability in God: thus the process of creation and history was not divorced from God's Being. So we can say that evolutionary theology and process theology are not foreign to the Christian tradition, because Christian theology has always insisted that God is not monolithic. Where it is not a crude anthropomorphism, pure monotheism is liable to become belief in a static and remote First Cause, almost irrelevant to the religious life.

(*ii*) Trinitarian theology, simply because it defies expression, was a constant warning against over-simple theologies, blasphemous in their attempts to pin down the Being of God. Religion is destroyed without mystery – indeed paradox. Faith and devotion depend upon the interplay of awe and familiarity, and the Christian doctrine of God as Father and Brother, Judge and Advocate, King and Servant, the one to whom we pray, the one with whom we pray, and the one who prays within us, has had an essential role in the worship and spiritual tradition of the church. It is instructive to read medieval literature like the writings of Julian of Norwich. Trinitarian theology is the traditional way of expressing the mystery of God and the inadequacy of our human attempts to express his Being whether in imaginative and analogical terms, or in abstruse philosophical definitions. It would be a serious impoverishment to lose this. We worship a mysterious, not an anthropomorphic God.

So, despite the objections raised, the future seems to lie with pluralism in christology. For some time now the church has been moving towards pluralism in the expression of salvation and atonement; because christology is so intimately linked with soteriology, sooner or later it must take the same path. Jesus Christ can be all things to all men because each individual or society, in one cultural environment after another, sees him as the embodiment of their salvation.[51] He becomes, as he did for Paul, the unique focus of their perception of and response to God.

NOTES

1. Developed particularly in Barnabas Lindars, *St John*, New Century Bible Commentary, Oliphants 1972.

2. J. L. Houlden, *The Johannine Epistles*, A. & C. Black 1973.

3. E.g. O. Cullmann, *The Christology of the New Testament*, SCM Press 1959; R. H. Fuller, *The Foundations of New Testament Christology*, Collins/Fontana 1965.

4. G. Vermes, appendix to M. Black, *An Aramaic Approach to the Gospels*, third edition, Oxford University Press 1967; R. Leivestad, 'Exit the Apocalyptic Son of Man', *New Testament Studies*, vol. xviii, 1971–2, pp. 243–67; J. A. Fitzmyer, 'The Contribution of Qumran Aramaic to the Study of the New Testament', *New Testament Studies*, vol. xx, 1974, pp. 357ff.

5. See note 3 above. A few of the other studies easily accessible in English include: W. Bousset, *Kyrios Christos*, Abingdon Press, Nashville 1970; H. Tödt, *The Son of Man in the Synoptic Tradition*, SCM Press 1965; A. J. B. Higgins, *Jesus and the Son of Man*, Lutterworth 1964.

6. See ch. 5 'Two Roots or a Tangled Mass?', pp. 187ff. below.

7. While it is true that 'Son of Man' could be an idiomatic phrase in Aramaic, referring to a human being or possibly a periphrasis for 'I', it is clearly used in the Greek gospels as some sort of eschatological title, at least in some contexts. This statement is therefore not inconsistent with my earlier remark.

8. Whether or not the Suffering Servant passages of Second Isaiah were understood messianically in pre-Christian Judaism has been a subject of much debate. Opposing views are represented by Zimmerli and Jeremias, *The Servant of God*, SCM Press 1957; and Morna Hooker, *Jesus and the Servant*, SPCK 1959. It seems most likely that Messiahship tended to have political success overtones in the New Testament period, but the idea of the suffering king was latent in the Old Testament texts, particularly the Psalms of suffering and possibly also Isaiah 53. Since the near-contemporary Maccabaean literature contains the idea that a martyr dying for the nation could expiate the nation's sins (see J. Downing, 'Jesus and Martyrdom', *Journal of Theological Studies* ns, vol. 14, 1963, p. 279), a positive understanding of the role of suffering was available, and not unnaturally associated with prophecies of an ideal king-Messiah, in the view of the kingly suffering motif referred to above.

9. Especially in Matthew's gospel; see W. D. Davies, *The Setting of the Sermon on the Mount*, Cambridge University Press 1964, and M. D. Goulder, *Midrash and Lection in Matthew*, SPCK 1974.

10. See ch. 5, pp. 87ff. below.

11. Bultmann and his pupils have been the main protagonists of this view. An easily accessible summary of their position is to be found in *Appendix III* in G. Bornkamm, *Jesus of Nazareth*, Hodder & Stoughton 1960. See also A. J. B. Higgins, op. cit., and R. H. Fuller, op. cit. Contrast the position of O. Cullmann, op. cit.

12. Implied in synoptic sayings like Mark 8.38; made explicit in John's gospel, e.g. 9.39–41. But note that the observations made in this sentence do not depend exclusively on the specific texts mentioned in the notes, but rather on the total impression created by the gospel material.

13. This is a possible interpretation of the incident of Caesarea Philippi (Mark 8. 27ff. and particularly v. 33). Cf. O. Cullmann, op. cit., p. 122, who argues that it certainly implies rejection of Messiahship.

14. Even though the 'realized eschatology' of C. H. Dodd has received justifiable criticism, the immediate imminence, and even presence, of the kingdom is certainly not absent from the gospel texts (e.g. Mark 1.15; Matt. 12.28; Luke 17.20; and

parallels and other examples). It is difficult to believe that it was *not* the core of Jesus' preaching. It is conceivable that Jesus himself was correcting the futurist and apocalyptic hopes of the people, reminding them, like the prophets of old, that *now* matters. Yet, he seems to have made use of current hopes to reinforce his message and provide it with sanctions. R. H. Fuller argues (op. cit.) that Jesus' own understanding of his purpose and person was in terms of the eschatological prophet, and this view is certainly attractive. However, the main point here is that, in view of the current assumption that prophecy had been dead for centuries and its arrival would herald the end, it was inevitable, whether or not Jesus claimed to be the fulfilment of prophecies, that his contemporaries should react to his message and authority in this way.

15. Although not advancing exactly the same point, an interesting comparison can be made here with E. Trocmé, *Jesus and his Contemporaries*, SCM Press 1973, who argues that different pictures of Jesus emerge from the different forms of material in the synoptic gospels, and these were the different impressions created on different groups with which he came into contact during his ministry.

16. It is instructive to observe the way in which Old Testament texts are used christologically in the Epistle to the Hebrews. Texts concerning the Lord (i.e. Jahweh) are taken to refer to Jesus (e.g. Heb. 1.10); and a text concerning mankind's status in creation is turned into a prophecy of the descent into flesh of God's Son, the heavenly man (Heb. 2.6–9). The use of collections of 'proof texts' in the early church is apparent in many parts of the New Testament. See e.g. Matt. 21.42; Mark 12.10; Luke 20.17–18; Acts 4.11; Rom. 9.33; I Peter 2.6–8. For discussion see B. Lindars, *New Testament Apologetic*, SCM Press 1961; C. F. D. Moule, *The Birth of the New Testament*, A. & C. Black 1962, ch. IV.

17. Cullmann, op. cit., p. 134; Fuller, op. cit., p. 230.

18. Implied by I Cor. 12.3 (as interpreted by Cullmann, op. cit., pp. 219ff.).

19. Col. 1.15–20. Cf. Prov. 8.22–31; Ecclus. 1.4; 24.3; Wisd. 725–26. See ch. 5 below.

20. C. K. Barrett, 'Pauline Controversies in the post-Pauline Period', *New Testament Studies*, vol. xx, 1974, p. 229.

21. Paul speaks of him as the 'image of God' (II Cor. 4.4; Col. 1.15), of his being in the 'form of God' (Phil. 2.6); and of God's fullness dwelling in him (Col. 1.20). These phrases imply a close relationship rather than identity (see note 23 below); and this is confirmed by the subjection of Christ to God (I Cor. 15.25ff.; 3.23; 11.3). It is sometimes said that he is called God in Rom. 9.5; II Thess. 1.12; and Titus 2.13; but it is more likely that the first is pious ejaculation unconnected with the syntax of the sentence; that in the second and third, the Greek is rather loose and in fact refers (in the former) to the grace of God plus the grace of the Lord Jesus Christ, and (in the latter) to the glory of our great God and of our Saviour Jesus Christ. (The Epistle to Titus is probably not the work of Paul anyway.)

22. Paul speaks of the 'man from heaven' in I Cor. 15.48. It is highly likely that when he uses phrases like the 'image of God', he thinks not only of the divine Wisdom, but also of perfect manhood, as man was created to be. This is particularly probable as an exegesis of Phil. 2.6, where there may well be a deliberate contrast between Adam, made in the image of God but tempted to be equal with God knowing good and evil, and Christ, also made in God's image (*morphē*) but humbling himself and not seeking equality with God. Cullmann, op. cit., pp. 174ff.

23. Rom. 1.3 and Phil. 2.9ff. *et al.* might seem to reflect an 'adoptionist' sort of Sonship and Lordship, but they may be pre-Pauline. Paul himself uses the title Son in a variety of contexts, but especially (*i*) of him being 'sent' to condemn sin in the flesh and to redeem men form the law, where his being born of woman and being in the likeness of sinful flesh is emphasized, and the point is his perfect obedience which destroys the power of sin and law over man (Gal. 4.4; Rom. 8.3); (*ii*) of his Sonship and our adopted Sonship (Gal. 4.4–7; Rom. 8.14ff.; note v. 29 where his chosen

ones are to be 'conformed to the image of his Son' (*summorphous tēs eikonos tou Huiou autou*); cf. Eph. 1.5 (even if Ephesians is not actually from Paul's hand, I have regarded it as sufficiently Pauline in its thought and language to be used in this connection, and there are further references below). He is the first-born of many brethren (Rom. 8.29; cf. Col. 1.15, 18); and we are his fellow heirs (Gal. 4.7; Rom. 8.17). Clearly Paul thinks of Jesus Christ being 'Son of God' in a special way (Rom. 8.32: he did not spare his own Son), but he is not the only potential son and he is sent as perfectly obedient man. As man he is God's image, Son of God in the sense that Adam and Israel were destined to be sons of God if they had not been disobedient. He is sent (perhaps) in the sense that the prophets and John the Baptist were 'sent' by God (born of woman, Gal. 4.4). However, the phrase 'man from heaven' used elsewhere suggests that his sending meant that he came from outside into the world and the flesh. But he is certainly sent as perfect man; his coming from outside does not imply any 'substantial' relationship with God. He was the first-born of all *creation* (Col. 1.15), who as God's agent obediently carried out God's predetermined plan for the redemption of all the children of God (Eph. 1.5–12). Even the most far-reaching phrase about 'all the fullness of God dwelling in him' (Col. 1.19; 2.9) is paralleled in Ephesians by a phrase concerning men: 'that you may be filled with all the fullness of God' (Eph. 3.19); and furthermore, the fullness of God *was pleased* to dwell in him (*eudokesen*); it was choice, will, purpose, election, rather than essential derivative nature.

24. E.g., the charges of Celsus: Origen, *Contra Celsum*, viii.12: If these men worshipped no other God but one, perhaps they would have a valid argument against the others. But in fact they worship to an extravagant degree this man who appeared recently.

25. See ch. 4 below; the prologue of St John's gospel (whatever may have been the origins and connotations of the Logos in that context) gave scriptural authority for the development. The chief exponents of this theology were the Apologists; but the idea of the Logos was taken up and developed in a philosophical way by Clement and Origen, and Logos remained the normal title by which reference was made to the pre-existent and incarnate Lord right up to and after the Arian controversy. On the Logos-theology, see e.g. J. N. D. Kelly, *Early Christian Doctrines*, A. &. C. Black, fourth edition 1968, ch. I and IV; E. R. Goodenough, *The Theology of Justin Martyr*, Jena 1923; G. L. Prestige, *God in Patristic Thought*, SPCK 1952; H. A. Wolfson, *The Philosophy of the Church Fathers*, Harvard 1964.

26. Origen, *Contra Celsum* provides valuable insight into the debates between rival schools; note especially i.10. The rivalry of different philosophical schools was in fact a commonplace of Christian apologetic and pagan satire.

27. The philosophers upheld an ultimate monotheism, while allowing polytheistic worship: e.g. Maximus of Tyre, *Dissertationes*, xxxix.5: The gods are one nature but many names. Cf. Celsus in *Contra Celsum*, v.45; viii.2. In Porphyry, grades of deity are expounded and fitting worship for each defined: *De Abstinentia*, ii.34–39. Alongside this, the stress on ethics (with metaphysics only a support to moral teaching) a stress which was characteristic of post-Aristotelian philosophy, meant that true worship of the Supreme God came to be seen in terms of virtue and gradual transformation into likeness of God until 'apatheia' of soul was achieved. The best example of this is to be found in Marcus Aurelius' *Meditations* (e.g. v.27, 33; vii.9), though here we see it in the framework of Stoicism. Maximus of Tyre, *Dissertationes*, xi, expounds the 'philosopher's prayer' as understood in Middle Platonism. Both Christian Platonism and Neoplatonism adopted these attitudes (e.g. Clement, *Stromateis*, vii.14, 31, 33; Porphyry, *De Abstinentia*, ii.34–5).

28. For a convenient exposition of the Platonist tradition in Jewish and Christian form, see H. Chadwick, 'Philo and the beginnings of Christian thought', in A. H. Armstrong (ed.), *The Cambridge History of Later Greek and Early Medieval Philosophy*, Cambridge University Press 1967.

29. These characteristics go back ultimately to Parmenides' One. In Philo and the Christian Platonists the identification with God is clear, and seems to have been used in Middle Platonism. For a convenient exposition, see E. F. Osborn, *Clement of Alexandria*, Cambridge University Press 1957, chs. I–III. For the attributes of God in patristic theology, see G. L. Prestige, op. cit.; and in Christian Platonism, H. Chadwick, op. cit. For the One in Neoplatonism, see A. H. Armstrong in *The Cambridge History of Later Greek and Early Medieval Philosophy*, and J. M. Rist, *Plotinus, The Road to Reality*, Cambridge University Press 1967.

30. Plato, *Republic*, 509B: The Good is beyond Being. This statement was not only taken up in the ultra-transcendent theology of Neoplatonism (see Rist, op. cit.), but is found in the popular Platonism represented by Celsus (*Contra Celsum*, vi.64) and Justin (*Dialogue with Trypho*, 4). Platonism distinguished between the One as a unity in itself and a One–Many, that is, a composite unity. In Philo, for example, God in himself was the One, and the Logos of God, containing the Forms, was the One–Many, and the principle of creation. In Neoplatonism, the One is transcendent, but Nous and Psyche are composite hypostases linking the One with the world. For examples of this and parallels with the Logos-theology of Clement of Alexandria, see S. R. C. Lilla, *Clement of Alexandria. A Study in Christian Platonism and Gnosticism*, Oxford University Press 1971; and E. F. Osborn, op. cit.

31. Gnosticism was criticized by Plotinus as well as Christian writers. Both Neoplatonists and Christians were fundamentally opposed to any form of dualism; evil was not 'in Being' and everything had its origin in God. Gnostic myths portrayed a fragmentation of and fall of the divine which was alien to the Christian and Platonic outlook. Yet there is a similarity in spite of this very important difference. Even the same terminology is employed: e.g. Basilides (according to Irenaeus, *Adversus Haereses*, i.19) speaks of an unbegotten Father from whom was born Nous from whom was born Logos.

32. E.g., Clement, *Strom.*, iv.25; Origen, *Comm. in Joh.*, i.20. See Osborn, op. cit.; Lilla, op. cit.; J. Daniélou, *Gospel Message and Hellenistic Culture*, vol. II of *A History of Early Christian Doctrine before the Council of Nicaea*, Darton, Longman & Todd 1973.

33. Augustine, *Confessions*, vii.9.

34. Athanasius, *De Incarnatione* is the classic exposition. See my 'Insight or incoherence? the Greek Fathers on God and Evil', *Journal of Ecclesiastical History*, vol. xxiv, 1973, p. 113.

35. In post-Nicene theology, the notion of Mediator is still found, but it has been interpreted. Now the God-Man is Mediator because he is at once *homoousios tōi patri* and *homoousios hēmin*. E.g., Theodoret, *Comm. on I Tim.*, J.-P. Migne (ed.), *Patrologia Graeca*, PG 82: 800A. This is clearly a quite different concept of mediation.

36. This was hardly original, belonging both to the philosophical and Christian traditions behind him. The real point was the conclusions he drew from it. For Arianism and the reaction, see e.g. Kelly, op. cit., ch. IX; Prestige, op. cit.

37. For a discussion of Eusebius' position, see G. C. Stead, 'Eusebius and the Council of Nicaea', *Journal of Theological Studies*, NS, vol. 24, April 1973, pp. 85ff.

38. Athanasius, *De Incarnatione*, 54.3.

39. Athanasius himself insists that we do not become *theoi* or *huioi* in the same sense as the Logos is *theos* or *huios* (e.g. *Contra Arianos*, iii.19–21); but he does not perceive that it is a fatal admission for his argument, which may have religious force, but is not strictly logical.

40. Athanasius is driven to say '*ta hēmon emimēsato*', *Contra Arianos*, iii.57. See the classic article by M. Richard, 'S. Athanase et la psychologie du Christ selon les Ariens', in *Mélanges des sciences religieuses*, IV, 1947, pp. 5–54.

41. A. Grillmeier, *Christ in Christian Tradition*, Mowbray 1965, presents a case for seeing the Antiochene position as derivative from the Alexandrian in the post-

Nicene situation. However, one suspects that Paul of Samosata at least must have had views somewhat akin to the later Antiochene approach, though his condemnation was hardly a good recommendation for his views!

42. Eusebius, *Vita Constantini*, iv.29; iii.15.

43. Basil, *De Spiritu Sancto*, xviii.44–5; Gregory of Nyssa, *Contra Eunomium*, i.19. Kelly, op. cit., p. 268.

44. E.g. Gregory of Nazianzus, *Orationes*, ii.41.

45. Traditionalists may react by saying 'What about the virgin birth?'. Quite apart from the difficulty of 'proving' such a story, as a literal statement of Jesus' origins, it is virtually inconceivable in the light of modern knowledge of genetics and reproduction. The matter is discussed at greater length in J. A. T. Robinson, *The Human Face of God*, SCM Press 1973, ch. 2.

46. Koestler, *The Act of Creation*, Hutchinson 1964, ch. XX.

47. These examples are particularly well emphasized by A. T. Hanson, *Grace and Truth*, SPCK 1975. His argument that humanity is the appropriate vehicle for divinity in the space–time context, and his use of biblical parallels to the suffering of Jesus, comes close to my position. However, he fails to see that all this implies that the traditional 'hard' distinction between God and man can no longer be upheld, and each man is potentially 'God incarnate'. The *ontological* uniqueness of Jesus cannot then be successfully defended.

48. I deliberately include the idea of God's death, since this highlights the 'mythical' and paradoxical nature of the Christian story. The fathers were nonplussed by the claim that God died on the cross, and tried to give an intelligible account of it; but this was to miss the whole point. I do not think it is possible to say exactly what is meant by God dying, but that it is an essential element in the saving story, I am sure.

49. This does not mean that I am suggesting as some do, that in Jesus 'myth' was 'actualized' in history, or that something happened in 'God's biography' when Jesus died on the cross. I am simply stating that as a matter of fact the story of Jesus has become a catalyst which has opened the eyes of those in the Christian tradition to this aspect of God as revealed in the world he created. That the same truth could be witnessed elsewhere is undeniable, e.g. in Jewish history.

50. S. G. F. Brandon, *The Trial of Jesus*, London 1968.

51. A. T. Hanson's study of the incarnation, *Grace and Truth* (see note 47 above), has come to my notice since the first draft of this paper. It is interesting that he makes a similar plea for admitting more than one expression of christology.

3

Jesus, The Man of Universal Destiny

MICHAEL GOULDER

A few years ago, the philosopher in my department, who delights to pull the theologian's leg, asked me if I had heard the one [1] about the Pope being told by the cardinals that the remains of Jesus had been dug up in Palestine. There was no doubt that it was Jesus – all the Catholic archaeologists were agreed. 'Oh,' said the Pope, 'what do we do now?' 'Well,' said the cardinals, 'there is only one hope left: there is a Protestant theologian in America called Tillich – perhaps you could get him on the phone?' So Tillich was telephoned, and the position was explained to him. There was a long silence, at the end of which the voice said, 'You mean to say he really existed?'

The anecdote is not less barbed for being, of course, apocryphal. In the eyes of philosophers, the Christian faith has become intellectually disreputable because it no longer asserts anything. Our fathers believed many things, accessible to all in the Bible. We don't believe in hell (most of us) or the devil or verbal inspiration, and when such ideas are derided we join in the laughter: 'did you really think we believed that?', we say. Even when the incarnation, or divine providence, or almost any view of the atonement is derided, the Christian is often found to be joining in too, perhaps rather uncomfortably: did you really think we believed that? 'Well,' says the philosopher, 'it sounds as if your faith is pretty elastic: can you get by without the resurrection, or the historicity of Jesus? Aren't you really a humanist, but without the honesty to say so?'

I will tell you a second story, this time a true one. Soon after being instituted to my first living, I went to visit a patient in hospital. I had to wait, and was shortly joined by two further

Christian ministers, the one a Congregationalist, the other (in my opinion at the time) of an even lower breed, completely without the law. There being nothing else to do, we fell naturally to theological disputation, and in the course of time the sister was somewhat startled to come in as my Congregationalist friend was saying, 'Well, one thing is certain; he didn't think he was the Second Person of the Trinity'. I found the remark doubly annoying – partly because I had always supposed that Jesus thought he *was* the Second Person of the Trinity (although wisely not mentioning the fact), and now it was said, it somehow had the ring of the obvious. And partly also I did not relish being enlightened by a minister not of the established church.

I have set the second tale alongside the first, because they seem to me to epitomize the double and conflicting pressure under which a thinking Christian lives today, especially if he be a minister of the gospel. Orthodoxy once provided a divinely revealed road round the mountain to heaven. Even a generation ago, despite the collapse of biblical literalism and other sections of the road, there seemed to be still a firm path round the mountain. Then, without our being aware of it, other sections of the way have been eroded, and we have suddenly realized it in odd conversations, as I did in Withington Hospital. So our way has come to include a few leaps over crevasses, and diversions over the scree. Come, says the friendly philosopher, your path leads nowhere, and will be the death of you: join me in a noble and resolute despair. My path will not take you to heaven, but it is a path through life where you can be a man, caring for the truth, and for your fellow men. But if we will not, or cannot, leave the church's way, there are siren voices behind us also, summoning us back to the safety of the mountain-hut of traditional belief. Is it so obvious that the time-honoured doctrines of God and Christ and salvation and judgment and authority and the rest are incoherent and implausible? Would we not do better to continue to believe as we were taught? But it is my belief (and that of my fellow-essayists) that we do not have to choose between the abyss of atheism and the fixity of traditional orthodoxy. There is a way forward: not the full broad road our fathers enjoyed, but a path still, which I will do my best to trace.

To believe the Christian faith is to believe something about Jesus, called Christ; and that seems to me inevitably to mean believing certain things about him as a historical person. History is a matter of probabilities, and no one in the present climate of learned scepticism can assert much as a historical probability without risk of contradiction. In an essay of this length all I can do is to state my

criteria, and leave the critic to dispute either them or their application: the literature on the matter is too enormous for me to debate
the criteria and conclusions of others, and I have severely limited
the footnote references. So then, I am using three hard criteria,
amplified by three softer criteria. Hard criteria (if correctly applied)
should give highly probable results, soft criteria rather probable
results. The hard criteria are:

1. *Coherence.* The account given must hang together: it is no use
claiming that Jesus was a Zealot, and then finding no trace of
Zealot teaching in the early church; or that the resurrection was a
forgery, unless it can be shown how the church survived the crucifixion.

2. *Accidental information.* Paul is trying to tell the Corinthians
that Jesus rose from the dead, and he says, 'He appeared to
Cephas': he tells us by accident that there was a man known as
Cephas, and this is therefore dependable. Detection, both criminal
and historical, is largely based on this criterion.

3. *Material told to the church's embarrassment.* We believe
Protestant lives of Cranmer when they tell us something to his
discredit, and Catholic lives when they tell us something to his
credit.[2] So Mark quite often tells us things about Jesus and the
apostles which Matthew and Luke omit or colour.[3]

The three soft criteria are:

4. *Material which Paul says was handed on to him.* Since Paul was
converted in the middle 30s, perhaps less than five years after
the crucifixion, what he was taught at his conversion is not likely to
have been badly distorted.

5. *Aramaic and Hebrew words.* Matthew usually, Luke always,
translates these: they cannot have been created by the Greek-
speaking churches, and are likely to be remembered from Jesus
himself.[4]

We may also give cautious credit to:

6. *Very widespread tradition,* at least for such general claims as
that Jesus was a man of love, which is evidenced indirectly in the
epistles as well as directly in the gospels. These six criteria are such
as a disinterested historian would bring to the task; and if we are
seeking historical probabilities, they must suffice us.

It seems to me that we can make twelve statements about Jesus
on the basis of these criteria:

(*i*) Jesus' career was based on a public preaching mission in
Galilee, of which the central message was that the reign of God,
promised by the prophets, had now been inaugurated. Such
statements are common to all four gospels (criterion 6); without

some such religious message no coherent account of Christian origins is possible (criterion 1); and whereas the church's interest lay in proclaiming Jesus, the Jesus of the synoptics proclaims the reign of God (criterion 3).

(*ii*) Jesus' belief that God's reign was beginning probably sprang from the conviction that John the Baptist's mission was divinely inspired. Again, all four gospels begin Jesus' mission with an account of John (criterion 6). There was a sect of John's followers (Acts 18.25; 19.3) which to some extent competed with the church; and Mark's view of the Baptist is sharply toned down by both Luke and John (criterion 3).

(*iii*) Jesus supported his proclamation by the performance of a large number of healings. It is not possible to persuade other people of so high a claim, and it is difficult to maintain confidence in oneself, unless there is constant backing for it (criterion 1). Healing stories take up a great deal of the account of the ministry in Mark, and much of the other gospels (criterion 6). They include Hebrew (*Ephphatha*)[5] and Aramaic words (*Talitha cumi*)[6] (criterion 5). Paul mentions that healings and miracles took place in the church, and he attributes this to the church's being the body of Christ (I Cor. 12.27f.): that is, an extension of Jesus' work in his lifetime (criterion 2).[7]

(*iv*) Jesus saw himself as the one through whom God's reign was being inaugurated. This is entailed by statements (*i*) and (*iii*). God's reign was prophesied as a time when the blind would see and the deaf hear, etc. (e.g. Isa. 35.4ff.); Jesus was proclaiming it, and Jesus was doing the healings. While Jewish expectations of the period take many forms (e.g. Messiahs of the line of David or Levi; Melchizedek; Enoch), there is almost always some inaugurating figure, God's representative;[8] so we have again a form of the coherence argument (criterion 1).

(*v*) It is likely that Jesus saw himself as (Davidic) Messiah. This was the most widespread of the conceptions of inaugurating figures, and it is the one best evidenced in the gospels (criterion 6). In part it would fit his ministry well, since Jesus saw himself as the leader designated by God over his incipient kingdom (statement *iv*). In part it would fit ill, because Messiah was seen as a warrior leader, destined to established a Jewish empire to exceed David's: and this Jesus was not. Such an ambivalence goes well with the Marcan account, where Jesus knows himself to be Messiah, but will not use the title, and bids his disciples say nothing of it. Mark's reticence is a confirmation of the veracity of his account.[9] The church's message, in Paul and Acts, is that Jesus was the Christ:

Mark thought so too, but you would hardly know it to read his gospel.

(*vi*) It is also likely that Jesus saw himself as (Danielic) Son of Man.[10] Daniel 'foretold' (by *ex post facto* prophecy) the overthrow of the heathen empires, pictured as a series of beasts, by God's kingdom, pictured as 'one like a son of man'. Sometimes in Daniel the beasts are the empires, sometimes their emperors; and this invited the same possibility for both God's kingdom and its ruler, especially as the phrase 'the son of man' had been applied to the king of Israel in Psalms 8 and 80. The Son of Man was an image better suited to Jesus than Messiah – partly because of its universal, numinous ring, whose mystery he could exploit; and partly because it solved the problem of dissonance. One can go about proclaiming for a while that God's reign has begun, and point in evidence to series of striking healings: but it must soon become clear that iniquity remains on the throne in the form of oppressive landlords and tax-gatherers, enslavements and crucifixions, and that no hint is being given of how this situation is to be reversed. A proclamation of God's kingship inaugurated, with Jesus as inaugurator, is thus incoherent unless it includes the message of temporary humiliation (criterion 1). This need the Daniel Son of Man supplies. How can God's reign have begun, and yet heathendom remain unmoved? The answer is given in Dan. 7: the reign of God would not be established easily – the one like a son of man must be given over to tribulations for a time and two times and half a time (half a week, whether of years or days), and only then exalted to God's presence and given the kingdom.[11] So Jesus saw his destiny according to Mark. He was the Son of Man, God's vicegerent on earth, with full powers to forgive sins and to revoke the fourth commandment: but as Son of Man, he expected to suffer and die, and after three days to be exalted to heaven and given his kingdom, which he would return to reign over in power. Not only is Jesus' self-understanding as Son of Man evidenced in all the gospels (criterion 6), and virtually required by the criterion of coherence (criterion 1): it is confirmed by the fact that it is never used by Paul. The Greek churches found it unpreachable: as in modern times, it requires a theological lecture to make it understood (criterion 3). Mark uses it despite its difficulty because history required it: and Matthew and Luke extend its use because of its numinous overtones.

(*vii*) It is likely that Jesus interpreted the term Messiah/Christ to imply a unique personal relation of Sonship to God. Messiah was to be a king of David's line, fulfilling the prophecies to David; and in the Old Testament the Davidic king was thought of as God's son

– 'I will be to him a father, and he will be to me a son', 'Thou art my son: this day have I begotten thee'. So it would be easy for Jesus to see himself in relation to God, not as his lieutenant, or his prophet, but as his Son; and we find evidence of this in the Aramaic expression which Jesus uses in Gethsemane, 'Abba', according to Mark (criterion 5).[12] The term was used in ecstatic prayer in the 50s (Romans and Galatians) by Christians holding themselves to be under the mantle of Jesus' unique sonship. Although there are a number of examples in Jewish literature of rabbis and other holy men being spoken of as God's sons, there is no serious parallel for the use of Abba in address to God, the term being normal for a human child to his father.[13]

(*viii*) What is remarkable about Jesus is his original interpretation of the kingdom as the reign of love. It was axiomatic to all Jews of the period, including those who taught Jesus, that God's will was expressed in the Law, and that when Messiah came Israel would keep the Law (if not as the precondition of his coming). Every iota of it was valid, and apparent discrepancies were all capable of reconciliation. Jesus saw himself as God's vicegerent, and as such he could do as he pleased. He pleased to act on, and to teach, the validity of the principle of love, and no other. When passages of the Law conflicted with this principle, he abrogated them. He healed on the sabbath, and said that the sabbath was made for man (a dangerous doctrine suppressed by Matthew); he spoke of marriage as indissoluble in defiance of Deut. 24; he overturned the dietary laws. He dined with the unclean, and welcomed them into his community, to the scandal of the pious. Jesus' originality does not consist in valuing love, for almost all his positive teachings can be paralleled in Jewish sources; it consists in seeing that there are occasions when love and the Law are at variance, and in taking responsibility to override the Law. It is difficult to think that such traditions are unhistorical. Not only are they widespread in the gospels (criterion 6), and an embarrassment to Christians trying to win over Jewry (criterion 3): but we should require some such scandal to make plausible the rejection of Jesus in his lifetime (criterion 1).

(*ix*) It is impossible to justify any stronger claims than these – to Jesus' sinlessness, or his *complete* devotion to God's will, or his *invariable* attitude of love. What we can say is that love is the normative mark both of Jesus as portrayed in the gospels and of the churches as portrayed in the epistles (criterion 6); and that it is difficult to reconcile this evidence had Jesus been a harsh or olympian or legalist Messiah (criterion 1).

(*x*) Jesus not only taught the primacy of *agape*, self-giving love; nor was it only, as the English poet was to say, that 'first he folwed it hymselve'. He also founded a community whose keynote it was, and it is in the perseverance of this community that Christians set their hope. Jesus' intention of founding a community is evident partly from his use of the title Son of Man (statement *vi*); for from Daniel on the Son of Man is thought of as a central figure with the ultimate community gathered round him, the saints of the Most High. But it is also evident from the fact that Jesus appointed a group of followers whom Paul refers to *en passant* as 'the Twelve' (criterion 2): for what can have been the point of constituting a group of twelve but that they should be the nucleus of a New Israel – as indeed they were understood to be by Matthew and Luke? Peter, similarly, was given the Aramaic surname Cephas, because Jesus took him to be in some sense a rock (criteria 2 and 5): whether he meant (as Matthew thought) the church's authority, or (as Luke thought) its pastor, we have a deliberately formed community either way. Paul, and other New Testament authors, took it that faith, hope and love were the essence of this community, and above all love, and it is difficult to think that in this they are wrong in seeing a continuity with Jesus (criterion 2). The widespread evidence of Jesus' acceptance of social outcasts into his community, in which they experienced acceptance by Jesus himself, and by those who had made less scandalous compromises with life, also tells in the same direction (criterion 6). In view of the biblical tradition, it was inevitable that this experience should be described in terms of the forgiveness of sins: we should wish to emphasize the positive side also – they found that being accepted and loved, they had a power to love others they had not known before.

(*xi*) Jesus saw his own death coming, and interpreted it as the means to a new relationship between God and his people. Such is probably inherent in Jesus' use of the Daniel Son of Man image (statement *vi*): he was to be exposed to tribulation for three days and a half as the prelude to his exaltation, and although the prophecies of Jesus' sufferings in the synoptics have certainly been embroidered, it is likely that a core of Jesus' own expectation underlies so widespread a tradition (criterion 6).[14] Paul was taught at his conversion that Jesus saw his death as destined and as meaningful (I Cor. 11.23ff.): on the night when he was betrayed, he interpreted the bread and wine of his last (Passover) meal as the symbols of the new covenant that his death would seal (criterion 4).

(*xii*) Jesus died on the cross, and for a period beginning two days later his disciples had experiences of seeing him, which convinced them that he was alive, raised from death and exalted to God's presence in power. Without such conviction it is impossible to explain the survival of the church (criterion 1); Paul was taught of it at his conversion (criterion 4); and it is the presupposition of every New Testament document (criterion 6). We are not obliged to accept the first Christians' supernaturalist account of what happened: indeed, as historians, we shall be bound to prefer a naturalist account if one can be offered, and this I shall attempt briefly below.

There is in human history a small class of people whom we may refer to as men and women of destiny. There is a groundswell to history, the changes of climate and technology, of birthrate and economic and social forces, which throw up new communities, new classes, new nations. These communities come to points of crisis, and at the crisis they may or may not produce a leader who expresses in his whole personality the community and movement of which he is a part. Such were Themistocles, Joan of Arc, Churchill. It is a part of such a person's life to know himself as destined for leadership at this moment. They believe themselves to be inspired. They hear voices. Churchill writes of his feelings at 3 a.m. on 11 May 1940, 'At last I had the authority to give directions over the whole scene. I felt as if I were walking with destiny, and that all my past life had been but a preparation for this hour and for this trial.' At such moments leadership is taken from those who, whatever their talents, do not incarnate the spirit of the people. The wily, venal, fissiparous rulers of the ancient Greek *poleis* gave way to the wisdom of Themistocles pleading union or slavery, and sent their combined fleets to Salamis. The demoralized courtiers of fifteenth-century France yielded place to a daughter of the people of faith and courage. The guilty men of Munich and the phoney war were forced to resign by the rising tide of disaster, in favour of a man who was later to say that he had but expressed the feelings of the British people at their moment of trial. In pointing to this class of men and women of destiny, I do not mean to assert an absolute distinction between them and a much broader class of men and women of vocation; whose background and abilities have been felt to be matched to the challenge of their life, and who have given of themselves in response. There is a continuum: but at the end of the continuum the perils are sharper, the gifts rarer, the sense of mystique indispensable. Only one who embodies and at the same time transcends the popular tradition, only one whose tradition is itself at the moment of flood, can do the work. Gandhi, Mao and Martin Luther King might qualify from the last generation.

The sense of destiny arises from the combination of extreme peril to the community with gifts of extreme rarity: in a slight peril many leaders would suffice, some from the stock of oligarchs in power already. It is this that defines the work of men of destiny: they are deliverers, saviours. The hosts of Xerxes have crossed the Hellespont, and he that stands will die for nought. The English hold a third of France, and the Dauphin is uncrowned. Britain is about to face her finest hour, alone against the unconquered Wehrmacht. India can be free. Black Americans have human rights. In all these cases the community is either in peril of enslavement, or in hope of liberation, and the hour is at hand when the issue must be decided.

In all the cases which I have instanced, the deliverance involved has been primarily of a political nature, though the whole freedom of the community's spirit is normally at stake along with the political kingdom. It is common for a religious freedom to be a part of this aspiration, and it may be a large part, as in the Dutch revolution under William the Silent, or the English under Cromwell. It was a very strong element with Gandhi and Luther King, but in all these cases the destiny has been the liberation of a particular people from a particular peril, and the same must be said of many purely religious men of destiny like St Francis or Luther or Ignatius. St Francis' work was the rebuilding of the thirteenth-century church, Luther's and Ignatius' the reforming of the six-teenth-century church. Like all great movements of the human spirit, these were to have repercussions for a large part of mankind, but they were understood by their founders to be *ad hoc* endeavours, called forth by the exigencies of the moment.

In Jesus' case, we have the same feeling: here is a man whose community's creative history stands at the parting of the ways. The legalism of the Pharisees, the violence of the Zealots, the opportun-ism of the Sadducees were all different denials of that creativity. A man of the people, he proclaimed a more excellent way, and drew behind him a movement. He felt himself under the divine 'must': his position in history was foretold in scripture. But in an important way Jesus was different. Both in intention and in effect, he was not the deliverer of a particular community, the saviour of a particular people: he was a man of universal destiny. He saw himself so: the Son of Man symbol which he applied to himself was such in Danielic prophecy – 'To him was given dominion and glory and kingdom, that all peoples, nations and languages should serve him; his dominion is an everlasting dominion which shall not pass away, and his kingdom one that shall not be destroyed' (Dan. 7.14). He was to be God's vicegerent, inaugurating God's kingdom that would round off human history. He was to be the ultimate deliverer, the saviour of mankind. In the sense that all men would be his subjects in a reign of humanity and responsibility, such a claim extends back into early Israelite thought, as in Psalms 47 and 87. For concrete evidence of Jesus' care for non-Israelites, we are dependent upon Mark's account of the Syro-Phoenician woman, much to the embarrassment of Matthew (criterion 3); and the less probable story of the Gentile centurion.

It is the faith of Christians that Jesus was the Christ, and insepar-able from that word is a confession of uniqueness. He was not just one of a group of men of universal destiny, with Mohammed, Gautama Buddha, etc.: he is *the* man of universal destiny. I do not intend to undertake the distasteful and unprofitable task of trying to show that the leaders of other world-religions have a less hon-ourable place than Jesus. Let their adherents make a case for them. Mine is a confessional statement. I see the growth of a community of self-giving love as the basic thrust of the will of God in human history, and I see that community as exemplified primarily in the church founded by Jesus. Christians do not need to deny the activity of God in other religions, or that they can learn from them; but they are bound to see their own movement as central, and its founder therefore as the one whose destiny transcends all others'. The crucial evidence upon which such faith rests is the impact upon the Christian of Jesus and the saints.

It is a part of the calling of men of destiny that they risk martyr-dom, and know it. Their movements draw upon them the hatred of the oppressors whom they defy, and their rare gifts of leadership make them conspicuous targets. Of those whom I have instanced, some who relied upon force, Churchill and Mao Tse-Tung, died in honour. Others, like Joan of Arc, and more especially the men of peace, Gandhi and King, risked betrayal and assassination, and died for their faith. Jesus belongs with these last; and it is this which makes sense of the Christian doctrine of the atonement. We are saved by being incorporated into the society of *agape* that Jesus founded; and that society could not have been effectively founded without the martyrdom of its founder. Jesus' death was, histori-cally, a high probability as the end of his life of self-giving love. To love as he loved was bound to evoke the hostility of the authorities; and this would, he saw (statement *xi*), end in his death, and so be the means to God's giving him the kingdom in power, the means of forging the new covenant that would replace Sinai for ever. Our acceptance of that covenant in the sacraments and life of the church

means that we are reconciled with God; and this happens increasingly as we forsake self-centred ways and give ourselves to others as
Jesus did. The church's experience is that we cannot do this by
trying, nor can we do it by meditating upon, and imitating Jesus:
but our salvation consists in our incorporation into his body the
church, where his spirit will breathe in us to live his life of love. We
are not saved merely from the consequences of lovelessness, as our
ancestors thought, whether from a literal or a metaphorical hell: we
are saved from lovelessness itself, and the meaninglessness of life
which that entails. To be saved is to love.

Alas for those whose task is the defence of the traditional doctrines of the atonement! Better Skid Row than the endless round of
empty speculations that run from the implausible to the irreligious:
the theories that point to demons more powerful than God (unless
he can cheat them), and those that posit a faceless justice more
powerful than God; those that make Christ a whipping boy, and
those that make him an international banker in merit, with
resources enough to pay off the world's balance of payments deficit.
Many such expositors end their labours with the complacent reflection, 'All these pictures are inadequate: we need them all to do
justice to the greatness of the facts': but rubbish added to rubbish
makes rubbish. Jesus' death is in fact but the crown of his life.
Gandhi knew that he could liberate India from the British only at
the risk of his life. He needed not only to go to prison, and to go on
hunger-strike, and to live with the outcastes. But he could only take
India over by compromises that would bring him enemies, enemies
fanatical enough to kill him. The cost of his achievement was not
only his sufferings throughout his life, but his final martyrdom.
Luther King could bring civil rights to the blacks of America,
similarly, only by risking his life. Not only must he be prepared to
be roughed up by southern policemen; he must also risk assassination – and the greater his success, the more likely did the assassination become. And so with Jesus. To live the life of love, to teach
love, and to found the community of love *entailed* the likelihood of
the cross. The tradition is that Jesus knew it from early on, and he
had divine prophecy to guide him as well as common sense. So we
do not need an atonement theory to explain what is already explained. We are saved into the community of love, the church,
which Jesus founded by a life of love that inexorably ended on the
cross. In this sense we may say, 'By his stripes we are healed', or
'There was no other good enough to pay the price of sin'.

Teachers of righteousness are in general a pathetic lot: for, as
Paul was quick to note, it is no use hearing what is good and

approving it, if you can't for some reason do it – and many a clergyman and social worker has learned the same lesson the sad way. Had Jesus merely lived and taught *agape* and died for it, it is difficult to think that his community would have lasted a fortnight. But by the completeness of his faithfulness unto death Jesus achieved unwittingly the destiny which he had followed all his ministry, the actualization of God's kingdom in a society of love that was permanent. For there are locked within the human psyche strong forces which an event of this quality can set in motion. There is a limit to the dissonance which man can tolerate.[15] Peter in particular had nailed his colours to the mast. He had left his home, his wife, his boat; his surname, Cephas, must imply some special degree of confidence that Jesus reposed in him (criteria 2 and 5); then came his denials – the story of Peter's disgrace was too embarrassing to be told if it were not true (criterion 3). He had boasted of his faithfulness though all others should fail; and then through a fatal twenty-four hours he had seen all that he believed in taken from him. He had slept, he had been thrice rebuked, he had run away, he had denied his master three times, he had only just escaped with his skin; and then his master had failed him, dying like any criminal. There is a type of human character, it has been often found elsewhere,[16] which does not break under such a series of blows, but which experiences a conversion. Instead of giving up its previous beliefs, and giving up the self-respect which is so vital to us, it casts about for a means of resolving the dissonance, while holding to its belief-system the more strongly. Arthur Koestler has given us an account of just such a conversion-experience in *Arrow in the Blue*,[17] in which he was turned from a half-hearted Marxist to a full-blooded evangelist for the Communist faith. On Easter Sunday morning Peter achieved the same type of resolution, a conversion experienced in the form of a vision. The amazing 'truth' dawned on him, to solve all his problems: Jesus was not dead after all – he had risen again, he was raised to God's right hand in heaven, he would soon return to establish his kingdom in power. Peter's experience was soon told to the others, and so great is the power of hysteria within a small community that in the evening, in the candlelight, with fear of arrest still a force, and hope of resolution budding in them too, it seemed as if the Lord came through the locked door to them, and away again. So was Jesus' life's work sealed. The experiences of Easter fused a faith that was to carry Jesus to divinity, and his teachings to every corner of the globe. It was by his integrity, through his ministry and in the Passion, that Jesus in fact brought about the conversions of Easter and the days following; and so involved the emotional as well as the rational element of man in the church, in a way that has continued through a chain reaction ever since.

To the first Christians these conversion visions seemed plainly to be miracles. Jesus was alive, for they had seen him; God had vindicated Jesus as his Son. The first traditions were all in the form, 'He was seen . . .' Half a century later Luke and John added stories that emphasized his materiality: how the disciples ate with him, and doubters touched him. A miraculous interpretation has become hallowed over many centuries, and it has become dear to many Christians. But it is but the last gap to be filled by the God of the gaps. Science, we used to say, hasn't explained the leap from monkey to man. Now, we often say, science has not explained the resurrection. Well, nor it has, completely: but, as I have suggested, there are psychological explanations for the 'appearances', and we do not lack ways of explaining the growth of the resurrection narratives. Are we wise then to make a miraculous explanation a last-ditch principle? We have been driven out of too many last ditches; and natural explanations, where they are at all plausible, are surely to be preferred on the basis of Occam's razor. Besides, a natural explanation is in line with all else that we have experienced about God. He works through nature, and he gives the responsibility for our world, including our church, to us.

In many ways the things which I have said about Jesus might be acceptable to a humanist. Humanists also believe in the primacy of love, and an unprejudiced humanist might be prepared to see and admire Jesus as the prime historical source for the first full teaching of love, and its realization in an ongoing human community. I have not, however, become a humanist, and my intention in using the phrase 'the man of universal destiny' is to safeguard the divine initiative in Jesus. For while words like vocation and destiny are commonly secularized so as to omit any reference to a calling or destining divine will, a Christian will not see them so. To him a man's destiny is that to which God destines him, and I understand Jesus to have been destined by God to establish the community of selfless love in the world. This notion of destiny will be understood in accordance with the notion of providence entertained by the Christian. Some more traditional Christians see God as in constant interaction with human living, calling each man to specific deeds in consequence of the ever-novel situations of life, offering the grace by which to do his will: as A. M. Farrer says, like the master oriental carpet weaver, who can include in his design the errors made by his pupils, so does the divine wisdom include the consequences of sin in his developing plan. For such a view of providence, Jesus' life was God's master-stroke. When the fullness of time had come, God revealed to Jesus his destiny; and Jesus was obedient, even unto the death of the cross – that is, he responded day by day to the ever-broadening vision of what this destiny was to demand of him.

Other less traditional Christians see God as in creative and sustaining relationship to the universe, but without *inter*acting, responding. He set the world on its path, including the built-in pattern of evolutionary development, including the rise of man with an inbuilt religious response to life, including the rise of some peoples with a sharper religious sense than others, and inevitably one – it happened to be the Israelites – with the sharpest sense of all. Once the world was on its way God did not interfere with it: but he surveys it with longing and loving care, triumphing in man's loving response, agonizing with his suffering. In such a world, with such an A-stream people as Israel, it was inevitably an Israelite on whom would fall the destiny to initiate the universal loving community; such a calling could not be exercised until a certain point of national maturity; and it then was open to any Israelite of sufficient devotion, courage and intensity of purpose to respond. The man who took up the challenge was Jesus.

It should be noted that on either view we may properly speak of the life of Jesus as the act of God. In the former case God acts upon Jesus by direct inspiration. General Montgomery won the battle of Alamein, but he was acting under the orders, and with the detailed co-operation, of General Alexander, who sent to England the telegram announcing that the enemy had been driven from North Africa. Charles II built St Paul's after the Fire of London, and so did Christopher Wren, and so did the latter's clerk of works. We are used to speaking of one enterprise as being performed by two different people, where the one is more directly concerned with the detailed decisions and actions, and the other with authorizing, inspiring, designing, enabling, etc.[18] In the latter case God acts indirectly in Jesus. In 1170 Henry II exclaimed, 'Who will rid me of this turbulent priest?': he did not command FitzUrse and the other three knights to kill Becket in Canterbury. It happened to be they who understood the king's command and obeyed. We do not dispute the Pope's justice in commanding Henry's flogging in penance, as well as in the excommunication of the four knights. It was the action of both.

In all this I have merely come full circle back to the primitive faith of the church, of Rom. 1.3f. and Acts 2 and 13, texts which I will expound in a second essay; to a christology of agency rather than of substance. In the later biblical period there arose, as I shall hope to show, a second christology, of the incarnation of a hypostasis of God; and it is this which was canonized, with all its problems, by the fathers in the creeds. The substance idea was a part of the world view of the later Roman Empire, and involves contradictions which cannot be resolved. My faith is not in the unity of substance, but in the unity of activity of God and Jesus; *homopraxis*, if a Greek word is wanted, rather than *homoousia*. Such was the understanding – so far as our documents take us – of Jesus himself, and St Peter: and it will provide a path forward round the mountain for the Christian of today.

NOTES

1. I see this anecdote has also been used by F. Borsch in *God's Parable*, SCM Press 1975, p. 1.
2. See J. Ridley, *Thomas Cranmer*, Oxford University Press 1962, pp. 1–12.
3. Caution is needed in applying this criterion. There may be things which embarrass us, or embarrassed Matthew and Luke, which did not embarrass Mark at all.
4. The foreign words may have been retained by Mark for use by Christian healers, but this would not imply their creation by him; cf. D. E. Nineham, *Saint Mark*, Penguin Books 1963, pp. 162, 204.
5. See J. A. Emerton, '*Maranatha* and *Ephphatha*', *Journal of Theological Studies*, vol. 18, no.2 1967, pp. 427ff. The same mood of the same verb comes in Isa. 35.5 (*tippathahna*), 'The eyes of the blind shall be opened, and the ears of the deaf *unstopped.*' Using the rare word *mogilalos* for the dumb man in the story, Mark shows that he thinks of it as a fulfilment of Isa. 35. If the Semitic word goes back to Jesus, it is evidence that he saw himself as fulfilling Isaiah's prophecy of the coming of God to save.
6. R. Bultmann suggested that such words were 'stylistic elements' in the telling of miracle stories (*The History of the Synoptic Tradition*, second edition, Blackwell 1968, pp. 213f., 222), but this does not seem to show that they are unhistorical. Their use in church healings might be rather limited.
7. Paul sees the apostles as Jesus' delegates, continuing the use of his authority; the prophets as inspired to speak as he spoke under God's inspiration; the teachers as continuing his teaching. On the other hand, speaking with tongues is new, a gift of the Spirit. For continuity in healing, cf. Acts 9.34, 'Aeneas, Jesus Christ heals you.'
8. An exception is I Enoch 1–36, 91–104.
9. Mark's reticence can be interpreted in a quite different sense, viz. that Jesus' Messiahship was an invention of the church, covered over by Mark with the device of a Messianic secret, divulged first by God and the demons, understood slowly by the disciples and finally by the centurion: cf. Wrede, *Das Messiasgeheimnis in den Evangelien*, Göttingen 1901, ET, *The Messianic Secret*, James Clarke 1971. For a recent criticism of this theory see E. Trocmé, 'Is there a Markan Christology?' in *Christ and Spirit in the New Testament* (ed.), B. Lindars and S. S. Smalley, Cambridge University Press 1973, pp. 8ff.: it is especially striking that Jesus' commands to silence are so often balanced by commands to proclaim later in the gospel.

Mark thought the mystery of the kingdom had to be first hidden and then revealed (cf. ch. 4); and it is easy to believe that his theory was rooted in what actually happened. For a full discussion see G. Minette de Tillesse, *Le Secret messianique dans l'Évangile de Marc*, Paris, 1968.

10. For recent defences of this highly controversial statement, see J. Coppens, 'Les Logia du Fils de l'Homme dans l'Évangile de Marc', in *L'Évangile de Marc* (ed.), M. Sabbe, Louvain 1974, pp. 487–528; cf. B. Lindars, 'Re-enter the Apocalyptic Son of Man', *New Testament Studies*, vol. 22, 1975, pp. 52–72. There is a good criticism of attempts (*a*) to dissociate Jesus from the use of Son of Man as a title (e.g. by G. Vermes, Appendix E to M. Black, *An Aramaic Approach to the Gospels and Acts*, third edition, Oxford University Press 1967); (*b*) to limit his use of Son of Man to this-world contexts (e.g. by E. Schweizer, *Erniedrigung und Erhöhung bei Jesus und seinen Nachfolgen*, ET 1960); or to future contexts (e.g. by R. Bultmann, *The History of the Synoptic Tradition*); in F. Borsch, *The Son of Man in Myth and History*, SCM Press 1967.

11. The one like the son of man is sometimes interpreted, e.g. by J. Barr in *Peake's Commentary on the Bible* (ed.), M. Black and H. H. Rowley, Nelson 1962, pp. 597f., as of the angel of God's people, rather than as the people itself (and its leader). But 7.26f. is in close parallel to 7.9–14, and the interpretation of the evangelists is plainly of the earthly leader's humiliation; so if Jesus used the concept, he is likely to have read it as they did.

12. It is often suggested, e.g. by D. E. Nineham, *Saint Mark*, p. 392, that the word was the church's 'reverent conjecture', derived from the Lord's Prayer. But it is more likely that the case is the other way round: that the Lord's Prayer is composed by Matthew from Jesus' prayers in Gethsemane and teaching on prayer (Mark 11.25) – see my *Midrash and Lection in Matthew*, SPCK 1974, pp. 296–301.

13. J. Jeremias, *The Prayers of Jesus*, SCM Press 1967; cf. G. Vermes, *Jesus the Jew*, Collins 1973, pp. 210–13. But Abba is not the same as 'Our Father in Heaven', and the single text Vermes offers (b Taan. 23b) does not provide an instance of God being addressed as Abba.

14. See above, note 9.

15. Cf. L. Festinger, *When Prophecy Fails*, Minneapolis 1956; *A Theory of Cognitive Dissonance*, Evanston 1957; W. Sargant, *Battle for the Mind*, London 1957.

16. S. de Sanctis, *Religious Conversion*, London 1927.

17. Koestler, *Arrow in the Blue*, London 1952.

18. Cf. G. D. Kaufman, *God the Problem*, Harvard 1972, ch. 6.

4

The Two Roots of the Christian Myth

MICHAEL GOULDER

I began the last chapter with an autobiographical confession: in my
early ministry I was still a trembling believer in Chalcedonian
orthodoxy – Jesus was God the Son, of one substance with the
Father, who came down from heaven. Trembling beliefs do not
alter themselves: they are reinforced daily by the repetition of the
liturgy. When I look back, I think that the firmest plank on which
my creed rested was the familiar passage in John 1, 'The Word
became flesh and dwelt among us . . .'. This was not alone, for there
were similar statements in Col. 1 and Phil. 2, and hints of the same
in many of the Pauline letters, and in Hebrews. Where had St John
got the doctrine from? Not from Jesus (my Congregational friend
was right thus far). Bultmann, I knew, had speculated about a
Gnostic Redeemer-myth, and others had spoken of the heavenly
man in Iranian thought, or the pre-existence of Wisdom in the Old
Testament: but none of these seemed very convincing, and they had
been criticized by respected scholars. The answer seemed plain:
John had the doctrine *by inspiration.* Just as a scientist, allowing his
mind to scan the phenomena of some unsolved problem, may hit
upon a plausible hypothesis causing him to cry *Heureka* in his bath,
so the apostle praying, or very likely pen in hand, struggling to
inspire his congregation to faith, suddenly saw with unmistakable
clarity the truth about Christ which had hitherto eluded him. He
was the Word of God, become flesh. The circumstances of John's
doctrinal development are misty; and mist, notoriously, tends to foster
mystery. But at least the inspiration theory was the best in the field; and
even if the expositors of incarnation-theology found it hard to achieve
clarity, better that, I thought, than demythologization.

Historical study is the implacable enemy of such a view of inspira-aion: when we remove the mist, we remove the mystery. It shows, I believe, two roots to the Christian myth, that is, the Christian account of what went on, goes on and will go on behind the scenes of this world. One is the Galilean eschatological myth, taught by Jesus and the earliest Christians; the other is the Samaritan gnostical myth, which is less well known, and to this I shall devote the central part of the present chapter. As with the account I have given of Jesus, we are forming a reconstruction of history, and such reconstructions can never be more than probable. There are other reconstructions which would point to the same conclusions on the doctrinal plane; indeed, my fellow-essayists had reached these conclusions by other routes, and may still prefer them. But this was the route that first convinced me, and I offer it in the hope that the reader may find it convincing also.

In the programmatic opening paragraph of Acts, Luke designates the advance of the church as being in four stages: in Jerusalem, and in all Judea and Samaria, and to the end of the earth. Six chapters are given to the Jerusalem mission (2–7), two to the Judean mission (8.26–40; 9.32–11.18), sixteen to the mission beyond Palestine (13–28): the Samaritan mission is confined to twenty-two verses (8.4–25). Two features of the Samaritan story are singular, and raise questions.[1] Why do the Samaritans have to be 'confirmed' by the apostles? Baptism elsewhere in Acts conveys the gift of the Holy Spirit without mention of the laying on of hands, and apostolic action is not required – Philip himself baptizes the eunuch without either in the same chapter. What was the real standing of Simon? Luke at first tells us that he claimed to be 'that power of God which is called Great', 'somebody great' (Acts 8.9f.); which seems to imply that Simon thought he was God incarnate. Later Luke appears to smooth such blasphemy into the relatively harmless statement that he was a magician. Perhaps the second was necessary to justify Simon's acceptance into the church, but the first was the uncomfortable fact evident (as we shall see) from his later history. As Luke was not obliged to include Samaria in his Proem, it looks as if the Samaritan mission was something of an embarrassment to him. It was important enough that it could not just be mentioned in passing, like the Galilean mission: but there were not any very satisfactory stories to tell about it – rather like a Marxist history of the Revolution, perhaps, dealing with Trotsky.

The impression that Samaria had been a success, but that there were aspects of the matter which it would not be edifying to mention, is confirmed by the comments of Hegesippus (*c.* AD 160), which are preserved in Eusebius:[2]

> After James the Just had suffered martyrdom ... Symeon was appointed bishop ... They used to call the church a virgin: for she had not yet been corrupted by vain teachings. But Thebuthis, because he was not made bishop, began secretly to corrupt her from the seven sects among the people (sc. the Jews) to which he himself belonged: from which came Simon (whence the Simonians), and Cleobius (whence the Cleobians), and Dositheus (whence the Dositheans), and Gorthaeus (whence the Goratheni), and the Masbothaeans. Springing from these the Menandrianists and the Marcianists ....

Hegesippus leaves Thebuthis' affiliations obscure, but there is no doubt about the five first-generation and various second-generation sects which he alleges him to have spawned. Simon is said to be a Samaritan by Luke, and Justin (himself from Samaria) names his native village as Gitto.[3] Cleobius is associated with Simon in the *Didascalia*;[4] Dositheus is a colleague of Simon in the *Clementines*[5] and many later texts, and is said to be a Samaritan by Origen[6] and others; Epiphanius couples the Gorathenians and Dositheans and Sebuaeans (thought to be the same as the Masbothaeans) as three of the four Christian Samaritan sects;[7] and Justin tells us that Menander was also a Samaritan, from the village of Capparetaea.[8] The heterodox sects in Hegesippus are all of them Samaritan in origin. It seems safe to say that there was a strong faction of Samaritan Christians in Jerusalem in the 50s, but that they failed to get their nominee appointed bishop after James' martyrdom, and in the decades that followed became the nucleus of fissiparous sects.

The extent to which Samaritan influence was at work in mainstream Christianity is revealed by the number of instances, especially in Luke–Acts and John, where there is a positive correlation between details in the Samaritan Torah and Targum against both MT and LXX.[9] Acts 7 is a particular instance often cited, but it would be a mistake to limit Samaritan influence to Stephen's speech: the Samaritan 'Messianic' text, for example, Deut. 18.15,[10] which was hardly so used by the rabbis, is cited under Peter's name at Acts 3.22 as well as at 7.37, and is referred to in John 1.21 and elsewhere. John in particular shows signs of Samaritan sympathy, as well as of detailed background. The greater part of chapter 4 is given to a mission by Jesus to a woman of Samaria, who is converted and brings her fellow-citizens to faith, in contrast with the much less successful dialogue with Nicodemus in the previous chapter. Worship on Gerizim is said to be a mistake, but so is worship at

Jerusalem: salvation is of the Jews, but Samaria's claims are worth refuting. At John 8.48 the Jews say to Jesus, 'Are we not right in saying that you are a Samaritan and have a demon?': this raises the suggestion that John's own church in Ephesus was accused by Jews of being infected with Samaritanism. In John 1, in place of the five first-called apostles of the synoptic tradition, Peter, Andrew, James, John and Matthew/Levi, we have an unnamed apostle, Andrew, Peter, Philip and Nathanael. The apostle Philip was believed by the Ephesian church in the 130s to have been Philip the evangelist of Samaria,[11] and Nathanael is promised that he will see the angels of God ascending and descending on the Son of Man, a clear reference to the vision of Jacob at Bethel, the Samaritan sanctuary.[12] Nathanael, for what it is worth, is a Hebrew form of Dositheus (Nathan = Dosi = give, 'El = Theos = God).

A word should also be said about the Epistle to the Hebrews. Jews certainly on occasion called themselves *Hebraioi*,[13] but the Samaritans, who were not *Ioudaioi*, use the name frequently: and this suggests that the epistle may have been addressed to Samaritan Christians. Such an idea finds confirmation in the otherwise curious fact that the sacrificial argument in the epistle is all drawn from the Tabernacle, not the Temple: for Samaritans had only the Pentateuch as their scriptures, and so honoured the Tabernacle, but abhorred the Jerusalem Temple. The heroes of faith in Heb. 11, similarly, up to the appendix ('The time would fail me to tell . . .'), cover the Pentateuch and the Book of Joshua, which were the biblical books acceptable to Samaritans; and precisely similar lists of heroes of knowledge are present in Samaritan sources.[14]

It was the unanimous and confident opinion of the fathers that the Samaritan teachers had been the first Gnostics,[15] and Irenaeus himself gives a considerable account of the Simonians,[16] and a few lines on the Menandrians,[17] which substantiate this. Menander and his disciple Satornilus taught in Antioch; another disciple of Menander, Basilides, settled and taught in Alexandria,[18] where, according to the Clementines, Simon and Dositheus had earlier spread their doctrines.[19] Hence there would seem to be a *prima facie* case from the New Testament and church tradition for claiming that the Samaritan Christians were a powerful section of the first-century church, and that their movement grew into Christian Gnosticism in the second. While this movement presented a challenge to Galilean Christianity everywhere, it would appear to have enjoyed a virtual monopoly in early times in Egypt and eastern Syria.[20] To read Acts, we might think that the church's mission went only north and west: but the rising curtain at the end of the second century reveals the church to us as a flourishing tree, with branches not only in Italy, Greece and Asia Minor, the fields of Paul's labours, but all over Syria and Egypt, the latter with a 'heterodox', gnostical, theology. It is the aim of this chapter to argue: (*a*) that our knowledge of Samaritan theology enables us to form a picture of the position that would be likely to arise in an encounter with Christianity; and (*b*) that the New Testament documents portray a dialectic, in which the primitive eschatological gospel reached a synthesis with just such a position.

Our principal difficulty with Samaritan studies is the late date of most of the evidence: except for the Samaritan Pentateuch and Targum, and occasional references in non-Samaritan sources, we are dependent on documents from the fourth century AD, notably the Memar (Teaching of) Marqah, and later. Some parts of Samaritan liturgies are old, but it is not safe to argue that Samaritans are conservative, and so not likely to have developed their beliefs. If we are to make any claims about first-century Samaritan teaching, therefore, we have either to show that the positions taken by Marqah and in the liturgies belong to the community's basic stance; or provide reasons for thinking that such positions were actually taken in the early period. In this connection the traditions about Simon are of especial interest to us, since he was a leading figure among those Samaritans who actually became Christians.

The break between Jerusalem and Samaria took place slowly over a period of centuries, beginning with the building of an independent Temple on Mount Gerizim in Alexander's time.[21] The Samaritans took over the Jewish Pentateuch, making a limited number of changes to the text. Much of the Pentateuch is old pro-Joseph material, and therefore raised no difficulties. Jerusalem is not mentioned, but Shechem and Bethel, the Samaritan sites, featured largely in Genesis; and in Deuteronomy worship is repeatedly commanded on Mount Gerizim and Mount Ebal, above Shechem. Joshua was accepted, as he distributed the land in Shechem, and renewed the covenant there. The troubles began, in Samaritan belief, when Eli moved the sanctuary to Shiloh; and the tendency of the D-histories, which is solidly anti-Northern from Judg. 17 on, made them unacceptable as scripture. Nor are the writing prophets much better: so the Samaritan Bible is the Pentateuch alone, and revelation is cut off with Moses. This basic difference from Judaism entails an important theological cleft. The Jews saw God as *active in history*: the prophets had descried his activity in blessing and chastisement in the past, and such activity continued into the present with rabbinic miracles and the Bath Qol, even though there were no more prophets to foretell it. To the Samaritans, God had *withdrawn from history*. The Moses–Joshua period was an era of his good pleasure (*rahuta*), when he had been active; the period since Eli was an era of his turning away (*panuta*), in which he did nothing. The community's hope rested therefore on the coming of a new age of good pleasure, when he would be active again. Not only are these concepts very widespread in Samaritan literature, and implied in some early texts;[22] but they are logically entailed by the rejection of the whole Jewish prophetic corpus.

It is possible, in the light of this, to understand the following five features of Samaritan theology:

1. Since God cannot be experienced through history, *he is experienced through revelation*, i.e. scripture. In the nature of the case some passages are more revelatory than others, and the chapters on which far and away the most Samaritan meditation was spent are Gen. 1 and Ex. 34. All Samaritan synagogue services open with the reading of Gen. 1.1–2.7,[23] which is especially revelatory of God's relation to the world. He is often thought of as the ultimate light, the source of all light in creation.[24] Marqah says, for example, 'Respond to the light within you, and it will develop until it is one with the Light'.[25] Ex. 34 is particularly significant as in it God reveals his name to Moses, and thus the final mystery to his people. Verses 6 and 7, 'The LORD, the LORD . . .', have been worn away in some Samaritan manuscripts by constant kissing.[26] The passage is repeated and referred to *ad nauseam* in the liturgies: e.g. 'You can grasp all in your hand with the secret of the sacred Name . . . Thy name is Forgiver of iniquity, transgression and sin, Merciful, Gracious and (All-)Seeing, Supporter, Healer, Bearer, Pardoner.'[27] Such an elaboration of the Ex. 34 text testifies both to the community's yearning for forgiveness, so that the period of displeasure may cease; and also to its attitude to scripture as a revelation of God's secret nature in eternity, rather than his present action.

2. It follows from this that God's revelation should often be spoken of as secrets or mysteries, and that there should be much talk of *wisdom and knowledge of God*. 'Let him who would have knowledge of God reflect';[28] 'from the works that thou hast made, those that have knowledge of thee know that thou art the God of them';[29] 'Teach me and make me wise, make me knowing and guide me.'[30] There is an elite, those who have knowledge – 'all wise men in their wisdom, all men of understanding'.[31] There are exercises by which this knowledge can be attained, or it may come by

dreams:[32] 'No man sees the Lord except through wisdom.'[33] The High Priest is expected to be a prime exponent of such wisdom.

A short passage from Marqah illustrates the gnosticizing tendency of Samaritanism:

We turn from this to matters that involve ourselves. Let us enquire of the origins of wisdom, why the sections of the law were not written with all of the twenty-two letters, but were in fact written with the absence of seven. I have already revealed them to you that you may understand (Tit, Nun, Simcat, Phi, Sadi, Qoph, Tau). As for there being seven, no more, nor less, it is good for us to enquire into this mystery. ... Their total amounts to 789, which is informative and instructive about a momentous matter, ... each bringing understanding to pass, because it speaks and makes itself complete with all knowledge, for knowledge is a light that shines in the heart (Memar, VI.2).

Even if these sentences are three centuries after the church's Samaritan mission, they cohere well with the basic Samaritan view of a God not known in his present providential activity, but in the revelation once given to Moses.

3. A God who, as we might put it irreverently, spends the centuries from Eli on sulking, is inevitably a remote God, and the Samaritans often speak of him by abstract names – Power, Truth, Mercy, Eternal Life, etc.[34] The name Power, for example, seems to lie behind Simon Magus' claim in Acts 8.10, to be 'the power of God which is called Great'.[35] The tension between the God who withdraws himself from history and the God who reveals himself through Moses, is expressed by a *dualism* of language in which God is spoken of as the Pristine God (*'Elah qamma'ah*), or the Divine One (*'Elahoth*), while his hypostasis which reveals is spoken of as the Glory. Marqah writes:[36]

Moses only expounded the holy scriptures when God commanded it. The Glory and the assembly of all the heavenly angels and the Pristine God were gathered together when he wrote with his own hands, while these stood and magnified the commandments and commanded what must be done. The Divine One appeared and established the covenant. The Glory appeared and magnified what was good. The angels came to magnify what was glorious and they were all assembled for Adam. The Divine One formed him and the breath of life was breathed into him. The Glory made him complete with a great spirit; the two of them were clad in two crowns of great light.

The strongly dualist note in this passage is evident from (*i*) the remarkable expression, 'the Pristine God', (*ii*) the mention of the Glory before him, with the angels between, (*iii*) the parallel activities of the Divine One and the Glory, especially in the creation of Adam, (*iv*) the expression 'the two of them' (*tereyon*), which can only refer to the Divine One and the Glory. In the first part of the passage the context is the giving of the commandments and covenant in Ex. 34 ('with his own hands', Ex. 34.1); in the second it is the creation of Adam in Gen. 2. In so strongly biblicist a religion as Samaritanism, we should look for an origin to such dualistic expressions in the Bible text, and the answer for Gen. 1f. is probably in the differing names for God. In the P creation story in Gen. 1 it is God (*'Elohim*) who makes/creates man; in the J. story in Gen. 2 it is the LORD God (*Yhwh 'Elohim*) who forms man and breathes into him the breath of life. Two accounts of creation, two names of God; hence a duality in the Godhead.

The Ex. 34 passage is cited in full by Marqah a little earlier,[37]

The LORD, a God merciful . . . to the third and fourth generation (6f.).

He comments,

When the True One proclaimed the first Ten (words) before him (Moses), the Glory repeated them before him. He (the Glory) responded and also proclaimed ten (words). When the True One proclaimed, he (Moses) was not permitted to proclaim, but when the Glory proclaimed, he was permitted to do so. The first of the Ten which the Glory proclaimed was *Yhwh*, and the last of them the word *'Emet* (i.e. Ex. 34.6b).

We have thus a second instance of dualist language in the same Ex. 34 context; but this time there is no double account, nor use of two names of God. It is likely that the dualist language is due to the curious phrasing of Ex. 34.5: 'And *Yhwh* descended in the cloud and stood with him there, and called by the name of *Yhwh*.' A literal reading of the text suggests a duality: the first *Yhwh* in the cloud will be the glory of the LORD in the cloud referred to in Ex. 24.15f., etc.; the second, on whose name the first calls, will be the True One, the Pristine God.

There are many later texts in Samaritan literature which stress the unity of the Godhead: how are these to be reconciled with the plainly dualist material in Memar Marqah VI.3? Similar tensions in biblical, and in other Samaritan, writings would suggest a slow triumph of monist orthodoxy. In Israel monotheism triumphed while leaving the earlier plurality of gods still visible in Psalms 82 and 89. A parallel in Samaritanism is suggested by H. G. Kippenberg.[38] In the early AD period Dositheus claimed to be the prophet like Moses; later Samaritan writing tends to suppress this claim, but frequently asks the polemical rhetorical question, 'Who is like Moses . . . ?' Perhaps similarly the very insistence on the unity of God in Samaritanism is due to the memory of an earlier Binitarian stream such as is visible here.

4. Now the point which is cardinal for our purposes is that Simon Magus took himself to be an *incarnation* of one person of this binity: there is evidence for this on a broad front, which throws the dating of the conceptions involved back to the 30s of the first century, and into that very section of the Samaritan community with which we are most concerned, the Samaritan Christians. I have already noted Luke's embarrassment with Simon's claim to be 'somebody great', 'that power of God which is called Great' (Acts 8.9f.). E. Haenchen comments,[39]

Luke rightly recognized in *megale* a title, whereas *tou theou* (cf. Luke 22.69) is a mere gloss, and misleading at that: thus the 'great power' is not *a* power of God, but the highest divinity itself. Simon was thus not just a pseudo-Messiah: he claimed to be far more.

Kippenberg shows that *heilah rabbah*, corresponding to *megale dynamis*, is a phrase from Samaritan tradition.[40]

Justin, himself a native of Samaria, writes:[41]

There was a Samaritan, Simon, a native of the village of Gitto, who in the reign of Claudius Caesar, and in your royal city of Rome, did mighty acts of magic. He was considered a god, and as a god was honoured by you with a statue, which . . . bore this inscription . . . 'Simoni Deo Sancto'. And almost all the Samaritans, and a few even of other nations, worship him, and acknowledge him as the first God; and a woman, Helena, who went about with him at that time, and had formerly been a prostitute, they say is the first Idea (Ennoia), generated by him.

Whether or not Justin had been deceived over the statue, which may have been in honour of the Sabine deity Semo Sancus, there is no gainsaying Justin's observation that in his day almost all the Samaritans in Rome held Simon to be a god, and worshipped him. Nor is Simon himself the only incarnation; for Helena is believed to be the incarnation of the first Ennoia. Thus Justin supports and amplifies the Lucan tradition about Simon, as Haenchen interprets it.

But could this not merely mean that Simon had taken over the Pauline conception of incarnation and applied it to himself? Well, hardly: for the term that he used of himself, as reported by Hippolytus, Clement of Alexandria and the Pseudo-Clementines, is not a Pauline term. Simon called himself the Standing One (*Stans, Hestos, Qa'em*); and it is plain that this mysterious title represented a claim to divinity. Clement writes[42] of Simon's followers who 'wish to conform their lives to the Standing One whom they worship'; Hippolytus[43] of 'He who stands, who stood and who will stand'; the Clementines of his 'being addressed as the Standing

One, meaning by this name that I shall not be dissolved, my body itself subsisting of divinity, so as to endure for ever'.[44] Hippolytus is thought to be citing from a Simonian tract, *Megale Apophaxsis*.[45] Now the origin of the title[46] lies before us in Ex. 34, the passage to which I have referred: 'And the LORD descended in the cloud and *stood* with him there, and proclaimed the name of the LORD.' So also Marqah, in the piece cited above: '(The Glory and the angels) stood *qa'mu*) and magnified the commandments and commanded what must be done.' Ten words are spoken of the name of the Divine One; but what is said of the Glory, as Marqah calls it, of Yhwh as it stands undifferentiated in Exodus? It is said that he stood by Moses. It is this hypostasis of God of which Simon claims to be the incarnation; and he takes the title from the classic Samaritan text on the nature of the Godhead; the very text which we find expounded in a binitarian sense by Marqah. So dualism and a doctrine of incarnation were accepted features of belief among some of the Samaritans who actually became Christians in the first decade of the church's life.

5. Samaritan expectations of the future were less developed than those of Jews at the turn of the era. Both Jewish and Christian sources in the main say that Samaritans *did not believe in the resurrection* of the dead,[47] often aligning them with the Sadducees in this respect. This is entirely credible because there is no thought of resurrection in the Pentateuch, and the doctrine was still a controversial innovation in Judaism, deriving its impetus from the experiences of the Maccabaean War and from the prophecy of Daniel, neither of which was a part of Samaritan life. The steady feature of Samaritan eschatology is a final age of God's good pleasure, associated with the Day of Vengeance and Recompense prophesied in Deut. 32.35f., 'Vengeance is mine, and recompense . . .' This was probably taken as it was written, in purely this-worldly terms. Elaborations on this continuous element are various, and in many cases probably later. The oldest concept is likely to have been that of 'the prophet like unto Moses', whose coming is promised in Deut. 18.15, 18;[48] for this text was inserted in the Samaritan Pentateuch after the Ten Commandments in Ex. 20, and Dositheus claimed to have been the prophet like unto Moses in the first century AD.[49] The disciples of both Simon and Dositheus interpreted their master's teachings not in terms of resurrection but of immortality: Simon would stand, he would not be dissolved;[50] Dositheus would not die.[51] The success of the Dosithean sect caused a revulsion, however, and Marqah never cites the text. In place of it we find the Taheb, probably to be understood as the Reformer, who is

a vague and somewhat colourless figure in classical Samaritan literature, and who only came into his own in later times;[52] or Moses is
thought of as returning himself to reveal the Tabernacle hidden on
Mount Gerizim;[53] or a place is found for Joseph.[54] We cannot
with any confidence suppose any of these last ideas to have had free
currency in the first century.

Now it is not difficult to see what kind of belief would be likely to
arise when Philip came to Samaria in the 30s with the story of
Jesus' life, death and resurrection. The cross was, as Paul says, a
stumbling-block to faith: and small wonder. The term *Christos*
means the anointed king of the line of David, and the function of
kings is to reign. When Messiah came, he would lead Israel to
victory, like General Sharon in the 1973 war, and establish the
Jewish empire from Morocco to Indonesia. Crucified Messiahs are
paradoxes, and hard to sell. The Petro-Pauline churches justified
the paradox by appeal to Daniel. The Son of Man in Dan. 7 had to
suffer, finally to suffer eschatological agonies for a time and two
times and half a time; then he would be exalted to God's right
hand, and given universal dominion. Jesus had suffered indeed, and
he had been three days in the tomb until his resurrection to God's
right hand: a few more years at the most, and he would come at the
Parousia, and judge mankind. So Mark and Matthew, and in the
view of many, Luke. Paul, a born theologian, revelled in paradox:
O the depth of the riches, both of the wisdom and the knowledge of
God! Christ redeemed us from the curse of the law, having become
a curse for us; his death was a sacrifice, the cancelling of the bond
that stood against us, a means of forgiveness for the sins done
aforetime, our Passover-sacrifice to bring us out of Egypt, he
became sin for us: and so on. His resurrection was God's vindi-
cation of him.

How could any of this cut ice in Samaria? David was not in the
Samaritan Bible; he was the arch-apostate who had set up worship
at Jerusalem. The Messiah was not a Samaritan concept;
Samaritans had not heard of Daniel or the Son of Man. Their faith
was in the restoration of the cult on Gerizim, not in one whose
death might be a sacrifice; and resurrection was, in all probability, a
foreign notion to them. It would be inevitable that, in a community
that thought in terms of a second hypostasis of the Godhead, and
of its taking form as a man, the Christian mission must sooner or
later lay claim to the fulfilment of such notions in Jesus, or fail.
Philip might begin by preaching Jesus as the prophet like unto
Moses, but in the end he must keep up with the Simon Magus's. He

cannot have spoken of him as a Jewish son of David, but ultimately as a Samaritan God become man: and in place of the primitive eschatology, the stress would now fall on a protology.

For the eschatologists the war is only half-won. Our forces have crossed to the west bank of the canal; there has been an unfortunate and apparently disastrous cease-fire; but empire shall be ours shortly. The eschatologist looks for more action. For the protologist this is not nearly so evident. The Great Power has come in the form of Jesus to reveal the truth, to give us knowledge of the Divine One. Through him, and through the Gerizim traditions, we know what lies behind the universe. We know the secrets of creation, and knowledge is what matters. This is eternal life, that we should know God and Jesus Christ whom he has sent. With his coming the age of good pleasure has been inaugurated, and we have already begun to share in his triumph. We have seen in him the Prophet like unto Moses who has instituted a new commandment. The Day of Recompense is still ahead, but already there is light, and we can walk in it. The protologist does not really need more action: he looks, like Mr Rabin, for a deeper knowledge of the war's having been won already.

Thus a Samaritan christology would tend to contribute five things to a hitherto Galilean interpretation of the significance of Jesus: (*i*) an emphasis on wisdom and knowledge as the primary fruits of conversion, rather than faith and love; (*ii*) the myth of Jesus' pre-existence in the Godhead, and of his incarnation; (*iii*) a 'glory'-ministry instead of a Son-of-Man ministry, with Moses instead of David as the type-figure; (*iv*) a minimizing of the cross and resurrection – Jesus should rather just go his way to the Father; and (*v*) a realized eschatology rather than a futurist eschatology. In addition, the emphasis on revelation of the mysteries transcending the world would tend to issue in a depreciation of this world, with ethical corollaries of both ascetic and antinomian kinds, as in second-century Gnosticism. All these emphases are characteristic of Paul's opponents at Corinth, and lie behind the controversies of the next two hundred years.

I turn now to the New Testament evidence, which seems to show these five Samaritan tendencies as the beliefs of Paul's opponents, and the source of the dialectic leading to the synthesis of classical orthodoxy:

1. One of Paul's most admirable qualities is his flexibility, his ability to steal the opposition's clothes while they are bathing. Do we need letters of commendation? Some do, but surely not the

founder-apostle. But, come to think of it, you yourselves are our letter of commendation, a letter from Christ written with the Spirit on tablets of human hearts. There is a trump for your ace. It is the same with the claims to wisdom and knowledge which caused the apostle to fret in I Cor. 1–3. 'Christ did not send me to . . . preach with eloquent wisdom . . . "I will destroy the wisdom of the wise, and the understanding of the understanding will I thwart". Where is the wise man? . . . Has not God made foolish the wisdom of the world? . . . I did not come proclaiming to you the testimony of God in lofty words or wisdom . . . my speech and my message were not in plausible words of wisdom.' Paul begins by contrasting his own simple preaching style with the eloquence and wisdom of the other missionaries, but soon moves over to attack worldly wisdom as a thing contemptible. But then, he bethinks himself, among the mature we do impart wisdom, although it is not a wisdom of this age or of the rulers of this age; we have received not the spirit of the world but the Spirit that is of God, that we might understand the gifts bestowed on us by God: and we impart this in words not taught by human wisdom but taught by the Spirit.

Paul will steal the other missionaries' wisdom, but their knowledge he will not touch, or not in I Corinthians. 'We know that "all of us possess gnosis". "Gnosis" puffs up, but love builds up . . . However, not all possess this gnosis' – some Christians believe that the meat really has been offered to idols, and their conscience is defiled. 'Take care . . . For if any one sees you, a man of gnosis, at table in an idol's temple', might he not be led to sin? 'And so by your gnosis this weak brother is destroyed.' 'Knowledge' does a lot of harm. 'If I have prophetic powers and understand all mysteries and all gnosis . . . but have not love, I am nothing' (8.1, 7, 10 and 11; 13.2). It is not mentioned among the three cardinal virtues. However, by II Corinthians Paul has appropriated knowledge as well as wisdom: 'But thanks be to God, who . . . through us spreads the fragrance of the knowledge of him (Christ) everywhere'; '(God) has shone in our hearts to give the light of the knowledge of the glory of God in the face of Christ'; 'by purity, knowledge, forbearance, kindness, the Holy Spirit'; 'Now as you excel in everything – in faith, in utterance, in knowledge'; 'we destroy arguments and every proud obstacle to the knowledge of God'; 'Even if I am unskilled in speaking, I am not in knowledge' (2.14; 4.6; 6.6; 8.7; 10.5; 11.6; cf. I Cor. 1.5). No doubt Paul would have drawn a line between the knowledge of Christ and the knowledge of all mysteries claimed by the others; and with his unquenchable love of paradox can glory in folly also – 'Let no one think me foolish; but' (come to think of it) 'even if you do . . .' But it seems plain that the two Samaritan categories, wisdom and knowledge, have been introduced into the church by his opponents, and finally accepted by Paul himself.

Once wisdom and knowledge were made at home in the church, they became a growth industry. By the early 60s Paul (if it is he) is praying that the Colossians may be filled with the knowledge of God's will in all spiritual wisdom and understanding (1.9f., 15ff., 25ff.; 2.2f., 8, 23; 3.9, 16). In Ephesians (1.9, 17f.; 3.3ff.) all is wisdom and insight, and knowledge of mysteries and revelation – a far cry from I Corinthians. The verbs *oida* and *ginosko* hardly occur in the synoptics: both come more than fifty times in John. The knowledge of God which John values is a personal one, and in this eternal life consists: but in Ephesians we are on the road to the knowledge falsely so called, with its mythologies and genealogies, against which the Pastorals were written; and, in time, Irenaeus' *Adversus Haereses*.

2. I Thessalonians was written about AD 50, before Paul had any contact with Samaritan theology, and the myth which he taught in Thessalonica was the straight Galilean eschatology. Jesus is God's Son (1.10), but this is not integrated into the picture, which is entirely concerned with his earthly life, his present activity in heaven and his imminent return: what may be called a take-off-and-landing myth. There are thirty-four references in the letter to Jesus, the Lord Jesus, etc., and of these perhaps six are to his earthly life, eleven to the Parousia and the other seventeen to his present life in heaven guiding the church, etc. There is no reference to the pre-existence, and there is considerable stress on the Parousia, which comes in every chapter casually as well as when it is the central topic in 4.13ff. Jesus was a man on earth, he has now been resurrected and has received authority, he will come again. It is no surprise that pre-existence is not mentioned, because it is inconceivable to a Jew: Messiah was the long-awaited scion of the line of David (or sometimes of Levi), to whom the covenant of eternal kingship was given in II Sam. 7.

That Paul inherited this belief from earlier Christians,[55] and believed it in an unassimilated way himself, is plain from two passages in Romans. Rom. 1.3f.: '. . . the gospel concerning his Son, who was descended from [literally, who came to be out of the seed of] David according to the flesh, and designated Son of God in power according to the Spirit of holiness, by his resurrection from the dead'. Jesus was the Messiah; that is, he came from David's seed physically (according to the flesh). In Rom. 9.5 he makes the same point, speaking of the Jews: 'of their race, according to the flesh, is Christ'. God did not by-pass the normal process of human generation in Paul's view: a man *is* the seed of his father in Jewish thought, the mother being merely the vessel in which the seed grows, and Jesus was of David's seed in the Jewish race according to the flesh. Paul sees the tension between his two beliefs, in the sheer humanity of the Christ of Jewish expectation, and in the Son of God whom Jesus in the tradition claimed to be. He thinks to resolve the matter by a two-levels view, *kata sarka* and *kata pneuma*. Jesus had always been the Son of God, but he had to be born *somehow*, and this is taken to be through the Davidic line on the father's side: the divine Sonship is then declared in power on Easter Day. The uncomfortable question of how the double paternity is to be reconciled is evaded by the empty two-levels formula. The assumption of Jesus' human ancestry runs all through Gal. 3, similarly. 'The promises were made to Abraham and to his seed. It does not say, "And to seeds", referring to many; but referring to one, "And to your seed", which is Christ' (Gal. 3.16). The argument falls to the ground if Jesus is not Abraham's seed.

Jesus' human ancestry does not feature in Col. 1 and Phil. 2: where does the developing incarnation doctrine come from? It begins, again, in I Corinthians. I Cor. 8.6: 'There is . . . one Lord, Jesus Christ, through whom are all things and through whom we exist.' Jesus was divine, and participated in creation. I Cor. 10.4: 'The Rock (in the wilderness) was Christ' – Jesus was divine, and was God's agent in the desert. I Cor. 15.47: 'The first man was of the earth, a man of dust; the second man is from heaven.' Adam was made from clay and came from this world: Jesus was divine and came to the world from heaven. II Cor. 8.9: 'You know the grace of our Lord Jesus Christ, that though he was rich, yet for your sake he became poor, so that by his poverty you might become rich.' Romans and Galatians were probably written between the two Corinthian letters, and both testify to a landing, Son-incarnate christology, as well as to a take-off, resurrected-Messiah christology. Rom. 8.2: 'God, sending his Son in the likeness of sinful flesh . . .': Gal. 4.4: 'When the time had fully come, God sent forth his Son, born of a woman.' If Jesus was sent, it looks as though he was there to be sent (though cf. Mark 12.2). Novel ideas take time to digest: when Paul is writing to incarnation-minded converts at Corinth, the new christology is drawn in, however briefly. In Romans and Galatians it is pushed into the background by more familiar notions. Even in Philippians, Paul's last letter, there seems to be a wavering in the logic. Christ Jesus was in the form of God and emptied himself, being born; and became obedient unto death, even death on a cross; therefore God has highly exalted him and bestowed on him the name which is above every name. But if he was in the form of God, did he not have the name which is above every name from the beginning? It looks as if a landing christology has been prefixed to, and not quite assimilated to, a take-off christology. But there is no reference to Jesus' human paternity in the captivity epistles: the more obvious dissonances have been put away.

All the evidence would seem to be explained by a Samaritan hypothesis: Paul appropriated the idea of Jesus' incarnation in the course of dialectic with the Samaritan missionaries in Corinth and Ephesus between 50 and 55. We know that a non-Pauline mission was active in these two cities in this period, led by Apollos. Luke tells us (Acts 18.24ff.) that Apollos came from Alexandria in Egypt, where Pauline Catholicism was not to be fully established for more than another century; that Paul's disciples Aquila and Priscilla found his doctrine wanting; that Apollos was an eloquent man (cf. I Cor. 1–2); that he came to Corinth with letters of commendation (cf. II Cor. 3). Paul, with much leaden-footed diplomacy, reveals that Apollos' mission had divided the Corinthian church in two (I Cor. 1–4). 'For when one says, "I belong to Paul", and another, "I belong to Apollos", are you not merely men?' Paul's disciples said with justice that his teachings were those of Cephas too (cf. I Cor. 15.5), and Apollos' disciples replied that they were disciples of Christ. So Paul is able to play the father, and to save everybody's face by speaking as if there were four parties, Paul's, Apollos', Cephas' and Christ's: but the truth keeps coming out – when it came to it, he was applying all this to himself and Apollos for your benefit, brethren, that none of you may be puffed up in favour of one against *the* other (4.6). The dialectic with the Samaritan-christology missionaries was a stormy one. Paul could work with Apollos (I Cor. 16.12); but his associates are referred to sarcastically as 'super-apostles' (II Cor. 11.5; 12.11) and 'false apostles' (11.11) by the time of the second letter. The identity of the rival missionaries comes out in 11.22: 'Are they *Hebrews*?' Paul does not use his natural and normal word of Jews, *Ioudaioi*; nor is there any sign of their interest in food-laws, circumcision, etc., the normal preoccupation of Jewish Christians. I have already mentioned that Hebrews was a name by which the Samaritans called themselves, for they were Hebrews but not Judaeans.[56] So we have a ready explanation of where the landing christology came from. But while the Samaritans were content with a landing-and-take-off myth, whereby Jesus is first incarnated and then returns to the Father, Paul insisted to the end on an imminent eschatology, thus providing the comprehensive scheme of a landing-take-off-and-landing myth, which reached its classic statement in St John.

The same ambivalence characterizes the three synoptic gospels as the later Paul. Mark's Jesus is no mere son of David (12.35f.); he is the Son of God (1.1), his Sonship being revealed at his baptism (1.11), and made known in his mighty works till at last it is evident to the centurion at the crucifixion (15.39). But at the same time he is human, and the Passion story dominates Mark in a way that ill befits a Samaritan God-Man. Matthew in the 80s resolves the problem of Jesus' origin with the aid of Isa. 7.14: his mother Mary was a virgin, and God, not Joseph, was his father, so that he was really God's Son from the beginning of his life. Even so this is not the christology of the Samaritans, and Philippians: Jesus is not God's Son eternally, but only from his conception. Luke shows honest traces of the old Galilean christology when he makes Peter say in Acts 2.22, 36, 'Jesus of Nazareth, a man attested to you by God . . . Let all the house of Israel know assuredly that God *has made him* both Lord and Christ' (cf. 13.23). Jesus was a man to whom God bore witness by the miracles: now he has by his resurrection made him Messiah – the same christology as underlies Rom. 1.3f. But in the opening of the gospel Luke follows Matthew in a virginal conception story, and both of them are then faced with the problem of what to do with the older Davidic sonship tradition. Matthew's solution is to fabricate a bogus genealogy back to David and Abraham, with *legal* paternity only in the final link with Joseph. Luke follows him, but has it both ways by extending the line on the father's side back to God also.

John, by about the year 100, with his Samaritan church-membership, goes the whole way. He puts together the two central Samaritan texts, Gen. 1 and Ex. 34: 'In the beginning was the Word . . . we beheld his glory.' There is no word of Jewish Wisdom. We have the full doctrine of the Samaritan binity, the Pristine God and the Glory. In Exodus the Glory proclaimed, 'The LORD, the LORD . . . abounding in steadfast love and faithfulness (*rabh-hesedh we'emeth*)': Moses did not see God (33.20f.), and what came of the vision was the Law and the Tabernacle. The Word became flesh and tabernacled among us, full of grace and truth;[57] we beheld his glory, glory as of the only Son of the Father. Grace and truth came through Jesus Christ. No one has ever seen God; the only Son, who is in the bosom of the Father, he has made him known, proclaimed him. The same duality is expressed by God and the Word from the

Gen. 1 context in a manner too obvious to need exposition. It is John 1 which has fixed Christian orthodoxy, and has given the incarnation in its substance form the status of revealed truth these two millennia.

3. Paul has little to say about the ministry of Jesus. The hints he gives in I Corinthians are of a human enough rabbi, giving instructions on remarriage and the support of his apostles, instituting the eucharist. The Galilean tradition comes through to us in Mark, where Jesus walks the earth of Palestine in full humanity, knowing fatigue, disappointment, fear and desperation. 'They took him with them as he was . . . he was in the stern asleep on the cushion'; 'O faithless generation, how long am I to be with you?'; 'What were you discussing in the way?'; 'Get (thee) behind me, Satan'; 'My soul is very sorrowful . . . Abba, Father, all things are possible to thee; remove this cup from me'; 'My God, my God, why hast thou forsaken me?' (Mark 4.37–38; 9.19, 33; 8.33; 14.34, 36; 15.34). The more scandalously human sides of Jesus' life are soon eroded by Mark's successors. They omit, they gloss, they substitute. Luke, to take a single example, omits Jesus' cry of despair on the cross for a more edifying Psalm-text, 'Father, into thy hands I commend my spirit'. But the full work of divinizing Jesus falls to John, who has no mere human being but the Word of God incarnated, striding an inch above the ground. As he sees Nathanael under the fig tree he knows him to be an Israelite without guile; he knows the Samaritan stranger to have had five husbands; he needs no one to bear witness of man, for he himself knew what was in man. When Peter in Mark had been with Jesus for months, perhaps years, he realized that he was the Christ: Andrew in John knows it in a night. Nathanael in a minute can cry, 'Rabbi, you are the Son of God! You are the King of Israel!' (John 1.49). In John Jesus' miracles are signs which manifest his glory. When the soldiers come to arrest him they draw back before the power of the Word of God and fall to the ground. John is almost, if not quite, a docetist. His Jesus weeps and is weary, but that is the limit of his humanity. He prays to impress the crowd (11.42), and says he is thirsty on the cross so as to fulfil the scripture (19.28).[58] The cross is his triumph, not his despair, and he can cry as he dies, '*Tetel-estai* (it is finished)'. We are on the road to the Asian Docetists of I John and Ignatius, whose Jesus walked a foot above the ground, and only seemed to be born and to die; to the Gnostic gospels where Jesus has no ministry, does nothing, but all is his words of revelation.

4. It is clear from I Corinthians that the rival missionaries soft-pedalled the cross: 'Christ . . . sent me . . . to preach the gospel, and

not with eloquent words, lest the cross of Christ be emptied of its power. For the word of the cross is folly to those who are perishing ... We preach Christ crucified ... I decided to know nothing among you but Jesus Christ and him crucified ... None of the rulers of this age understood this; for if they had they would not have crucified the Lord of glory' (1.17–18, 23; 2.2, 8). The cross, which Paul had been insistent upon as the centrepiece of his theology, was an embarrassment to the Samaritans, and they had minimized it, concentrating on the wisdom which Christ came to reveal. The same tension underlies much of II Corinthians, in part directly (5.14–21), in part indirectly, because Paul believed that the Christian, and especially the apostle, must share Christ's sufferings and become like him in his death.

Although Paul preached the cross, he lacks any clear theology of it. Rather he expounds it in a series of striking images: Christ was put forward as a *hilasterion*, Christ became a curse for us, he was made to be sin, he disarmed the principalities. To the synoptics the paradox of the cross was soluble via Daniel: the Son of Man must suffer, and after three (and a half) days be exalted to God's right hand. It is not till Hebrews that the Pauline wing of the church achieves a full theory of the death of Jesus. The sacrificial notions implicit in Romans are now expounded in terms of the heavenly high priest, whose offering is once for all. The Samaritan Christians, or Hebrews, who had no cross in their gospel, are berated for their dullness of hearing: it is time to leave elementary things and press on to solid food for the mature, the doctrine of the high priest of Melchizedek's order. The Samaritan incarnation doctrine has been absorbed by the Pauline author ('a Son, whom he appointed heir of all things, through whom also he created the world'), the point of whose letter is largely to bring them Paul's understanding of the centrality of the cross. As usual, Samaritan doctrines show through in John, where the cross is the hour of Jesus' glorification, his going his way to the Father. John remains a Pauline Christian at heart with his full account of the Passion, however. It is only in the Gnostic gospels, like Thomas, that we have no passion or resurrection story: Jesus came merely to reveal the truth.

5. Paul's first surviving letter, I Thessalonians, contains references to the imminent return of the Lord in every chapter, and an extended account of the doctrine in chapter 4. Philippians, probably his last letter, contains two references to 'the day of Christ' in the exordium (1.6, 10), and closes in the happy confidence that 'the Lord is at hand' (4.5). He never lost his faith in the

primitive Galilean eschatology. In these Macedonian churches the matter was not in dispute: it is, once more, in Corinth and Ephesus, that Paul has to argue with a different view.

He opens I Corinthians with an assertion of the Galilean eschatology: 'I give thanks ... that you are not lacking in any spiritual gift as you wait for the revealing of our Lord Jesus Christ; who will sustain you to the end, guiltless in the day of our Lord Jesus Christ' (1.4, 7 and 8). He closes the doctrinal part of the letter (chapter 15) with a description of the last things in detail. This was 'of first importance' (15.3): but in the meantime other teachers have argued that it was a mistake – 'How can some of you say that there is no resurrection of the dead?' (15.12). We are reminded of the persistent tradition among the rabbis and the fathers[59] that the Samaritans denied the resurrection of the dead. But Paul's Corinthian opponents could certainly subscribe to a realized eschatology, if not to a future resurrection: the time of God's good pleasure had arrived already. 'Already!', cries the apostle. 'Already you are filled! Already you have become rich! Without us you have become kings!' (I Cor. 4.8). Realized eschatology is bunk, and draws his most biting sarcasm. With time the Samaritan preaching of wisdom and gnosis in Corinth in the 50s grows into the gnosis falsely so-called in Ephesus half a century later, whose leaders have erred concerning the truth, saying that the resurrection is past already (II Tim. 2.18). It is no surprise if the same denial of a future resurrection, and the same confidence that the gnostic, pneumatic man has been raised, is reigning already, marks both communities.

The imminent future eschatology is the mainspring of Mark and Matthew, and (*pace* Conzelmann)[60] is still a large force with Luke. But by the year 100 it has, to the clear eye of John, lost its plausibility, and the Samaritan alternative asserts its attractiveness. 'He who believes in him is not condemned: he who does not believe is condemned already'; 'This is the judgment, that the light has come into the world, and men loved darkness rather than light'; 'Now is the judgment of this world, now shall the ruler of this world be cast out' (John 3.18, 19; 12.31). The whole apocalyptic discourse of Mark 13 is omitted, and in its place comes the Johannine Farewell Discourse. It is not now primarily the returning Jesus but the Spirit who will come to you and be in you. Christians will not visibly reign with Christ, but whatsoever they ask the Father in his name, he will give it them. John, like the Samaritans, still believes in a future judgment, but the emphasis now falls elsewhere. Realized eschatology was to have a great future from Ephesians and John to Dr Dodd: the future eschatology lost its credibility at the turn of the century, and was given to euthanasia by II Peter's doctrine that a thousand years = one day (II Peter 3.8 = Ps. 90.4). The removal of imminence deprived it of meaning.

The Samaritan theory has the advantage over all other suggestions known to me in a number of ways. We know that the Samaritans were an established religious community for centuries BC, and do not have to posit proto-gnostics sprung from some Qumran-like group, or from further afield. Even though we lack much BC documentation, we can still infer the outline of their beliefs with some confidence from their basic stance towards Judaism, and we have adequate traditions about Simon. We know that they were a strong force in the early church, and one name by which they commonly called themselves, Hebrews, is the one used by Paul's rival missionaries in Corinth in the 50s. There is plentiful evidence that these 'Hebrew' missionaries introduced new doctrines to the Corinthian and Ephesian churches in at least five areas: a stress upon wisdom and knowledge, the teaching that Jesus was God become man, a glorifying and de-humanizing of his earthly life, a soft-pedalling of the cross and the substituting of a realized for a future eschatology. I have given reason to think that these tendencies would be natural in a group of Christianized Samaritans, whose creed already embraced revelation, wisdom and knowledge as central concepts, and the incarnation of divinity, and who denied resurrection. Such a theory not only seems to explain satisfyingly the main dialectic of the New Testament documents, but also the evolution of one wing of the church into full-blown Gnosticism in the second century; a movement whose first writings seem all to be Christian, and whose origins are now widely believed to be from the periphery of Judaism, while being, in a curious way 'metaphysically anti-Semitic'.[61] It all hangs together in a rather convincing way.

Historical study does not disprove divine activity: it just renders the old inspiration model implausible. Here we have a Galilean eschatology which none of us believes, because Jesus did not return in the lifetime of anyone standing by: and a Samaritan protology, which none of us believes because the inference of a second divine being from Ex. 34.5 is (for us) a cranky speculation. When we see them put together in the dialectic of the first century, the idea that the combination of them is revealed truth falls apart. I do not mean that their combination was apart from the mind of God, for clearly the creation of a myth believable through the ancient and medieval worlds was of crucial importance to the establishment of the church. What I mean is that it is not believable today, and that our generation is called to formulate its christology anew. As Catholic Christians we shall wish to give authority to the experience and belief of Jesus himself and his first followers, and much of this (I have suggested in the last chapter) is open to us. But the incarnational speculations introduced into the church by Simon Magus and his fellow-Samaritans seem to me entirely dispensable.

NOTES

1. For further details see E. Haenchen, *The Acts of the Apostles*, Blackwell 1971, pp. 300–8.

2. Eusebius, *Ecclesiastical History (HE)*, IV.22.

3. Justin, *I Apol.*, 26.

4. *Didascalia* 6.8; see also *Apostolic Constitutions*, vi.8.1, vi.16.12. These and other texts noted below are conveniently collected in S. J. Isser, *The Dositheans*, Leiden 1976.

5. Pseudo Clement, *Homilies*, 2.22–4, *Recognitions*, 2.7–12; Isser, op. cit., pp. 19ff.

6. Origen, *Hom. Luc.*, 25; Isser, op. cit., pp. 27ff.

7. Epiphanius, *Panarion*, 9–12; Isser, op. cit., pp. 39ff.

8. *I Apol.*, 26.

9. There is a bibliography in C. H. H. Scobie, 'The Origin and Development of Samaritan Christianity', *New Testament Studies*, vol. 19, 1973, pp. 390ff. Some of the more impressive cases are given in M. Wilcox, *The Semitisms of Acts*, Oxford 1965.

10. Deut. 18.18–22 is inserted at the end of the Ten Commandments in the Samaritan Pentateuch. The text is interpreted messianically in Josephus, *Antiquities*, 20.97, 169 (J. Jeremias, '*Moyses*', *TDNT* IV, pp. 85ff.), and in one late rabbinic reference, Pes. de R. Kah., Pisqa 13 (112a). H. J. Schoeps, *Theologie und Geschichte des Judenchristums*, Tübingen 1949, p. 90, suggests that it was suppressed through Christian use: but why not (far wider and earlier) Samaritan use? J. M. Allegro, 'Further Messianic References in Qumran Literature', *Journal of Biblical Literature*, vol. 75, 1956, pp. 182ff., claims 4Q Test. as evidence of its use at Qumran, but the messianic reference is obscure.

11. Eusebius, *HE*, V.24.2, 'Philip, one of the twelve apostles, who has fallen asleep in Hierapolis, as have also his two daughters who grew old in virginity, and his other daughter who lived in the Holy Spirit and rests at Ephesus' – cf. Acts 21.9.

12. H. G. Kippenberg, *Garizim und Synagoge*, Berlin/New York 1971, pp. 188ff. I have found Kippenberg to be the most careful and dependable guide on many Samaritan questions.

13. Cf. W. Bauer, *Lexikon*, ad voc. But the 'synagogue of the Hebrews' at Corinth may be a Samaritan synagogue.

14. Cf. Marqah, *Memar* VI.2, ed., J. Macdonald, Berlin 1963, Isser advances other arguments for a Samaritan relationship to Hebrews on p. 142, note 54.

15. The first to state so is Justin, *I Apol.*, 26.

16. *Adversus Haereses*, i.23.1–4.

17. Ibid., i.23.5.

18. Ibid., i.24.1.

19. *Homilies*, 2.22.2–4. Cf. J. M. Fennelly, *The Origins of Alexandrian Christianity*, unpublished thesis, University of Manchester 1967.

20. W. Bauer, *Orthodoxy and Heresy in Earliest Christianity*, ET, SCM Press 1972, pp. 44–60.

21. Kippenberg, op. cit., pp. 48–59.

22. Listed in Kippenberg, op. cit., p. 367.

23. Kippenberg, op. cit., p. 205.

24. J. Macdonald, *The Theology of the Samaritans*, SCM Press 1964, p. 119.

25. Ibid., p. 106, citing Marqah.

26. A. F. von Gall, *Der hebräische Pentateuch der Samaritaner*, Giessen 1918, app. crit. ad loc.

27. I. Lerner, *The Special Liturgies of the Samaritans for their Passover . . .*, unpublished thesis, Leeds 1956, pp. 264, 292.

28. A. E. Cowley, *The Samaritan Liturgy*, London 1909, p. 69, 1.12.

29. Ibid., p. 492, 1.3f.

30. Lerner, op. cit., p. 243.

31. Cowley, op. cit., p. 491, 32.

32. Macdonald, op. cit., p. 306.

33. Ibid.

34. Ibid., pp. 73, 98, 115.

35. Cf. Haenchen, *Acts*, ad loc., p. 301.

36. Memar VI.3, Macdonald's edition, I.135; II.221.

37. Ibid., Macdonald, I.135; II.220.

38. Kippenberg, op. cit., pp. 316ff.

39. Haenchen, *Acts*, p. 301.

40. Kippenberg, op. cit., pp. 328–49.

41. *I Apol.*, 26. Note the Samaritanism, 'the first God'.

42. Clement of Alexandria, *Stromata*, II.xi.52.

43. Hippolytus, *Refutatio*, VI.13, 17.1f.

44. Pseudo-Clement, *Recognitions*, 2.7.1.

45. So G. Kretschmar, 'Zur religionsgeschichtlichen Einordnung der Gnosis', *Evangelische Theologie*, vol. 13, 1953, pp. 354–61. It is disputed by R. McL. Wilson, *The Gnostic Problem*, London 1958, p. 100.

46. Other explanations are offered by H. Leisegang, *Die Gnosis*, Stuttgart 1955, pp. 62ff., and by Isser, op. cit., pp. 138ff.; but the references to Ex. 33.21 and Deut. 5.28(31) are to the 'standing' of Moses and not the divinity. *Qa'em* occurs as an epithet of God in Samaritan liturgy, Isser, op. cit., p. 140.

47. Strack-Billerbeck, *Kommentar*, I, pp. 548f., 551f.; Origen, *Comm. Matt.*, xvii.29; Epiphanius, *Panarion*, 9.2.3f.

48. See Kippenberg, op. cit., pp. 306–27.

49. Ibid., p. 326.

50. *Recognitions*, 2.7.1.

51. Origen, *Comm. Joh.*, xiii.27.

52. Kippenberg, op. cit., pp. 276–305.

53. Ibid., p. 326, 234ff.

54. Ibid., pp. 255ff.

55. R. Bultmann, *Theology of the New Testament*, ET, SCM Press 1952, p. 49, and following commentators, take Rom. 1.3f. to embody an earlier credal formula.

56. Paul only uses the expression 'Hebrews' in one other passage, Phil. 3.5, in a precisely similar controversial context.

57. For a recent and effective justification of this equivalence, see A. T. Hanson, 'John i.14–18 and Exodus xxxiv', *New Testament Studies*, vol. 23, 1976, pp. 90ff.

58. I am indebted to the Rev. David Cook for this suggestion.

59. See previous note.

60. H. Conzelmann, *Die Mitte der Zeit*, Tübingen 1953.

61. H. Jonas, 'Delimitation of the Gnostic Phenomenon', in *Le Origini dello Gnosticismo* (ed.), U. Bianchi, Leiden 1967, p. 102.

5

Two Roots or a Tangled Mass?

FRANCES YOUNG

1. Introduction

In the previous chapter Michael Goulder has presented a specific theory which accounts for the rise of incarnational belief. It provides a very good example of the kind of hypothetical reconstruction which is possible. The chief objection to this sort of theory is that exclusive concentration on one or two specific sources inevitably involves ignoring evidence of parallels and coincidences found elsewhere, and thus fails to do justice to what seems to have been a highly complex and syncretistic situation in this particular period of Graeco-Roman civilization, especially on the borderlines of Judaism.

In this chapter no specific theory is advanced. This is simply an attempt to present samples of the kind of evidence at hand which could be relevant, and to outline some of the other theories which have been proposed. For all the material available to the scholar, the gaps in our knowledge are still more extensive than the areas filled in, and the precise implications of much of the evidence is open to considerable dispute. Yet, while it may be admitted at the outset that there seems to be no exact parallel to the Christian doctrine of incarnation, and certainly not in indisputably pre-Christian material, the indications are that christological confessions about Jesus evolved from a vast range of expectations and concepts, images and speculations that were present in the culture of the age and society in which the church was born and matured. Scholarship has not yet found enough pieces of the jigsaw to reconstruct a totally convincing picture of the sources and development of christological belief, but it is certain that the jigsaw is there to be played with; or, to change the analogy, we may not be able to identify confidently two and only two roots of the Christian myth, but roots there were, even if they appear more like a tangled mass whose full unravelling is probably not possible in the present state of knowledge. Let us dig around and see what comes to light.

2. First Probings

Round about the year AD 248 Origen, who may be described as the first great Christian scholar, undertook to compose a reply to an attack on Christianity written some seventy years previously by a pagan named Celsus. Amongst other things, Celsus had poured scorn upon the idea that Jesus was Son of God, miraculously born of a virgin. The character of the arguments for and against the Christian position is very illuminating:

(*a*) Celsus regarded Jesus as one of *many* frauds, who only impressed the gullible. The sole reply that Origen could offer was that his so-called fraud had had considerable success, whereas the followers of Simon Magus or of Dositheus were reduced to a mere thirty faithful.[1] The debate assumes more than one claimant to divine origin, amongst whom it was impossible to decide except by the 'Gamaliel test': 'If this doctrine be of men, it will be overthrown, but if it be of God, you will not be able to overthrow it' – a text Origen himself quoted.[2] It was not a bad argument in the syncretistic atmosphere of the Hellenistic world where faith was 'directed to divine power rather than divine personalities' (i.e. the believer cared more about the 'success-rate' of a god or his prophet than his precise identity or character);[3] yet in the thought-world of today, it would surely be more natural to look for historical causes to explain how the claims for one survived the demise of all the others. At any rate, the controversy reflects a cultural atmosphere in which such claims could find root and might thrive. Celsus indeed points to many prophets in Palestine wandering about saying 'I am God, or a son of God, or a divine spirit'.[4]

(*b*) Celsus' main argument against Christian claims for Jesus were variations on the theme that he was not a very proper divine visitant; he was just not what one would expect an incarnate god to be like; ichor not blood flows in the veins of the gods; a god would not have been born or have died in the normal way; a divine being would have foreseen the terrible death plotted for him and would have used his power to avoid it; and so on. Such arguments imply a cultural climate in which *docetic* incarnation was an acceptable possibility. To claim that a god visited the earth in human *disguise* would have caused no surprise and little comment. What Celsus was determined to assert was that 'no God or child of god has either come down or would have come down' [5] in the sense that the Christians meant; but in the sense in which Apollo and Asclepius 'came down' with oracles and miracles, Celsus not merely admits such a possibility but refers to the witnesses' insistence that Asclepius was 'not a phantom': 'a great multitude of men, both of Greeks and barbarians, confess that they have often seen and still do see not just a phantom but Asclepius himself healing men and doing good and predicting the future'.[6]

(c) Origen replies to attacks on the notion of the virgin birth by appealing to parallel pagan stories: 'In addressing Greeks, it is not out of place to quote Greek stories, lest we should appear to be the only people to have related this incredible story. For some have thought fit (not in respect of any ancient stories and heroic tales, but of people born quite recently) to record as though possible that when Plato was born of Amphictione, Ariston was prevented from having sexual intercourse with her until she had brought forth the child which she had by Apollo.' [7] Clearly Origen lived in a society in which such stories were current, and the notion of divine paternity was by no means peculiar to Christian circles.

If we look around the religious world in which Celsus and Origen lived, we find further confirmation of this kind of outlook. Two writers exemplify this particularly clearly.

In the satirical works of Lucian of Samosata, we meet examples of the religious fraud or charlatan. Lucian lived through the latter part of the second century AD and was contemporary with Celsus. We shall briefly consider two of his characters – Alexander of Abonuteichos and one Peregrinus, otherwise known as Proteus; typically, Lucian enjoys playing upon the fact that he had the name of the mythical old man of the sea who kept changing his form.

These two characters are not Lucian's inventions. That Alexander existed and established a new cult centre and a famous oracle is confirmed by archaeological evidence. Gems, coins and inscriptions corroborate what Lucian tells us, and show that the mystery-cult he founded had widespread influence and lasted at least a century. Both Alexander and Proteus are mentioned in other ancient sources: for example, Athenagoras, the Christian apologist, discusses statues of them both which were supposed to give oracles and perform cures.[8] Many people were clearly taken in by these men, even if Lucian himself was not.

Proteus' main claim to notoriety was his self-immolation by fire at the Olympic Games in AD 165. The whole incident was clearly set up as an imitation of the myth of Heracles' apotheosis. Advance publicity spoke of Proteus being about to depart from among men *to the gods*, borne on the wings of fire;[9] and prior to the event, according to Lucian, he manufactured myths and oracles suggesting that he was to become the 'guardian of the night': a verse prophecy from the Sibyl was produced bidding men that, when Proteus 'kindleth fire in the precinct of Zeus ... leapeth into the flame and *cometh to lofty Olympus*' (the mythical home of the gods), they should pay honour to 'him that walketh abroad in the night-time, greatest of spirits, throned with Heracles and Hephaestus'.[10] The story went that 'when the pyre was kindled and Proteus flung himself bodily in, a great earthquake first took place, accompanied by a bellowing of the ground, and then a vulture, flying out of the midst of the flames, went off to heaven, saying in human speech with a loud voice, "I am through with the earth, to Olympus I go" '.[11] This account Lucian claims to have deliberately initiated, and goes on to mock the credulity of his contemporaries by recounting how he met an old man a little later who claimed to have seen the transfigured Proteus since his cremation, and to have witnessed the vulture flying out of the pyre.[12]

Earlier in his narrative, as a counterblast to the propaganda on behalf of Proteus' divinity, Lucian reports a debunking speech which gives an extremely unsympathetic account of his life as a wandering prophet, affirming that the reason why he originally left his hometown was that he had to flee from charges of parricide and other crimes. Amongst other stages in his dubious career, we are told, Peregrinus, on arrival in Palestine, joined up with the Christians.[13] 'He was prophet, cult-leader, head of the synagogue, and everything all by himself . . . and *they revered him as a god . . . next after that other whom they still worship, the man crucified in Palestine . . .*' There follows an account of how Peregrinus was arrested for his faith, and while in prison became virtually an object of pilgrimage and amassed great wealth in the process. The Christians Lucian regarded as peculiarly gullible: 'If any charlatan or trickster, able to profit by occasions, comes among them, he quickly acquires sudden wealth by imposing upon simple folk.' On his release, Peregrinus flourished on Christian funds until even these supporters were eventually offended.

Lucian's account thus throws interesting light upon the Christian image in the late second century – Christians were known for their charity and for their willingness to die as martyrs; but his main purpose is to poke fun at the fact that simple people were so easily induced to revere exceptional prophets as gods. That Lucian certainly misunderstood the attitude of Christians to martyrs only proves the point for non-Christians; and the actual apotheosis is entirely of pagan inspiration. Lucian alludes not only to the stories of Heracles' ascent to the gods by fire, but also to the deification of Asclepius and Dionysus 'by grace of the thunderbolt'; and to the strange stories about the death of the philosopher, Empedocles [14] (for which see below).

Lucian's other impostor, Alexander of Abonuteichos, is even more instructive since there is even less question of direct Christian influence, misunderstood or otherwise; the Christians are mentioned, but rather more sympathetically, being linked with the Epicureans as Alexander's atheistic opponents. Lucian's *exposé*, including accounts of deliberate trick questions and so on, was written approximately ten years after Alexander's death in the 180s.

According to Lucian, Alexander obtained a tame serpent and attached to it a false human head. He chose Abonuteichos as a likely site because the nearby Paphlagonians were known for their credulity, staring at any travelling musician or fortune-teller 'as if he were a god from heaven'.[15] He proceeded to organize prophecies of the appearance of Asclepius and an oracle saying:

Here in your sight is a scion of Perseus, dear unto Phoebus (i.e. the god Apollo)
This is divine Alexander who shareth the blood of the Healer (i.e. the god, Asclepius);[16]

then he engineered the birth of a tiny serpent from an ostrich egg, and the apparently wondrous birth was followed by apparently wondrous growth; for a few days later Alexander seated himself on a couch clothed in apparel suited to a god and took into his bosom the large, tame snake with the false human head. The snake became known as Glycon, the new incarnation of Asclepius. By various tricks Alexander produced prophecies and prescriptions for cures, and projected himself as the prophet who gets answers to prayers. Asked whether Alexander was a re-incarnation of Pythagoras' soul the oracle answered:

No, Pythagoras' soul now wanes and waxes at other times;
His, with prophecy gifted, takes its issue *from God's mind.*
Sent by the Father to aid good men in the stress of the conflict,
Then to God it will return, by God's thunderbolt smitten.[17]

That many believed him and that the cult of Glycon was a long-standing and wide-ranging success is quite clear; it is also likely that

Alexander's claims should be interpreted in some kind of incarnational sense.

Alexander of Abonuteichos was a pupil of a Pythagorean philosopher, Apollonius of Tyana. The *Life of Apollonius* by Philostratus is the most frequently cited parallel to the life of Jesus presented in the synoptic gospels. This work was composed some thirty years earlier than Origen's book against Celsus; it was commissioned by the Empress and based upon some genuine letters of Apollonius, some other available documents and evidence gleaned by the author on his travels. Apollonius was a neo-Pythagorean philosopher who was admired for his asceticism, was devastatingly critical of contemporary religion, especially the practice of sacrifice, and performed remarkable cures. The story told by Philostratus makes much of his virtue and piety, his miracles, his visit to the Brahmans in India and his brilliant defence against charges of wizardry and black magic before the Emperor. Several features of this narrative are of interest from our point of view.

(*i*) The first is the story of his miraculous birth which includes his mother's vision of Proteus, 'in the guise of an Egyptian demon. She was in no way frightened but asked him what sort of child she would bear. And he answered, "Myself." "And who are you?" she asked. "Proteus," answered he, "the god of Egypt." '[18] Alongside this story,[19] Philostratus reports that there was a spring sacred to Zeus near Tyana, and 'the locals say that Apollonius was the son of this Zeus, though the sage called himself son of Apollonius' (Apollonius had the same name as his father).

(*ii*) Philostratus calls Apollonius *daimonios te kai theos*.[20] In this period people believed in gods and demons as two ranks of higher beings; so Apollonius is being described as one with supernatural attributes. Furthermore, in his defence-speech, Apollonius not only defends himself against charges of wizardry, but also the charge that he is like a god, and that men regard him as a god.[21] He refuses to be ranked with Empedocles on this score (see below).

(*iii*) At the end, a series of mysterious reports are given about the uncertainty of his death; one tells how he entered a temple and a chorus of maidens was heard singing, 'Hasten thou from earth, hasten thou to heaven, hasten'; his remains were never discovered and no one ventured to dispute that he was immortal. Furthermore, he continued his teaching after his death; for he appeared to convince a doubter that the soul is immortal and that he was himself alive.[22]

These items of evidence have been variously assessed. Apollonius and Alexander have been treated as the chief examples of the 'divine man' phenomenon in the ancient world, miracle-workers and prophets who were regarded as visitants from another realm; it was this phenomenon, it is claimed, which accounts for the development of incarnational belief in the Gentile Christian communities. Others have treated most of these cases, and also the evidence in the *Contra Celsum* concerning prophets claiming to be god or a son of god, as post-Christian parody of Christian claims about Jesus; in particular, the *Life of Apollonius* is regarded by some as a consciously contrived rival to the gospels, focusing on a more congenial and respectable philosopher than the barbarian Jesus of Nazareth. In fact the very considerable differences between this *Life* and the gospels makes the theory that Philostratus wrote a deliberate imitation somewhat weak; and we have evidence in Eusebius that no overt comparison was drawn between Apollonius and Jesus until the time of Diocletian, nearly 100 years after Philostratus wrote the *Life*.[23] Yet we do have to allow for the fact that all the evidence we have considered so far is nearly 200 years later than the New Testament period and belongs to a situation in which Christian claims were more and more before the attention of the public; the atmosphere was possibly affected by Christian influence. So we turn to the question: can we trace this kind of attitude back two, three or more centuries?

3. Digging Deeper into the Past

The ancient world had a remarkable cultural continuity. From Plato to Augustine is a period of nearly 900 years; yet Augustine felt he belonged to the same world with the same heritage as Plato. In a mere 200 years, then, we should not expect to find a very marked degree of cultural change – certainly not so great as the cultural changes which have taken place during the 200 years of American independence. Yet it would be totally unscientific to ignore the question of chronology. The evidence we have considered is some of the clearest and most graphic available, but we must look for earlier clues to justify any claim that this kind of cultural climate can be read back into New Testament times.

There are a number of clues which are of considerable importance:

(*a*) Origen did not invent the currency of the story of Plato's miraculous birth; it is also mentioned a few decades earlier by Diogenes Laertius, the pagan author of the *Lives of the*

Philosophers, and he cites as authorities Speusippus' book *Plato's Funeral Feast*, Clearchus' *Encomium on Plato* and Anaxilaides' *On Philosophers II*.[24] Clearchus was a pupil of Aristotle who was a pupil of Plato; but more impressive is the fact that Speusippus was the son of Plato's sister Potone. The story of Plato's divine parentage must go back well before New Testament times.

Nor should we imagine that only Plato attracted such legends. Diogenes also reports stories implying the miraculous birth or death of other philosophers, attributing his information to sources well pre-Christian like Heraclides of Pontus, a pupil of Plato, or Hermippus, a collector of *Lives* who lived around 200 BC. Two of the philosophers around whom myths of incarnation and deification clustered were the presocratics Pythagoras and Empedocles. According to one version,[25] Pythagoras was the incarnate son of Hermes who though refused immortality, was allowed the miraculous facility of remembering a long series of incarnations; but his disciples were supposed to have claimed that he was the Hyperborean Apollo, a fact mentioned not only by Diogenes,[26] but also by Aristotle, to whom is attributed the additional information that Pythagoras had appeared to many and came to heal men.[27] The full development of such legends is to be found in the *Life of Pythagoras* by Iamblichus, the Neoplatonist philosopher who belongs to the early fourth century AD, but it is clear that much of the material originated long before the New Testament period. As for Empedocles, one of the surviving fragments of his teaching reads: 'All hail! I go about among you an immortal god, no more a mortal';[28] his claims became almost a literary commonplace, appearing as we have seen in both Lucian and Philostratus. Stories of healing, of rain-making and magical feats are coupled with reports that people responded by *worshipping and praying to him as to a god*.[29] Diogenes gives various different versions of his 'death', one of the most persistent stories being that he threw himself into the fiery craters of Mount Etna in order to confirm belief in his divinity.[30] But the story told by Heraclides was that Empedocles disappeared one night; afterwards someone claimed to have heard a loud voice in the middle of the night calling Empedocles and when he got up he saw a bright light in the heavens; and on failing to find any trace of him, his associates decided that 'things beyond expectation had happened to him and it was their duty to *sacrifice to him since he was now a god*'.[31]

(*b*) However, Diogenes' evidence only takes us to pre-Christian times at secondhand; so it may be felt that further confirmation is needed. We can move back further by looking at the works of Plutarch.

Plutarch lived during the late first century AD, but while he is contemporary with the writings of much of the New Testament literature, he was certainly remote socially from the Christian movement. He too reports the story about Plato's birth, and the following comments follow: 'I do not find it strange if it is not by a physical approach, like a man's, but by some other kind of contact or touch, by other agencies, that a god alters mortal nature and makes it pregnant with a more divine offspring. . . . In general (the Egyptians) allow sexual intercourse with a mortal woman to a male god, but in the contrary case they would not think that a mortal man could impart to a female divinity the principle of birth and pregnancy, because they think that the substance of the gods consists of air and breath (or spirits), and of certain heats and moistures.'[32]

The prevalence of miraculous birth narratives is further confirmed by Plutarch's most famous work, his collection of *Lives*. Here we find divine genealogies and stories of the supernatural begetting the founders of cities and outstanding rulers. We may briefly consider Alexander the Great and Romulus.

(*i*) Alexander's claims to divine descent go back to his own lifetime, and inscriptions and other sources confirm that Plutarch's statements are not based on recent legendary accretions. So it is that Plutarch regards it as beyond question that Alexander was a descendant of Heracles on his father's side and from mythical heroes of Troy by his mother.[33] He is less confident about the various versions of his birth, though he feels constrained to pass them on. The night before his parents consummated their marriage, the bride was said to have dreamed that a thunderbolt (presumably originating from Zeus) fell upon her womb;[34] such a claim might find confirmation in a story narrated by Plutarch later on, to the effect that a Syrian prophet greeted Alexander as *pai Dios* which Plutarch takes as a foreigner's mistake for *paidion*, a familiar greeting, but Alexander, he reports, interpreted it as 'Son of Zeus'.[35] The most persistent legend, however, with varying detail in different versions, attributed Alexander's conception to a god in the form of a serpent with whom his mother, Olympias, was espied sleeping; Philip ceased to sleep with her, convinced that she was the partner of a superior being, and an oracle implied that it was Zeus Ammon,[36] from whom Alexander later claimed descent. Furthermore, serpents were associated with the worship of Dionysus, son of Zeus, and the description, 'new Dionysus', came to be associated with Alexander soon after his death, though probably not before.[37]

(*ii*) As in the case of Alexander, so for Romulus, Plutarch reports a number of different versions of his birth and descent. Rather than survey these, we may consider the one which is also found in the work of the Roman historian, Livy, which takes us back to an even earlier date, namely, a little before 25 BC. Livy tells how the vestal *virgin*, Rhea Silvia, was raped and gave birth to twins, of whom it was said that their father was Mars, the god of war.[38]

Romulus, however, is just as interesting for the legendary accounts of his end. Again Plutarch produces several versions, one of which is found in Livy's earlier work. During a review of the army, a sudden storm enveloped all in thick cloud and when it passed over Romulus was no longer on earth. 'All with one accord hailed Romulus *as a god and a god's son*, the king and father of the Roman city, and *with prayers* besought his favour that he should graciously be pleased to protect his children for ever.' A little later one of the noblemen claimed to have seen Romulus descend from the sky with a command: 'Go and declare to the Romans the will of heaven that my Rome shall be the capital of the world; so let them cherish the art of war, and let them know and teach their children that no human strength can resist Roman arms.' So saying, Romulus departed on high.[39]

(*c*) Livy belonged to the great age of Roman literature inspired by the peace and success of the Empire under Augustus. That gods could descend among men and ascend back to their heavenly abodes appears in other literature of approximately this period. Baucis and Philemon entertained Jupiter and Mercury without realizing they were visited by gods in mortal form; here was an ancient myth re-told by Ovid round about AD 8 in his poetic collection of *Metamorphoses*[40] (i.e. miraculous changes of form narrated in the myths of Greece and Rome). This is a reminder that the appearance of gods to men on earth was the stock-in-trade of mythology and poetry from Homer onwards. How seriously these mythological narratives were taken is an open question, but that some people were far from sceptical is proved by the story in Acts 14.11ff., where Paul and Barnabas are taken for appearances of Hermes and Zeus (the Greek gods with whom Ovid's Jupiter and Mercury were conventionally equated).

The association of contemporary men with divine appearances is particularly marked in the case of rulers. Roughly at the time of Jesus we find the following examples:

(*i*) In 60 BC Cicero wrote to encourage his brother who was then governor of the province of Asia; the Greeks of Asia were to be so impressed by the incorruptibility of their governor, he suggested, that they would think that some great figure of past history or even a divine man from heaven had dropped down into their province.[41]

(*ii*) 40 BC Vergil wrote an eclogue addressed to the consul, Pollio, associating the arrival of a Golden Age with the birth of a child. The eclogue was later interpreted as a Messianic prophecy by Christians, though it cannot have had that sense in Vergil's own mind; precisely what, or rather whom, Vergil had in mind is much discussed. In this eclogue he speaks of the child consorting with gods and heroes and ruling the world in peace; he calls the child 'dear offspring of the gods, thou hast in thee the making of a Jupiter'.[42]

(*iii*) The court-circles around the emperor Augustus, during whose reign Jesus was born, wrote poetry celebrating the fact that he had been sent by the gods and even suggesting that he was a god come to earth. Horace, writing about 30 BC addressed his second Ode to Augustus:

Whom of the gods shall the people summon to the needs of the falling Empire ... To whom shall Jupiter assign the task of expiating guilt? ... With form changed may you, winged son of gentle Maia (i.e. Mercury), appear on earth as a young man, ready to be called the avenger of Caesar; late may you return to the skies, and long be pleased to dwell with the people of Quirinus (i.e. the Romans);

and the last verse makes it plain that Augustus is addressed as Mercury incarnate.[43]

While it is true that these examples should probably be treated as literary conceits with no very serious meaning, they do serve to remind us that such language was current at the time of Jesus, especially for rulers; indeed, the apotheosis of members of the imperial family became so absurd in the first century AD that it was an obvious target for satirists, notably in Seneca's *Pumpkinification* (*apocolocyntosis* for *apotheosis*) *of Claudius*, written soon after the death of that Emperor in AD 54.

We have, then, some grounds for tracing back the attitudes evidenced in Origen's debate with Celsus to an earlier date in the Graeco-Roman period, indeed to the time roughly contemporary with Jesus and the rise of the Christian movement.

4. Some Possible Theories

In the previous section allusion has been made to general background features which carry this atmosphere even deeper into the past, namely (*i*) the traditional mythology, particularly that concerned with the 'immortals', gods like Heracles, Dionysus and Asclepius, who attained immortality and divinity after living first as exceptional men, and (*ii*) the fact that Rome inherited the language of the ruler-cult from the Hellenistic dynasties in Egypt and Syria. It is this material coupled with the evidence presented earlier which has, not surprisingly, given rise to a number of theories tracing the origins of christological belief to the general Hellenistic religious and mythological environment. Each of the theories has been seriously questioned in detail, partly on grounds of sparsity or lateness of evidence, partly because none provides an exact analogy to Christian claims about Jesus. Yet it is important to realize that there is at least sufficient evidence to have produced each suggestion as a serious possibility, and the total impact of the evidence has led to widespread acceptance of the view that it was the Greek-speaking Gentile converts who transformed Jesus, the Jewish Messiah of Palestine, into an incarnate divine being. Since such a development was inconceivable, it is said, in the context of Jewish monotheism, only the syncretistic pagan environment can account for its origin.

(*a*) *The ruler-cult.* In his fascinating book *Light from the Ancient East*, Adolf Deissmann[44] collected together a number of representative inscriptions and papyri to show that early Christian titles for Jesus are closely paralleled by the imperial cult. An Asian inscription of 48 BC speaks of Julius Caesar as 'god manifest, offspring of Ares and Aphrodite, and common saviour of human life'. A marble pedestal from Pergamum bears the inscription: The Emperor Caesar, son of a God, god Augustus, overseer of land and sea. In these two examples alone we have the Greek words THEOS (god), THEOU HYIOS (son of god), SŌTĒR (saviour) and EPIPHANĒS (manifest, appearing). In the Oxyrhynchus papyri Augustus is described as THEOS and KYRIOS (lord), and many ostraca refer to Nero as KYRIOS. The virtual synonym DESPOTĒS is rarely used of Jesus, but BASILEUS (king) is a very obvious example of terminology common to emperor-worship and early christology. Even more interesting is the fact that it is not only titles that are common but also other associations, notably the words EUANGELION (gospel) and PAROUSIA (advent): e.g. (*i*) a stone from the market-place at Priene reads: But the birthday of the god (namely the Emperor Augustus) was for the world the beginning of EUANGELION because of him; (*ii*) Papyri and ostraca from Ptolemaic Egypt refer to the raising of contributions to make a presentation to the king at his PAROUSIA, that is, during his imperial tour; advent-coins were struck for Nero's visit to Corinth; and years could be dated from an imperial visit or parousia: one inscription reads, 'in the year 69 of the first parousia of the god Hadrian in Greece'. The alternative word EPIPHANEIA (epiphany) is also found for an emperor's visit.

From the time of Alexander the Great, kings and emperors had received divine honours. Were they regarded as gods incarnate? Some of the evidence concerning Alexander we have already glanced at, and certainly the Hellenistic kings represented themselves as Zeus and Apollo on their coin-types. Rulers of Hellenistic and Roman times had their statues erected in temples alongside other gods, and as we have seen Augustus was hailed by one poet as Mercury in human form. Literary and archaeological evidence seems to present a coherent picture, though precisely how significant these facts are from a religious point of view is much debated. A. D. Nock points out (*i*) that there is little indication of the ascription of any supernatural efficacy to rulers when dead, and even less of genuine prayers being offered to divinized rulers dead or living; and (*ii*) that most of the terminology applied to divine rulers is vague and it is not usual to find notions of the incarnation of a definite deity in a human frame continuing throughout a particular life-span: the rulers were EPIPHANĒS not throughout their careers but by specific manifestations of power, especially in war, though sometimes through miracles or healings.[45]

Nevertheless, the divine language used of the ruler so closely parallels titles accorded to Jesus in the New Testament that it cannot be regarded as entirely without significance. According to Josephus, Jews suffered all sorts of torments rather than confess, or even seem to confess, that Caesar was their master; for God was their only DESPOTĒS.[46] In a similar way, it is clear that the early Christian confession of Christ as KYRIOS was regarded as excluding Caesar-worship: bishop Polycarp's persecutors may have regarded it as a simple thing to say KYRIOS CAESAR, but it was not so for Polycarp himself; still less would he curse Christ.[47] It is with some plausibility that this situation is read back into the New Testament and used to interpret texts like I Cor. 12.3: 'No one speaking by the Spirit of God ever says, "Jesus be cursed" and no one can say "Jesus is Lord" except by the Holy Spirit.' Jews and Christians alike paid pagans the compliment of taking their religious language about Caesar seriously. The early Christians' confession of Jesus as Lord can be seen as a deliberate antithesis to the imperial cult: the real King and Lord is Jesus who, like Caesar, was God manifest on earth, and the Lord and Saviour of men.

(*b*) *Divine men.* Nowadays, however, the ruler-cult is usually regarded as being 'a negative stimulus rather than a model'[48] and more stress is put upon the general concept of the 'divine man' in the Hellenistic world. The hypothesis is not infrequently advanced that the early Gentile communities basically subscribed to a *theios anēr* (divine man), christology and Mark, almost certainly the earliest gospel, is then supposed to have utilized or perhaps corrected a source or tradition which presented Jesus as a 'divine man', that is a man endowed with superhuman miracle-working powers.

The character of the 'divine man' was admirably reconstructed by L. Bieler; in his book, *Theios Anēr*,[49] he collected and organized an enormous amount of material purporting to show that in the ancient world certain individuals were regarded as belonging to a class 'between gods and men', commonly described as *theios* or by other characteristic expressions. Typical motifs and biographical features are associated with these figures, along with similar accounts of their wisdom, exceptional powers and remarkable activities. Some of the best examples we have already utilized in this chapter. Superficially an extremely impressive picture is presented, but it has a number of weaknesses: a mass of evidence from Homer to the Middle Ages is pressed into service with little respect for chronology, and the material is over-schematized, giving the impression that the features described appear in amalgamation with greater frequency than is in fact the case. Further, to turn the expression *theios anēr* into a kind of title is a dubious procedure. That *theios* was a very general adjective with no incarnational overtones is clear from the fact that in a later period Christian saints and fathers could be so described: God's grace or spirit was enough to make a man or the scripture 'divine'. In pagan and Christian usage, the adjective could take the comparative form, 'more divine', or the superlative form, 'most divine'; thus in common parlance, men and things could have degrees of divinity. It was an honorific epithet and could be used in a variety of contexts. It is therefore true, as many have pointed out, that *theios anēr* is by no means a fixed expression and there is no such thing as a specific and defined class of people commonly called 'divine men'.[50] The adjective *theios* by itself conveys little more than the sense 'inspired'.

Yet for all the criticisms, the existence of striking analogies to christology cannot be totally dismissed. We are confronted not just with the fact that anyone regarded as exceptional or outstanding in personality, power or status could be called *theios*, but with the fact that miraculous birth-stories, legends of extraordinary disappearace at death, acts of salvation and healing, deification and appearances from on high were not infrequently associated with such figures in that miraculous birth-stories, legends of extraordinary dissapearance but 'son of Helios' or 'son of Zeus' was very much more common. Where did these titles and motifs come from? It is pretty clear that they were borrowed from ancient mythology,[51] the myth of Hercules being particularly influential.[52] In Stoic circles especially, Hercules became the ideal of manhood, overcoming evil and establishing world-wide peace, triumphing over death by his invasion of Hades and ultimately achieving immortality for his virtue; we find the dramatic presentation of these themes, along with the traditional mythological motifs, in the tragedies of Seneca written in the mid-first century AD. Christian apologists had to reckon with Hercules, Asclepius and Dionysus as potential rivals to Christ; in the second century, for example, Justin Martyr had a rather ambivalent attitude to the parallels, dismissing them, on the one hand, as deceitful fabrications by evil demons designed to reduce the Christian story to a 'mere tale of wonders like the stories told by the poets', and yet on the other hand using them to take the sting out of pagan mockery of Christian claims.[53]

According to Plutarch, Alexander believed that although God was the common father of all mankind, still he made peculiarly his own the highest and best of them;[54] the kinship of men with gods became a philosophical commonplace, and it was generally believed among philosophers that the polytheistic gods were originally deified men, as the myths of the 'immortals' made clear. Whatever the weaknesses of the *theios anēr* theory, it cannot be denied that in the case of exceptional men, especially rulers and philosophers (who may be regarded as the inspired religious leaders or prophets of the Hellenistic world), the myths of the 'immortals' were utilized to express a sense that they belonged, or had attained to a superior race and another realm; and since it is convenient to refer to this phenomenon by some agreed shorthand, the term *theios anēr* will continue to serve the purpose.

Moreover, one cannot dismiss out of hand the view that something of the same kind happened in the case of Jesus. There are, to take but one example, general similarities between Livy's account of Romulus and some synoptic narratives about Jesus: a virgin birth, conception by a god, a remarkable career, no trace of his remains after death, an appearance after death to commission his successors, the offering of prayers to him. It would be impossible to make a convincing case for direct influence; but people living at roughly the same time do seem to have produced mythological accounts with parallel motifs.

5. Objections and Alternatives

So far we have concentrated upon depicting a particular kind of atmosphere widespread in the ancient world in which any one with exceptional powers was liable to receive divine honours from a responsive populace. This provides an instructive context for considering the rise of christological belief, even though specific theories deriving christology from this background have failed to prove entirely convincing; this is partly because of the difficulty of showing any direct influence, but also because no one knows quite how seriously to take many of these professions of belief and worship: the ruler-cult seems to have become a half-mocked convention performed solely for political reasons and probably not affecting the bulk of the populace, and the traditional mythology could certainly be treated with scepticism at least by the educated.

As an alternative hypothesis, then, the origins of christology have been attributed to the more esoteric religious phenomena of the Graeco-Roman world, to rites and deities which certainly did call forth personal devotion. To explore the various possibilities in detail here would be to expand this chapter into a book, quite apart from the difficulty that the issues are somewhat clouded by lack of agreement concerning definitions and precise distinctions within a range of apparently related material and ideas. One important hypothesis concerns the parallels between the early Christian community and what is known of the practices and terminology of the mystery-religions, in which, it seems, salvation was imparted to the initiates through mystical identification with a dying and rising god. Another focuses attention on parallels with the revelations of the Hermetic literature. These phenomena have been associated with a general religious atmosphere in the ancient world described as 'gnosticism', and the Pauline incarnational language has then been explained by reference to the so-called 'Gnostic Redeemer-myth', the coming of an archetypal, heavenly figure into the world to reveal the secrets of the universe and the destiny of spiritual man. These theories have been widely influential, but none has proved generally acceptable. This is partly for chronological reasons (it is just as likely that Paul influenced Gnostics as *vice versa*); partly because of the nature of the evidence which is open to a variety of different interpretations and is fragmentary, diverse or non-existent, with the result that the supposed parallels can be regarded as hypothetical reconstructions in the minds of modern scholars corresponding to no historical reality; and partly because alternative sources can often be plausibly proposed.

Rather than enter into this highly complex and debated area, it seems more worth while to admit that there is a considerable objection to all the various hypotheses so far mentioned, namely that they depend upon a dramatic 'paganization' of the gospel at a very early date, a development which seems improbable given the Jewishness of Christian origins and the evident fact that Paul and the other New Testament writers maintained many Jewish prejudices and attitudes. The gospel spread among Jewish communities scattered around the empire, or among close associates of the synagogue, and the early church was only divorced from its Jewish roots after bitter internal controversy and outright rejection by the majority of the Jewish people. Judaism was therefore the context of early Christian origins, and Judaism in this period was resistant to pagan influence: for with the successful Maccabaean revolt in the early second century BC, most religiously influential Jews had rejected once and for all any assimilation to the dominant syncretism of the Hellenistic world: they were prepared to die rather than let the one true God be diluted by equation with Zeus or anyone else. No other being could be worshipped and no son of God was *really* a son of *God* in the Hebrew tradition. Hence the superficial attractiveness of the view that christology as we know it could never have flowered on Jewish soil, that it has a natural basis in Hellenistic syncretism and only the Gentile expansion of the church can account for the rise of incarnational belief. But this is to overlook the fact that the Jew, Paul, is our first witness to the belief that a supernatural agent of God entered the world in Jesus Christ. Could Paul, with all his Jewish prejudices, with his evident training in Jewish theology and exegesis – could such a man have been influenced by Gentile mystery-religions or some other pagan belief? Increasingly it has seemed improbable. In proposing the view that it was by analogy with Lord Serapis that Jesus was worshipped as Lord, Bousset stated:

No-one thought this out and no theologian created it. ... They would hardly have dared without further ado to make such a direct transferral of this holy name of the Almighty God. ... Such proceedings take place in the unconscious, in the uncontrollable depths of the group psyche of a community; this is self-evident, it lay as it were in the air, that the first Hellenistic Jewish communities gave the title *kyrios* to their cult-hero.[55]

But this hardly appears an adequate explanation given the deep-seated rejection of polytheism and heathen myths among Jews of the period; at least within the first-generation church, such a development seems very unlikely, and the continuance among Christians of Jewish apologetic traditions and polemic against polytheism and syncretism throughout the patristic period shows the strength of the church's attachment to its inherited past.

Such is the objection. The question is, how valid is it? After all, there did develop in Christianity doctrines which tended to undermine in a rather embarassing way this monotheistic emphasis. Perhaps this fact should encourage us to enquire whether the Judaism from which Christianity sprang was so monolithic and impervious to pagan influence as has been suggested. Subtle influences often master conscious resistance. Clearly it now becomes imperative to probe more deeply into the character of contemporary Judaism, and to consider the question whether the development of the incarnational idea is conceivable within that context.

6. Fresh Probings

As we turn to investigate the Jewish area, our enquiry needs to focus on a number of related questions: Were Jews in fact totally unaffected by the kind of atmosphere depicted earlier? Were there not movements in Judaism analogous to Hellenistic mysticism and gnosis? Was Judaism committed to an unalloyed monotheism, or were there speculations about other supernatural beings? Were phrases like 'son of God' always used with implications quite different from those in the pagan world? The last seems to be a good question with which to start.

(*a*) Was the expression 'Son of God' used in a totally different sense in a Jewish context? It was certainly not a description alien to Judaism, nor was it impossible for a Jew to envisage God addressing certain individuals as 'son'. So many studies have been devoted to the title 'Son of God' in the Old Testament and intertestamental literature that it seems best simply to summarize some of the more important points and comment on their implications.

(*i*) Such expressions are commonly used in Jewish literature to describe Israel, and they appear in the Old Testament (e.g. II Sam. 7.14 and Ps. 2.7) as descriptions of the king. They possibly figured as a description of the ideal King-Messiah in pre-Christian expectation. This is clear in II(4)Esd. 7.28, but this text may not be unaffected by Christian influence; a text discovered at Qumran seems likely to settle this debated point, though it is very fragmentary:

[. . . But your son] shall be great upon the earth [O King! All (men) shall] make [peace], and all shall serve [him. He shall be called the son of] the [G]reat [God], and by his name shall he be named. He shall be hailed (as) the Son of God, and they shall call him the Son of the Most High . . . etc.

The square brackets indicate the uncertain and fragmentary character of the text, but as Fitzmyer comments, there is no doubt that the titles 'Son of God' and 'Son of the Most High' are applied to some human being in the apocalyptic setting of this text of the first century BC.[56]

(*ii*) In the intertestamental literature, the works of Philo and the rabbinic material, such expressions are used of the righteous and wise man, or of Israelites who do the will of God. 'Be like a father to orphans . . . you will then be like a son of the Most High'; so reads the Greek text of Ecclus. (Ben Sira) 4.10 and the rediscovered Hebrew text reads 'God shall call you Son'.

(*iii*) Such expressions are associated with certain rabbis, and in particular with Hanina ben Dosa, a miracle-working charismatic of first-century Galilee. It is this figure which provides G. Vermes with his illuminating parallel to Jesus: a heavenly voice referred to 'my son, Hanina', just as the heavenly voice at Jesus' baptism designated him as 'my beloved son'.[57] This and other figures of Palestinian Judaism, like Honi the circle-drawer, bear some resemblances to the wonder-working *theios anēr* discussed earlier, and with both types, terms appear which imply some kind of divine sonship.

(*iv*) In both the Old Testament and later Jewish literature such expressions are used in reference to heavenly, angelic beings and to supernatural mediators. Philo describes his Logos as Son of God and first-born. We shall be exploring these supernatural mediating figures further.

In general it can be said that for Jews a son of God was a being of god-like qualities or one specially called and designated by God for a particular task. It is possible that we should draw a distinction between ideas about *the* Son of God and other sons of God, but if so, the distinction is not one of nature but one of function. *The* Son of God, whether human or angelic, would be the unique pre-destined fulfiller of God's promises; but sonship could equally well belong to other angelic and human beings. God's creatures were all regarded as potentially his sons, becoming so by response to his will and purpose. Certainly the idea that divine sonship meant that God was literally involved in a sexual-biological process was offensive to Jewish thought, however frequent in Hellenistic mythology. In Jewish traditions from the Old Testament on, there were miraculous birth-stories, but they did not posit the absence of a human father; rather the emphasis was upon the inability of the mother to bear a child without divine intervention. Two plausible hypotheses have been advanced for the appearance in the Christian birth-narratives of a form of miracle unprecedented in Jewish tradition: (*i*) Vermes has argued that 'virgin' could well have originally meant one too young for child-bearing, just as Sarah, Hannah and Elizabeth were too old or infertile, and then the explicit denial of Joseph's role is to be understood as a 'paganizing' development of the legend based on misunderstanding of the Greek word 'parthenos' in a narrowly, literal sense;[58] or (*ii*) such a development is more often attributed to the belief that Isa. 7.14 had been literally fulfilled, in which case a purely Jewish origin of the story is possible.

Whatever the answer to that problem, it seems clear that even if direct pagan influence is impossible to substantiate, there are *prima facie* parallels, apart from legends of divine paternity, between the Jewish and Hellenistic treatment of both rulers, actual or ideal, and prophets, saints, charismatics or miracle-workers as 'divine' or 'sons of God'.

(*b*) Were Jews unaffected by Hellenistic myths of apotheosis and deification? A number of hints suggest that some were not entirely impervious to the surrounding cultural atmosphere, though admittedly their tentative use of this sort of language was coupled by a certain embarrassment. At the same time, some indigenous development in this kind of direction seems to have been inspired by the biblical stories of the assumption of Enoch and Elijah directly to heaven.

We may consider first the legends about Moses. In his *Praeparatio Evangelica*, Eusebius preserves some extensive fragments from Jewish apologists of pre-Christian times. These include quotations from a romance about Moses written by Artapanus in the first century BC. Not only is Moses presented as a miracle-worker and law-giver, but he becomes the teacher of Orpheus and, 'deemed by the priests (of Egypt) worthy to be honoured like a god, was named Hermes, because of his interpretation of hieroglyphics'.[59] This tendency to treat Moses as a *theios anēr* finds further confirmation in Josephus. Josephus fought for his country in the Jewish War 66–70, but then became convinced of the futility of the cause, gave assistance to the Romans and spent the rest of his life trying to explain the Jews to an unsympathetic Gentile audience. In his *Antiquities*, he describes Moses as last seen discoursing with, and about to embrace, Eleazar and Joshua, when 'a cloud suddenly stood over him and he disappeared in a certain valley, although he wrote in the holy books that he died, which was done out of fear, lest they should venture to say that, because of his extraordinary virtue, he went to God'.[60] Elsewhere Josephus mentions the fact that some people thought that Moses 'had been taken to the divinity',[61] and the story is certainly reminiscent of the passing of Romulus.

A little earlier than Josephus, we find similar hints in Philo, an Alexandrian Jew who remained loyal to his origins while deeply versed in Hellenistic philosophy. His *Life of Moses* ends with the suggestion that the account of Moses' death appears in books he was supposed to have written himself because 'when he was already being exalted . . . ready at the signal to direct his upward flight to heaven, the divine spirit fell upon him and he prophesied with discernment while still alive the story of his own death . . .'; his literal death and burial, contained in scripture, is married to an ascension described earlier in terms which are characteristically 'intellectual' and yet seem to imply an exceptional translation: 'the time came when he had to make his pilgrimage from earth to heaven, and leave this mortal life for immortality, summoned thither by the Father who resolved his twofold nature of soul and body into a single unity, transforming his whole being into mind, pure as the sunlight'.[62]

Such hints that Jewish understanding of Moses was in varying degrees affected by Hellenistic motifs might be attributed in the case of the writers mentioned to an apologetic interest. But there is also the apocalyptic work called *The Assumption of Moses*; what survives of the text is more like a Testament and it seems to assume that Moses died in the normal way, but there are patristic references to this work which suggest more explicit descriptions of an assumption to heaven. Besides this, there are a few signs in rabbinic material of a tradition that Moses ascended to heaven: 'Some say Moses did not die, but stands and discharges above the (priestly) ministry'; 'Three went up alive to heaven: Enoch, Moses and Elijah.'[63] A later Hebrew book describes Moses' transformation into an angel, following the pattern of the Enoch traditions which we shall examine shortly.

Jewish speculation along these lines centred around the three characters just mentioned. In the case of Elijah the development

seems to have been 'indigenous' and very little trace of Hellenistic
influence can be shown; yet the analogies remain striking. According to II Kings 2.11, Elijah ascended to heaven by chariot of fire
and whirlwind. In two of the books of the Apocrypha the Elijah
tradition is elaborated: according to I Macc. 2.58 he was taken up
into heaven because of his great zeal for the law, and in Ecclus. (Ben
Sira) 48, we find a magnificent hymn addressed to Elijah, who is
honoured as a miracle-worker, raising the dead and standing up
against kings and princes. The most interesting point, however, is
the hymn's central section (48.9–10): 'You who were taken up by a
whirlwind of fire, in a chariot with horses of fire; you who are ready
at the appointed time, it is written, to calm the wrath of God before
it breaks out in fury ... and to restore the tribes of Jacob.' This
notion of Elijah's return before the day of the Lord goes back to
the prophet Malachi (Mal. 4.5.); and subsequently the phrase,
'... until Elijah comes' recurs as many as four times in the
Mishnaic tractate, *Baba Metzia*, as well as elsewhere in Rabbinic
literature. That Elijah lives as a supernatural being and can intervene on earth is assumed in the Babylonian Talmud, where he is
often introduced into stories, sometimes in disguise to aid the oppressed people of God: e.g. according to *Taanith* 22a, Rabbi
Beroka Hozaah used to frequent the market-place at Be Lapat
where Elijah often appeared to him, and there follows an example
of an edifying discussion between the two concerning who will have
a share in the world to come; and in the previous section of the
same tract, a story is told about Elijah arriving in disguise to dis-
suade a council from deciding to exterminate the Jews. Such
activities are those of angels or gods, and whether or not connections can be traced, the latter story has certain parallels with
Homeric myths.

For the history of speculation about Enoch we have more complete documentation in a series of Enoch-books, which belong to
the world of apocalyptic and esoteric Jewish mysticism. It is perhaps significant that in the course of the series we move from the
apocalyptic visions of the *Ethiopic Book of Enoch* (*I Enoch*) to
descriptions in the later texts of heavenly secrets which have a
definite Gnostic ring. This seems to support the view now
frequently canvassed that Gnosticism, so far from being the 'radical
Hellenization of Christianity' as Harnack thought, in fact originated
in Jewish circles. The esoteric tradition has left traces within the
Talmud itself, where there are hints of secret and dangerous teachings about creation and the Merkabah, the chariot-throne of God
first described in the visions of the prophet Ezekiel.[64] Further light

has been thrown on these speculations by some relatively unknown and largely unpublished Hebrew texts of uncertain date,[65] amongst which is to be found the so-called *Hebrew Book of Enoch* (*III Enoch*), one of the few texts published with translation and full commentary.[66] The difficulties in dating are illustrated by the fact that this text has been placed as early as the third century AD and as late as the eighth century.

The development of the Enoch figure in the texts we have available is strongly suggestive of a kind of deification. According to Gen. 5.24 'Enoch walked with God; and he was not, for God took him'. The apocalyptic book known as *I Enoch* is possibly pre-Christian; here Enoch becomes one who 'saw the vision of the Holy One in the heavens' as well as other typically apocalyptic manifestations, and then eventually he is translated into the heaven of heavens where he saw the throne itself surrounded by angels, 'the holy ones of God'. A slavonic text known as *II Enoch*, belonging probably to the beginning of the Christian era, develops his travels through the heavens in a more gnostic–mystical way and explicitly describes his transformation into an angel; but the most striking development is to be found in the *Hebrew Book of Enoch*. In this work 'Metatron, the angel, the Prince of the Presence' leads Rabbi Ismael to a vision of the Merkabah and in response to his questions explains that he was once Enoch who was taken up on the wings of the Shekinah to the highest heaven where 'the Holy One, blessed be he' transformed him into the greatest of the angels, a process described in graphic imagery, emphasizing his cosmic size, his garment of light, his crown of glory and his fiery nature. Thus, Metatron, a heavenly being of obscure name and origin, but one well-known to the bearers of rabbinic traditions, is identified in this text with the translated man, Enoch.

However, for our purpose, it is not simply Enoch's metamorphosis which is of interest, but the unusual relationship between Metatron and God himself. Metatron *sits* in heaven, unlike any other except God. The Rabbis played this down, suggesting that as heavenly scribe he had to sit;[67] but in *III Enoch* he sits on a throne which is described as 'like the throne of glory'.[68] In other respects too he appears accoutred like God, and he acts as God's ruler over all the powers of heaven. All the other angels 'fell prostrate when they saw me. And they were not able to behold me because of the majestic glory and beauty of the appearance of the shining light of the crown of glory upon my head.' God revealed all his secrets to Metatron, and 'he called me "the lesser Jahweh" in the presence of all his heavenly household; as it is written (Ex. 23.21), "For my name is in him" '.

Clearly such a picture of Metatron, along with his identification as the translated man Enoch, is remarkably close to Paul's affirmations about Jesus, that he sits at God's right hand (Rom. 8.34) and that 'God has highly exalted him and bestowed on him the name which is above every name (i.e. God's name), that at the name of Jesus every knee should bow, in heaven and on earth and under the earth, and every tongue confess that Jesus Christ is Lord (the title by which God is known and addressed), to the glory of God the Father' (Phil. 2.9–11). However, when we read elsewhere in *III Enoch* that certain heavenly beings are excluded from Metatron's jurisdiction, namely the 'eight great princes, the honoured and revered ones who are called Jahweh by the name of their king' (i.e. probably archangels whose names are compounds of God's name), we should perhaps hesitate to insist that the text provides an exact parallel. On the other hand, the story of Metatron's *de*thronement, which we find in Rabbinic texts and also as an addition to the text of *III Enoch*,[69] while clearly intended to reduce the force of the Metatron speculation and eliminate its dangers, actually highlights its potential implications; for both versions associate Metatron's dethronement with the account of an apostate rabbi who on seeing the Merkabah and Metatron enthroned in glory said, 'Indeed, there are two Divine Powers in heaven'. Perhaps then we are justified after all in seeing here a close parallel to Christian affirmation about Jesus, all the more remarkable in what is clearly a post-Christian text, whatever its exact date. It suggests the presence of certain inherent tendencies which were usually suppressed in opposition to Christianity.

So far our examination of Jewish sources suggests three things: (*i*) that, in spite of differences, there are parallels between the Jewish and Hellenistic use of phrases like 'Son of God'; (*ii*) that Hellenistic mythological motifs were on the verge of affecting the expressions of at least Greek-speaking Judaism, even though a certain reserve is persistently maintained; and (*iii*) that some exceptional individuals ascended at least to angelic status; and this feature, I suggest, is more like pagan apotheosis than might appear at first sight. For pagan philosophers in this period regarded all gods, new or old, as lesser beings below the Supreme God in a heavenly hierarchy, and Jews believed likewise in a heavenly hierarchy of lesser beings, namely the angels, below their one and only God. The difference was to a fair extent one of terminology coupled with disagreement over whether the lower 'deities' should be worshipped or not, and in this debate the Christian Origen upheld a more Jewish position than some of his fellow-believers when he affirmed that Christian worship, though offered *through* the Son, should be directed *solely* to the Father.

(c) Speaking of angels, we are reminded that these supernatural beings were themselves described earlier as 'sons of God'. The nature and function of these heavenly beings is clearly the next subject requiring examination.

Throughout the Old Testament there are stories of God acting through angels or messengers; he is several times seen with a heavenly council (e.g. Ps. 89.7 and Job 1) and monotheism was reached less by eliminating other divine beings than by subjugating them to Israel's one, almighty God. By the time of Daniel and the intertestamental literature, an elaborate angelology with named archangels associated with particular functions is beginning to be established. The midrash on creation in the book of Jubilee makes room for the creation of the angel-world with a hierarchy of different ranks. A number of Old Testament passages were taken to refer to these beings as 'sons of God' (e.g. Gen. 6.2, 4; Deut. 32.8; Ps. 29.1), and *I Enoch* in particular makes constant reference to the angels as the holy sons of God or the children of heaven.

In Jewish legend and apocalyptic speculation, these supernatural figures are envisaged as coming down to earth, often in disguise as men. With the descent of Jupiter and Mercury to visit the unsuspecting Baucis and Philemon we may compare Abraham's entertainment of divine guests (Gen. 18); that this was understood, in the New Testament period, as an unperceived angelic visitation is indicated by, for example, Heb. 13.2: 'Do not neglect to show hospitality to strangers, for thereby some have entertained angels unawares.' As an example of the kind of story developed, we may take the book of Tobit, a Jewish romance reflecting the conditions of the Babylonian Diaspora around 200 BC, though purporting to be a tale of the exile centuries before.

Tobit is depicted as a good, faithful Jew who had the misfortune to go blind. In response to prayer, God sent the angel Raphael to heal him (3.17), and also to succour an afflicted young woman who had seven times lost a husband on her wedding-night through the activity of a hostile demon. So it happened that Tobit decided to send his son on a journey to reclaim some money deposited years earlier, and Raphael accompanied him disguised as Azarias son of Ananias, a man hired as guide and servant (5.4). Through Raphael's advice and help, Tobias claimed the young woman as wife and dealt with the demon; then he successfully accomplished his mission and returned to cure his father's blindness. When Tobit and his son came to reward Azarias, he declared: 'I am Raphael, one of the seven holy angels who present the prayers of the saints and enter into the glory of the Holy One' (12.15). The descent of heavenly beings to intervene in earthly affairs, often to render assistance, is clearly a feature of both pagan and Jewish legend, and certainly pre-dates both the New Testament and the earliest traces of a Gnostic descending redeemer.[70]

To dwell further upon the role of angels in apocalyptic and elsewhere clearly lies outside the scope of this chapter. However, it is important to consider the way in which angel-speculation is linked with the activity of God in the last days. In particular we may focus upon an interesting fragment from Qumran which has some remarkable connections with the New Testament, and with the Epistle to the Hebrews in particular. To the uninitiated reader, quotations from the text would be obscure and over-lengthy, so an interpretive summary will have to suffice. The central character of the piece is Melchizedek, who is described as 'the heavenly one', and as the one who executes God's judgment. He judges Belial and takes vengeance on his wicked spirits, while being assisted by other 'heavenly ones'. This inaugurates the time of salvation, and Melchizedek's activity is portrayed, largely in texts and words drawn from Isaiah, as proclaiming liberty, making atonement for all the children of light and bringing good tidings to Zion. There are some grounds for linking this Melchizedek speculation with the archangel Michael;[71] but Fitzmyer[72] has argued that the text seems to present a figure *above* the angels to whom God delegates his prerogatives of judgment and mercy on the great Day of Atonement at the end of time. There are parallels with the functions of Enoch and the Son of Man in the Ethiopic apocalypse. In both cases, a heavenly being becomes God's vicegerent at the Last Judgment; in both cases speculation about an obscure human figure from the early part of Genesis is connected with one above angels and archangels. Perhaps it is not so surprising after all that the Epistle to the Hebrews can argue for the transcendent uniqueness of the one after the order of Melchizedek, the one superior to the angels, while insisting upon his perfect manhood; patristic exegesis remained uncertain whether the Melchizedek of Genesis was a human or angelic being.[73]

Two points seem important: (*i*) it is clear that eschatological speculation revolved around not just a human Messiah-Son of God, but also a possible supernatural agent, perhaps a superangelic Son of God or Son of Man who would act for God at the Final Judgment. What has happened in christology is the merging of these two eschatological perspectives. (*ii*) Some uncertainty as to whether this supernatural agent is an angel or more than an angel surrounds the Jewish texts, and this is paralleled both in Philo's treatment of his Logos (see below) and in the persistent tendency of Christian texts to treat the Son of God or the Logos as an angel or archangel, a tendency which lasted right up to the Arian controversy. In the early Christian work *The Shepherd of Hermas*, there are six instead of seven archangels with a 'mighty man in their midst', namely the Son of God; and in a pseudo-Cyprianic treatise, the Lord is described as creating seven angels, one of whom he determined to make his son. Christology was certainly related in some way to Jewish angel-speculation.[74]

In fact, the closest parallel to Christian belief found anywhere belongs to this context. It is in a Jewish apocryphal work known as the *Prayer of Joseph* which is now lost to us apart from quotations in the works of Origen.[75] In it Jacob says, 'I, Jacob and Israel, who speak to you, am an angel of God and one of the principal spirits. I, Jacob, am called Jacob by men, but my name is Israel, for by God was I called Israel (which means) "the man who sees God", because I am first-born of all living things that receive their life from God.' By this complex claim we are introduced to a being with angelic and human aspects, who is yet beyond the angels in being the first-born of God. There follows an extraordinary passage which seems to imply that in the famous wrestling-match at the brook Jabbok (Gen. 32.24), two archangels Israel and Uriel, both in incarnate form and both apparently claiming to be Jacob, contended against each other. 'Uriel, the angel of God, came out and said: I have come down upon earth and dwelt among men'; Jacob, however, asserted his superiority, unmasking Uriel and revealing himself as 'Israel, the archangel of the power of the Lord and the *archistratēgos* (top-general) among the sons of God ... the first of those who serve before the face of the Lord.' Thus the human progenitor of the nation Israel is seen as an incarnation of a superangelic being. The parallel is all the more striking in view of the hints in the New Testament of an underlying assumption that Jesus summed up all that Israel was elected to be, and founded a new Israel, the church.

(*d*) 'The Christian hope has its roots in Palestine; Christian theology and above all christology have theirs in Alexandria.'[76] Such was the conclusion of A. D. Nock, one of the greatest experts in the religious scene of the Graeco-Roman world. What led him to this judgment?

Twice we have alluded to another heavenly being known as 'Son

of God', namely Philo's Logos. Philo, whose description of Moses
we have already considered, was roughly contemporary with Paul,
and like Paul, he wrote in Greek. His Judaism, though orthodox in
practice, was theologically coloured by a sympathetic understanding of Greek philosophy and possibly Hellenistic mystery-religions.
At the same time there are undoubted links with Palestinian traditions and rabbinic exegesis. That Judaism, in spite of its ex-
clusiveness, could become considerably Hellenized in its thinking
while still recognizably itself, is made patently clear by Philo's
works. Other evidence suggests that he should not be regarded as a
totally isolated figure, but rather as the most outstanding example
of a tradition of religious thinking and apologetic which had a wide
currency in Greak-speaking Judaism outside Palestine.

The Logos-doctrine of Philo is highly complex and it is impossible to do more than draw attention to a number of points which
are particularly striking in relation to christological development.

(*i*) The Logos doctrine entails a kind of binitarian view of God,
an acknowledged distinction between God transcendent and God
immanent. 'When scripture says that God made man in the image
of God, it means he made him in the image of the "second God",
who is his Logos. For nothing mortal can be made in the likeness of
the most High One and Father of the universe.'[77] The intelligible
world, Plato's Ideas, came into being in the mind of God, and, as
his Logos (Reason, Word), provided the pattern for creation; but
the Logos is more than a pattern, since it is the immanent bond
which pervades the whole and keeps the multifarious creation in an
unbreakable unity.[78] Thus the transcendent God is related to the
world through the mediator, his Logos.

(*ii*) The Logos is not only 'God' but also 'Man', and men aspire
to be children of 'God's Man, who being the Word of the Eternal
must himself be imperishable'.[79] 'They who live in the knowledge
of the One are rightly called "sons of God", as Moses also acknow-
ledges when he says, "You are sons of the Lord God" (Deut. 14.1)
"God, the one who begat you" (Deut. 32.18), and "Is he not your
father?" (Deut. 32.6). But if there is any as yet unfit to be called a
son of God, let him press to take his place under God's first-born,
the Word, who is the "eldest" (a word conveying both priority and
status) of the angels, as it were an "archangel" (literally, the ruling
angel).'[80]

(*iii*) This heavenly or ideal Man/Logos is the prime image of God
who has direct access to realities rather than being dependent upon
instruction. He therefore imparts revelation. He also acts as God's
'viceroy'; for God, the Shepherd, 'leads his hallowed flock in accord-

ance with right and law but setting over it his true Word and first-born son'.[81]

Philo's writings were preserved and cherished by the church, and provided the inspiration for a sophisticated Christian philosophical theology – indeed, in many respects he certainly anticipated formal christological exposition. Even if he does not identify his heavenly Logos-Man with a particular historical figure – for all men participate in him in varying degrees, just as other particulars participate in a Platonic 'idea', yet he certainly provides a pre-Christian picture of a heavenly intermediary being of the kind Christians were to identify with Jesus. The frequent analogies to the language of the Johannine· prologue and the Colossians hymn about the cosmic Christ have not passed unnoticed, and his participatory language is akin to Pauline and Johannine expressions of 'adopted sonship', 'being in Christ', 'dwelling in him and he in us'. Yet it is impossible to establish that his writings were known to any of the authors of the New Testament books (except possibly the author of *Hebrews*), and it is highly unlikely that the sophisticated philosophy of Philo himself had any direct influence on the early development of incarnational belief.

Behind Philo, however, is the wider world of Hellenistic Judaism, a world of which we know tantalizingly little because most of the evidence has been lost. Yet it seems highly likely that Saul of Tarsus came under influences similar to those behind Philo, and in particular, both seem to have been inspired by the so-called 'hypostatization' of Wisdom.

In the book of Proverbs, alongside straightforward sayings suggesting the value of wisdom and knowledge, Wisdom appears in a strongly personified form, 'crying aloud in the street . . .', calling and rebuking men who refuse to follow her. For most of the book this seems to be merely a graphic way of speaking, and Wisdom is apparently contrasted with the strange woman, the harlot who leads young men astray, no doubt a personification of folly. In chapter 8, however, we seem to have something more. Wisdom again calls to men, but here what she calls is a long list of her virtues and accomplishments, and then a description of how she was possessed by the Lord in the beginning, how she was brought forth before creation, and acted as his 'child' or perhaps 'assistant' (the interpretation is uncertain) when he marked out the foundations of the earth. This is often regarded as still merely a graphic way of speaking, a view supported by parallel expressions in the book (e.g. 2.6; 3.19, etc.); yet the character of this poem is strongly suggestive of the 'Isis-aretalogy', texts in which the mystery-goddess

Isis is depicted summoning men and proclaiming her own virtues and accomplishments in the first person. It is not without plausibility that W. L. Knox sees here an interpolation which was a deliberate attempt in the Ptolemaic period to baptize, as it were, into the Jewish traditions, the female figure of Isis with all her attractions.[82]

Whatever its origins, this picture of Wisdom as issuing from God and acting as his agent is further developed in Ecclus. (Ben Sira) 24. Here she is created before all things, and in the congregation of the Most High, she proclaims herself as dwelling in high places; 'my throne is in the pillar of cloud'. The distinctive point in this aretalogy is her coming to dwell in Israel as the Torah.

So far we have looked at material which is certainly Palestinian in origin, and where the implications of the personification can be variously assessed. By contrast, the Greek *Wisdom of Solomon* (chapter 7) takes up these traditions and turns Wisdom into a kind of Stoic Logos, the immanent Spirit of God, 'pervading and penetrating all things by reason of her pureness', the 'breath of the power of the God, and a clear effluence of the glory of the almighty . . . an effulgence of everlasting light, an unspotted mirror of the working of God and an image of his goodness . . .' Some of these very phrases reappear in Hebrews 1.3 in relation to the Son.

In this development it looks as though an attribute of God, his Wisdom, has become a quasi-independent being acting as God's agent. It is clear that Philo's Logos is of a similar character; God's Mind or Reason is projected forth as his creative Word. But this kind of idea is not confined to Hellenistic Judaism. In rabbinic texts, Ben Sira's identification of Wisdom and Torah is pursued, and Torah seems to become a 'hypostatized' divine figure; God's Name, his Memra (word), and above all his Shekinah (presence) are treated as somewhat indirect manifestations of his transcendent holiness, so much so that they almost receive an independent existence. Surprising as it is, such ideas seem not to have been regarded as an affront to monotheism; presumably prior to their association with the concrete figure of Jesus they were only dimly perceived as personal, and Jewish scholars can reasonably defend the rabbis from 'Christianizing' interpretations. Yet, interestingly enough, some of the names of those concretely envisaged beings, the archangels, suggest the personification of divine attributes; Gabriel – might of God, Phanuel – face of God.

From this material it is clear that for Jews speculation about quasi-divine mediators was 'in the air'. What happened in christology was that they were all superseded by the Risen Christ who thus inevitably became pre-existent from before the foundation of the world.

7. Conclusion

It has not been my intention to suggest that any of the evidence presented in this chapter, or indeed any of the theories outlined, makes it possible to reconstruct a definitive account of the rise of incarnational belief in the early church. Subtle objections and rival interpretations of the texts are always possible. What I have tried to do is to show that the cultural atmosphere of the ancient world, pervading not only pagan circles but also various Jewish traditions and, as far as we can tell, affecting many social and intellectual strata of society, was conducive to the development of this idea. It is to the general syncretistic state of religion in the relevant period that we must look for an explanation of the rise of this doctrine.

So the only conclusion I wish to press is that the theological position discussed in this book does not depend upon any specific theory proving to be impervious to scholarly criticism. Michael Goulder's suggestion in the last chapter is a fascinating and plausible reconstruction if only because, more adequately than most other specific theories, it utilizes known influences on the early church at the time with which we are primarily concerned; but it is not indispensable for the general thesis that the idea of incarnation was culturally dependent. Indeed it should by now be apparent that some of the features of Samaritan theology to which he draws attention were in fact widespread elsewhere; for, as we have seen, insistence upon God's transcendent remoteness can be paralleled in texts from Hellenistic and rabbinic Judaism; and the tendency to 'hypostatize' God's attributes, especially Wisdom, could produce a similar 'binity' alongside the same protests on behalf of monotheism, as in Philo. In addition we may note that the sense that God had been absent for a long time was also felt by Jews of this period. For, like the Samaritans, the Sadducees rejected all books apart from the Pentateuch; and those who accepted further revelation in history believed that the Holy Spirit had departed from Israel after the last prophets, Haggai, Zechariah and Malachi, or even that it had never been present in the Second Temple.[83] Many Jews, then, lived in hope of a God felt to be remote or absent; some looked for an imminent apocalyptic irruption, supposedly predicted in the distant past when prophecy was still alive; others were beginning to look for gnosis and spiritual revelations rather than intervention in history. In other words, Samaritanism shared certain tendencies of Jewish theology in the Hellenistic age; indeed, while admitting the obscurity of Samaritan origins, we may observe that a plausible case can be made for its appearance during the early Hellenistic period as one of the many forms of Judaism which began at this time to lead a tense and sometimes openly hostile co-existence (another example being the sect at Qumran).[84] Hellenization of Judaism was not uniform, and the different groups reacted and developed in various ways. Indeed, it is perhaps a general point in favour of Michael Goulder's position that the persistent accusations of Jews against the Samaritan sect was directed at its syncretistic character, a charge made all the more plausible if II Macc. 6.2 is correct in suggesting that the Samaritans co-operated with Antiochus' Hellenizing policy. For if this assessment is at all fair, it is not unlikely that Samaritans were at least partially the vehicle of syncretistic influences in the early church.

For syncretism, both outside the confines of mainstream Judaism and in varying degrees within it, must be seen as the broader context within which specific theories need to be evaluated. There does not seem to be a single, exact analogy to the total Christian claim about Jesus in material which is definitely pre-Christian; full scale redeemer-myths are unquestionably found AD but not BC. Yet it is surely true to say with A. D. Nock that 'the impact of the figure of Jesus crystallized elements which were already there'.[85] There seem to be four basic elements:

(*i*) The use of phrases like 'son of God'; such were undoubtedly current, though admittedly with a wide range of implications, and applied to both human and superhuman beings.

(*ii*) The apotheosis or ascent of an exceptional man to the heavenly realm; we have been able to trace examples in both Greek and Jewish traditions.

These two elements were brought together in the claim that Jesus was the Messiah-Son of God, risen from the dead and ascended to become God's 'right-hand man' in heaven.

(*iii*) Belief in heavenly beings or intermediaries, some of whom might descend to succour men; one of whom might act as God's vicegerent in judgment at the end of time; and the first of whom could have been God's instrument in creation.

Once the Risen Christ took his place in heaven, it is scarcely surprising that he ousted or demoted all these figures in the Christian imagination, while taking over many of their functions and thus becoming pre-existent.

(*iv*) The fourth essential element is the idea of the manifestation of the chief of these heavenly beings on earth in a genuine incarna-

tion. Given the combination of the first three elements, it seems the
natural and logical outcome. However, it is here that the analogies
become inadequate. Pagan mythology could envisage a docetic
incarnation; Jewish legend could envisage the coming of an angel in
disguise. The association of historical or contemporary personages
with the appearances of the gods was occasionally made, but hardly
seems to have been taken seriously. Is it any wonder that the first
Christian heresy was docetism? The distinctive characteristic of
mainstream Christian belief is its inability to stray too far from the
historical reality of Jesus of Nazareth, a man crucified under
Pontius Pilate. The rapid appearance of Christian Gnosticism and
the subsequent problems of defining christology, problems which
have never been entirely resolved, show that this anchorage in history, though constantly asserted, has been permanently insecure as
long as the significance of this Jesus has been interpreted according
to categories supplied by the supernatural speculations of the
Graeco-Roman world.

   Whether or not we can unearth the precise origins of incarnational belief, it is surely clear that it belongs naturally enough to
a world in which supernatural ways of speaking seemed the highest
and best expression of the significance and finality of the one they
identified as God's awaited Messiah and envoy.

NOTES

Notes have been mostly confined to identifying passages actually quoted. Translations follow the Loeb Classical Library where it is available, apart from occasional
changes introduced by myself. Other translations used include: H. Chadwick, *Contra
Celsum*; E. H. Gifford, *Praeparatio Evangelica*; the Soncino edition of *The
Babylonian Talmud*; H. Odeberg; *III Enoch*. Other texts (e.g. Qumran) are quoted
from the secondary sources referred to.

1. Origen, *Contra Celsum*, i.57, the Simonians number thirty; ibid., vi.11,
Dositheans under thirty.
2. Ibid., i.57.
3. A. D. Nock, *Essays on Religion and the Ancient World*, ed., Zeph Stewart,
Oxford University Press 1972, vol. I, p. 35.
4. Origen, op. cit., vii.9.
5. Ibid., v.1.
6. Ibid., iii.24.
7. Ibid., i.37.
8. Athenagoras, *Legatio*, 26.
9. Lucian, *The passing of Peregrinus*, 4.
10. Ibid., 29.
11. Ibid., 39.
12. Ibid., 40.

13. Ibid., 11–16.
14. Ibid., 4.
15. Lucian, *Alexander the false-prophet*, 8–9.
16. Ibid., 11.
17. Ibid., 40.
18. Philostratus, *Life of Apollonius*, i.4.
19. Ibid., i.6.
20. Ibid., i.2.
21. Ibid., viii.7.
22. Ibid., viii.30–end.
23. Eusebius wrote a treatise against an attempt by Hierocles to turn Philostratus' *Life* into a rival gospel; he provides a critique of Philostratus' claims for Apollonius. See appendix to Loeb Classical Library ed. of Philostratus.
24. Diogenes, *Lives of the philosophers*, iii.2.1.
25. Ibid., viii.1.4–5.
26. Ibid., viii.1.11.
27. According to Aelian, *Varia Historia*, ii.26.
28. Diogenes, *Lives*, viii.2.66.
29. Ibid., viii.2.59ff. and 70.
30. Ibid., viii.2.69.
31. Ibid., viii.2.68.
32. Plutarch, *Table Talk*, viii.1.2.
33. *Alexander*, 2.
34. Ibid.
35. Ibid., 27.
36. Ibid., 2–3.
37. A. D. Nock, op. cit., pp. 134–52.
38. Livy, *Annales*, I.4.
39. Ibid., I.16.
40. Ovid, *Metamorphoses*, VIII.626–721.
41. Cicero, *Ad Quintum fratrem*, I.i.7.
42. Vergil, *Eclogue*, iv.
43. Horace, *Odes*, I.2.
44. Adolf Deissmann, *Light from the Ancient East*, ET, L. R. M. Strachan, Hodder & Stoughton 1927. For the following material see pp. 342ff.
45. A. D. Nock produced many studies of ruler-cults, the most important being in the posthumous collection cited above. For these remarks see p. 841 (vol. II) and p. 152 (vol. I).
46. Josephus, *Jewish War*, VII.x.1.
47. *Martyrdom of Polycarp*, 8.
48. Martin Hengel, *Son of God*, ET, John Bowden, SCM Press 1976, p. 30.
49. L. Bieler, *Theios Anēr*, Vienna 1935 and 1936.
50. See W. von Martitz, *Hyios* in TDNT, VIII, p. 339.
51. C. H. Talbert, 'The concept of immortals in Mediterranean Antiquity', *Journal of Biblical Literature*, vol. 94, 1975, 419ff.
52. Arnold Toynbee, among others, has popularized the parallels between Hercules and Jesus; see *A Study of History*, Oxford University Press 1939, vol. VI, pp. 465–76. M. Simon, *Hercule et le christianisme*, Paris 1953, is a more cautious historical study.
53. Justin, *I Apology*, 54ff. and 21ff., for these two different viewpoints.
54. *Alexander*, 27.
55. W. Bousset, *Kyrios Christos*, ET, John Steely, Abingdon Press 1970, p. 146.
56. J. A. Fitzmyer, 'The contribution of Qumran Aramaic to the study of the New Testament', *New Testament Studies*, vol. 20, 1974, pp. 382–407.
57. G. Vermes, *Jesus the Jew*, Collins 1973. See particularly p. 206.

58. Ibid., p. 218ff.
59. Eusebius, *Praeparatio Evangelica*, 9.27.
60. Josephus, *Antiquities*, 4.8.48.
61. Ibid., 3.5.7.
62. Philo, *Life of Moses*, II.288–91.
63. J. Jeremias, *Mōysēs*, TDNT, IV, p. 855.
64. *Hagiga*, 11b, 13a, 14b.
65. G. G. Scholem, *Major trends in Jewish Mysticism*, New York 1946, ch. 2; and *Jewish Gnosticism, Merkabah Mysticism and Talmudic Tradition*, New York 1960.
66. Hugo Odeberg, *3 Enoch or the Hebrew Book of Enoch*, Oxford University Press 1928.
67. *Hagiga*, 15a.
68. This and the following quotations will be found in *3 Enoch*, 10–14.
69. *Hagiga*, 15a and *3 Enoch*, 16.
70. That we do not need to posit Gnostic sources for the descent–ascent pattern is argued by C. H. Talbert, 'The myth of a descending–ascending redeemer in Mediterranean Antiquity', *New Testament Studies*, vol. 22, 1976, pp. 418ff., where further examples will be found.
71. M. de Jonge and A. S. van der Woude, '11Q Melchisedek and the New Testament', *New Testament Studies*, vol. 12, 1966, pp. 301–26.
72. J. A. Fitzmyer, 'Further light on Melchisedek from Qumran Cave 11', *Journal of Biblical Literature*, vol. 86, 1967, pp. 24–31; republished in *Essays on the Semitic Background of the New Testament*, Chapman 1971.
73. M. de Jonge and A. S. van der Woude, op. cit.
74. J. Daniélou, *The Theology of Jewish Christianity* (*A History of Early Christian Doctrine*, vol. I), ET, J. A. Baker, Darton, Longman & Todd 1964, pp. 122–3, and all of ch. 4: 'The Trinity and Angelology'.
75. Origen, *Comm. in Joh.*, 2.31.
76. A. D. Nock, op. cit., vol. II, p. 574.
77. Philo, *Qu. in Gen.*, IX.6.
78. *Plant.*, 8–10; *Fuga*, 112; *Qu. in Ex.*, II.118.
79. *De Conf.*, 41.
80. *De Conf.*, 145.
81. *De Agric.*, 50ff.
82. W. L. Knox, 'The Divine Wisdom', *Journal of Theological Studies*, vol. 38, 1937, pp. 230–7; and *St Paul and the Church of the Gentiles*, Cambridge University Press 1939, ch. III.
83. E. Schweizer, *Pneuma* in TDNT, VI. pp. 385ff.
84. R. J. Coggins, *Samaritans and Jews. The origins of Samaritanism reconsidered*, Blackwell 1975.
85. A. D. Nock, op. cit., vol. II, p. 932.

PART II

Testing the Development

6

The Creed of Experience

LESLIE HOULDEN

There is not one christology in the New Testament, there are many. By now it has almost become common knowledge that if you look at the New Testament writings from any point nearer than a distant mountain, you can distinguish a number of different pictures of Christ. In fact you will find that each writer has his own and you may even decide that one of them, Paul, shifted his viewpoint within the writings which expose his mind to us. Not that the pictures do not have much in common; so great is the overlap that the many Christian generations, which looked at the matter with synthesizing rather than analysing gaze, saw only contributions to a harmonious whole, whose outline the terms of later orthodoxy had picked out and defined. But today many of us are analysers, for good or ill. It would take too long to say why we are: we must accept our lot, bequeathed to us by the Enlightenment, and make the most of it. Still, the fact that our eyes are trained to distinguish rather than harmonize need not make us blind to the claims of unity. Of course the writers all (except James?) unite in seeing Christ as the key that unlocks all doors where God is concerned, the clue to the discovery of all secrets. And we can sketch a shared background within whose terms they all expressed those great, dominating convictions.

The first task, having admitted the variety, is to decide how to evaluate it. At one time, it was usual to take the titles of Jesus as the basis of analysis. One investigated their background, Jewish or Greek, and arrived at their sense. Then one moved from book to book, examining the use, dropping the sense into the mind of the sacred writers one by one. The focus has changed. It has come to seem wooden to suppose that the titles were so univocal, perhaps over a wide geographical area, that they could perform a closely similar role in book after book.

So the basis of analysis is now, more commonly, the individual writer, though the titles retain a place, as the chief tool of exploration. There is something humanly more sensitive and literarily more satisfying about this. When I am told what 'son of God' meant in the first century, the matter remains abstract until I hear to whom it meant it. So we set out to identify the picture of Jesus each writer saw, and we describe the christologies by reference to the titles in which the writers express them. We give an account of the christology of Paul by telling how he uses terms like Christ, Son of God, Lord, and wisdom with reference to Jesus. We compare him with John by noting that for John other titles and images also play a part and that the proportions differ. So we distinguish and relate the various New Testament pictures of Jesus. The ingredients both vary and coincide, but each account has its own outline, its own consistency and its own message. To this writer, then to that, this was what Jesus signified. By distinct combinations of information, speculation, conviction and piety, Jesus had come to mean these things, and these were the ways to express them.

As basis or as tool, the titles have become the staple element of scholarly analysis. Though not exhausted, perhaps in principle that vein has been mined enough. Moreover, this approach leaves something of a gap when it is a question of how christology may now be expressed: on what lines and by what reasoning does one put in new ways those ancient teachings, supposing one is not content simply to reproduce them? Other ways of analysing the thought of these writings are worth seeking, even though we may tread less surely. But before we look for signs of promise in this direction, let us dig into a fundamental question.

What is the status of the accounts of New Testament christologies which are offered to us? We take the writings of Paul. We set out, let us say, his use of 'Lord'. He uses it this number of times, in these syntactical contexts: so far we are on secure ground. We move on to the contexts of sense in which he uses it and we classify them, attempting to link them with our knowledge of the word's meaning elsewhere. The ground is now less secure, but nevertheless we build up a useful and identifiable picture, as we then go on to link 'Lord' with other titles Paul employs. In these later stages, imagination plays a necessary role, enabling us to shape a pattern, prepare a structure, which we modify as the enquiry progresses.

But what is the status of this pattern? In arriving at it in our own minds, then perhaps laying it out for others in speech or writing, what do we suppose we have achieved? It is our account of the christology of Paul; but what relation does it bear to anything which ever occupied the apostle's mind? And if I get as far as being aware of the gap between my picture of his thought and his own, as far as being baffled and tantalized by it, can I either profit from these emotions or do anything to bridge the gap?

The profit in the emotions lies in the feeling of them. All I can do towards bridging the gap is to perceive it. Both are better than to attribute a false objectivity to my account of his thought. They establish his autonomy while allowing me still to look at him and form my impression of him.

These considerations create an atmosphere of fragility in which to assess our account of (in our example) the christology of Paul. They put emphasis on its being our account of that christology, not that christology itself. They impose a reticence upon what seems at first to have the makings of solid objectivity. As we set about our counting and classifying, we seem to make a steady advance into measurable territory, which, once occupied, is ours. So we find it hard when we discover that talk of occupation is inappropriate for what we have done.

It is salutary to acknowledge the limitations inherent in our task, not only because they are there, but also because they seem more obvious in other approaches and we may feel discouraged, thinking – falsely – that along the conventional lines of enquiry they do not apply.

Thus, instead of working with the titles of Jesus, we may set out to distinguish one New Testament writer's belief about Jesus from another's by reference to their degree of closeness to renewed personal vision. In order to explain, let us boldly dogmatize. For some people, particularly at the start of a new religious movement, existing terms are inadequate to express experience. Only new words (or non-words, as in glossolalia) or new uses of old words will serve. Experience of God has been transformed by the arrival of new ingredients or by an impulse which rearranged the elements in existing patterns of thought. Clearly Jesus was such a new ingredient and agent of rearrangement. We may describe his felt effect as the revitalizing and reshaping of people's sense of God. There was heightened awareness of God's reality, God's claims, God's promises, God's power. Those affected now knew God differently from before.

The content of that new sense of God is not for the present our concern. What matters is the intimate link between experience and words: vivid experience leading to reminted words. We shall not be surprised that in such circumstances the same agent, Jesus, produced varied patterns of words; not surprised at imprecision, inconsistency, incoherence. Indeed, there will be a tendency for orderliness of language to be somewhat at the expense of brilliance and to arouse suspicion that experience has been considered in detachment before being tidied into words.

Is it then possible to separate this stage of theological creativity from another stage which may quickly follow or go alongside? We may name the first experiential, the second credal. At the second stage, the link between experience and statement is weakened, lengthened and altered. Weakened, in that the experience is now often second-hand and imitative, taught rather than inspired, a duty rather than an irresistible impulse, and flatly descriptive rather than brilliantly revelatory. Lengthened, in that a process of reflection, ordering and systematization has intervened. The surging spring of inspiration has turned into a controlled flow of thought. Altered, in that a new spirit has come into the process. Considerations of policy, institutional needs, such as come from teaching and worshipping, and external pressures, such as surrounding society exerts, clothe the hitherto naked and unselfconscious development with garb which may at first be felt to impede movement but is soon welcomed for its comfort.

In the New Testament there are examples of both stages, especially in christology and related areas of belief, for here was the central focus of early Christian attention. The two stages are not divided neatly by time, the first occupying so many years, the second supervening; though the first is more prominent at the beginning. Nor are they divided neatly between the books. Paul belongs more to the first stage, though he has strong elements of the second and some of them are inherited from Christians before him; while we may assign the writer of the Pastoral Epistles largely to the second. So though we may speak broadly of two *stages*, we may do better to speak of two kinds of expression, two approaches, which will occur in certain types of religious situation.

There is a strong element of post-Kantian consciousness in distinguishing the two approaches at all, and we need to reckon with the fact that those involved in writing early Christian books would surely have been aware of no such distinction. If Paul had survived to scrutinize the Pastoral Epistles and had felt moved to repudiate them, he would not have thought or said that it was because they had shifted intolerably from the experiential to the credal mode. And if we were in a position to explain to Paul that we considered him creatively imprecise and vividly imaginative in capturing his experience in new words, he might not take it as a compliment. On the contrary, both Paul and the Pastor would doubtless make the same claim: to be stating the factual truth about God and Jesus in their work for mankind.

But we find that claim inaccurate. No thoughtful modern man, however attached he may be to the Christian faith in its New Testament expression, would fail to distinguish between a level of fact and a level of imagery in Paul's work: yes, he may say, I can gladly echo Paul in saying that I am justified by God through Christ, but of course I know that both he and I are using imagery whose pedigree is ascertainable and which approximates to experience. God is not precisely that, he is like that. We have no reason to suppose that Paul would have appreciated any such distinction. It is true that Christians are often inclined to attribute greater straightforwardness of sense to central christological terms like 'Lord' or 'Son of God' than they do to terms like 'justify'. But only a modest effort of reflection is required to see that here too there is a context of imagery and concepts which conditioned early Christian use and, however highly we rate them in our own expression of faith, an element of approximation in their capacity to describe him to whom they point. To speak of Jesus, or in another use of the term, a Christian believer, as 'Son of God' is to use an analogy from human sonship which, if we decide that it is not too historically conditioned for continued use, we need to delimit as well as exploit; and the same is true of 'Lord', however uncritically it has been so commonly embraced.

So if (let us suppose) Paul was unaware of a distinction between descriptive, factual statement and imagery, as categories in which theological language might be placed, and so unaware that the former is always inappropriate, that is no reason why we should not venture to rescue him. And if he would not have recognized our distinction between experiential and credal modes of religious language, that is no reason why we should not recognize it on his behalf. But has the distinction any practical implications?

It has considerable implications for our understanding of both the way in which christological statement in the New Testament was arrived at and its point of reference.

Consider again the credal mode. In so far as he who formulates statements about Jesus in this mode leans upon inherited tradition rather than fresh conversion, feels loyalty to formulas rather than an impulse to struggle for new ways of expression, then he is likely to be at all levels involved in an allegedly descriptive and factual use of religious language. As he speaks of Jesus as 'Lord' or 'Son of God', not only will he reckon to be speaking factually (if only for want of awareness that any other option is open to him), but there will be no way by which we can point to other levels of awareness, concealed from him but open to scrutiny from our standpoint. They simply do not exist. The credal type of statement is then open only to repetition and reaffirmation – or else to flat denial. Dealing in allegedly factual statements about God or Jesus, it cannot be radically reinterpreted and is best dealt with simply by handing it on. It shuns creativity and invites tenacity.

But once conclude that descriptive, factual statement about God is to be disallowed, and the credal mode is done for. If the statement that Jesus is 'Son of God' or 'Lord' is once recognized as analogical, then the man who rests all on its being factual and descriptive can only be accounted mistaken. His belief is not what he thought it was and he has nowhere to turn. (So the man who believes in the imminent end of the world *solely* as a factually predicted event and whose belief is then falsified by the passage of time must abandon his belief and perhaps also attachment to the authority which backed it. It is a sign of how little such belief was *merely* predictive in the early church that falsification did not lead to the collapse of faith; however little those concerned would have been able to put it so, their belief was a way of expressing far more about God (a faith in his power, the ultimacy of his control) than just that he would wind up the world one day soon.)

Belief after the experiential mode offers other prospects. Unsatisfactory as supposed description its verbal expression may often be – it is liable to imprecision and inconsistency. But it is in close touch with the springs of religion: it leads us to the place where man most deeply responds to God. The point of interest is now that moment when someone first found himself impelled to say of Jesus, as the only appropriate response – 'Son of God'. That this term (or 'Lord' or 'Messiah' or 'Son of Man') was drawn out of him tells us, once we know its current sense (or in most cases, senses), something of the experience to which Jesus gave rise.

We should note that it was *religious* experience – that is, experience concerning God. Jesus evoked or produced significant new convictions, not primarily concerning himself (however much they presented themselves in that form), but concerning God. The titles attached to him because he was the novel, tangible element; but he was in fact the agent whereby experience of God was enlarged and transformed. In this sense *christo*logy is essentially parasitic upon *theo*logy, most clearly so where belief is set in the experiential mode. In the credal mode it is less clearly so: one can always describe one part of a picture while ignoring the rest, and some accounts of the significance of Jesus have had this character. But in the creative beginnings of the Christian faith it was not so. As a doctrinal innovator, Jesus was strictly the servant of God.

The titles of Jesus were then at the experiential stage not labels attached to his person but oblique statements about God. Each of them spoke of a way in which God had been freshly illuminated and the relationship with him transported to a new level. To take the 'lowest' and the 'highest' of them: if one regarded Jesus as a prophet, it signified a newly vivid expectation, aroused by him, of divine guidance or revelation; if one regarded him as 'wisdom', it signified (in certain contexts) a transformed vision of the created order, its status and its potentiality. To take the point of deepest effect: if one contemplated him as the crucified one, it led, by tortuous paths of scriptural imagery and insight, to a newly profound sense of the whole range of human experience as within God's grasp.

But, supposing this analysis to have any validity, does it lead us anywhere in our attempts to speak of Jesus now, taking account of the factors which now affect such speech? Notice that what we have done is to prise open that lid of words which, in the New Testament, lies upon the earliest stirrings of christological thought. Like the heavy lid of a great chest, it snaps back into place the moment we withdraw effort. But we must try to maintain the effort (largely of imagination) long enough to gain a new view of the task facing us. If we have reservations about what we have called the credal approach, not simply because formulas of the past become obsolete but fundamentally because such a use of language is improper concerning God, then we may be led to formulate the christological question thus: what must I say about Jesus when as a result of him, by innumerable routes, I have been brought to that experience of God which has been my lot and privilege? The resulting answer may be far from traditional words, but it will avoid the obstruction of technicality, it will have a refreshing realism, it will reach out towards spirituality, and it will be, strictly, theological. It may also turn out to bypass some of the traditional questions and draw the sting of anxiety which they so often retain: in what sense was Jesus unique? how was he both divine and human? how was he God incarnate? To use the bypass may strike some as being an evasion of the city; to others it is a way of reaching the destination more quickly.

Christians agree about the centrality of Jesus for all that concerns

man's relationship with God and understanding of him – and
everything that hangs thereon. They also agree (though you would
not always think it) in holding to the deep and intimate involvement of God with the world and the human race of which he is
creator. It would be odd to wish to attach oneself to the Christian
cause if one did not share that kind of understanding, that kind of
spiritual sense.

But is 'the centrality of Jesus for all that concerns man's understanding of God' an allowable equivalent for or development of the
relevant christological statements of the Nicene Creed or the
Chalcedonian Definition? And is 'the deep and intimate involvement of God with the world' an allowable interpretation of what
is at stake in the statement that 'the Word was made flesh'? Many
will hold that they are not: perhaps because they are wedded, for
good reasons or bad, to what we have styled the credal approach to
belief; perhaps because they think that too much of the spirit and
substance of traditional statement has been lost. The new
statements are in no reasonable sense 'equivalents' of the old, even
if they draw out some of their meaning. Some of those who take
this view may find themselves at a loss to know how such
equivalence may in any case be evaluated: on what basis may the
words of one age be carried into the speech of another?

Others (rarer beings) may applaud the new statements but not
share the concern for equivalence with ancient faith: let us speak
now as we can, telling in straightforward words what we can now
believe, leaving old words to old times, respected, known, built
upon, but left in their place.

Others still may wish to pursue the matter further. They will feel
the force of the historical and linguistic sensitivity which has
brought the traditional formulas into question and subjected them
to new brands of scrutiny. They will know the pressure of general
truth which makes certain ways of thought, implicit in the old
words, outmoded and unbelievable. They will also know that if the
Christian message is to make its way in the diverse and multiform
worlds of discourse now before it, it must strive harder for clarity
and intelligibility; and that the deepest levels of spiritual integrity
must be discovered and tapped. To that end the identifying in plain
terms of the earliest experience of God through Jesus may contribute, by sowing seeds in Christian minds which now seek to respond
to him in words of their own.

7

The Christ of Christendom

DON CUPITT

The Eastern theologian John of Damascus (*c.* 675–749) once used a very curious argument in favour of icons. Ironically, it was because he was living under Muslim protection before Islam became generally iconoclastic that he was able to defend icons from within Islam at a time when it was not safe to defend them inside the Empire. John replied to the criticism that icons are unscriptural by admitting the fact, and adding that you will not find in scripture the Trinity or the *homoousion* or the two natures of Christ either. But we know *those* doctrines are true. And so, having acknowledged that icons, the Trinity and the incarnation are innovations, John goes on to urge his reader to hold fast to them as venerable traditions delivered to us by the fathers. If they were lost, the whole gospel would be threatened.

He was not the only one to use this argument: Theodore the Studite (759–826) adopted it too. It brings out an odd feature of Christianity, its mutability and the speed with which innovations come to be vested with religious solemnity to such an extent that anyone who questions them find *himself* regarded as the dangerous innovator and heretic. An amusing example from our own day is the assurance with which the church praises and defends 'the family', so that almost the first principle of Christian ethics is respect for the family and dutiful performance of one's assigned role in it. Yet the gospels are still canonical, and it appears from the gospels that Jesus was highly critical of the family for strong religious reasons. For him, the call of the kingdom was away from family roles, not into them. The idealization of the family is a modern cultural creation, which the churches have validated, and now no modern bishop would dream of publicly endorsing Jesus' views about the family.

It is perfectly possible for an opinion to be firmly believed to be orthodox, traditional, conservative and Catholic, when it is in fact of very recent origin. Yet the suggestion that the classical doctrine of the incarnation belongs, not to the essence of Christianity, but only to a certain period of church history, now ended, will certainly startle many people. Nevertheless, I believe it is true. To begin at the end, there was a certain moment in the nineteenth century when the old Chalcedonian 'orthodoxy', a view of Christ which had prevailed for fifteen hundred years, began to crumble from within. The last really able defence of a fully orthodox doctrine of Christ in Britain was H. P. Liddon's *The Divinity of our Lord and Saviour Jesus Christ* (1865). The leader of the next generation, Charles Gore (1853–1932), found himself unable to continue the tradition.

It is important to remember that Gore really was an insider, for in these matters the thoughts of insiders are far more decisive than the thoughts of outsiders. In 'background', education, career and allegiances Gore was everything that the old bourgeois England, now passing away, thought a great churchman should be. As such he was of course no timeserver, but a thinker, an Anglo-Catholic, and a socialist, albeit of a very pale pink colour.

In his youth Gore seems to have been deeply influenced by reading Sir John Seeley's *Ecce Homo*, which had appeared in 1865. *Ecce Homo* was a pioneer in a *genre* still popular, the sentimental and by scholarly standards fictitious life of Jesus. Yet Gore, to the end of his life, thought it had real historical value, and it is remarkable to find him still praising it in 1927.[1] He belonged to a generation in which classical 'Mods and Greats' followed by private study of the Greek Testament and the fathers still seemed a sufficient education for a theologian. He was no radical in biblical criticism and knew nothing of rabbinic Judaism. And for him, *Ecce Homo* brought out something about the reality of Jesus' human life which the church had 'obscured'.

Gore's seniors, men like Liddon and E. B. Pusey, were contemptuous of *Ecce Homo*, and it is not immediately obvious why Gore was so impressed. He knew perfectly well, and always insisted, that the church had ever taught Christ's full humanity. He says rather priggishly that only divine providence could have led the fathers so firmly to emphasize Christ's manhood 'in an age when the general tendency of Catholic thought was certainly not humanitarian'.[2] And Gore never *intended* to break with orthodoxy, for he really did believe in the incarnation. He never believed that Jesus was a man with human hypostasis ('person' in the technical sense, roughly equivalent to 'individuating principle' or 'distinct logical subject-of-predication', and rather narrower in meaning than 'individual spiritual substance'). Gore believed that in Jesus there was only one person, and that the person of the Word of God. So Jesus was not a man living a human life, but the divine Word living a human life. Gore did not learn from Seeley that Jesus was a man after all. Seeley led him to think that what had been lost was a full imaginative realization of what it was for the divine Word to have actually lived a *fully* human life.

Liddon asserted, and set out to prove, that there is no difference between history and dogma, that the Jesus of the gospels really was the Byzantine Christos Pantocrator, 'the God whom we believers adore'.[3] Gore would not say that there was a real conflict between the Jesus of the gospels and the Christ of conciliar dogma, but he admitted a real distinction, and in effect a certain tension; and that was what mattered for the future.

His first manoeuvre was in line with Anglican tradition. He asserted that the old formulae (two natures, each entire, united without confusion in one divine person, coessential with Deity in his divine nature and with us in his human nature) did not contain any explanation of the incarnation, or analysis of its content, but merely defined certain limits to orthodox systematic thought and banned certain deviations from it. They set out not the content but the criteria of Catholic faith in Christ. They were not premises for dogmatic construction but rather boundaries within which it must keep.

Gore was making a form/matter distinction. To know the Word Incarnate you must do more than learn the definitions. You must read the gospels, guided by them. The dogmas prescribe the form, and the gospels provide the matter, of Christian knowledge of the incarnate Lord.

But if this were a sufficient answer, there would be no problem. The difficulty is, as Gore well knew, that if the orthodox dogma is internally incoherent it cannot function as a hedge, limit or boundary, because it fails to mark out and enclose any intelligible space for the Christian mind to move in. Gore was driven to tamper with the definitions in order to make them enclose such a real space.

Gore was not a philosophical theologian, and he did not phrase his questions in any very precise or technical form. He did not ask how one can distinguish, in God, between person, nature and attributes belonging to that nature. He did not ask, in a technical way, how one can intelligibly affirm that a single subject, the divine

Word, possesses three sets of attributes, the set which comprise his
divine nature, the set which comprise essential human nature and a
set of contingent human attributes, when some of the attributes in
the first set appear to be incompossible in a single subject with some
in the other two sets. He certainly did not ask how that being *can*
be 'fully human', the metaphysical subject of whose life is not
human, but divine. He did not put the matter in quite these technical terms. But he did implicitly raise such questions by the way he
posed the particular issue of the incarnate Lord's human knowledge and consciousness.

Some commentators give the impression that Liddon had taught
that Jesus was virtually omniscient, whereas Gore felt obliged to
admit the limitation of Jesus' knowledge. This is misleading. What
happened was that Gore found he could no longer hold together two
things that Liddon *had* held together. Liddon, following tradition,
declared that 'His Single Personality has two spheres of existence;
in the one it is all-blessed, undying and omniscient; in the other it
meets with pain of mind and body, with actual death, and with a
corresponding liability to a limitation of knowledge'. But, says
Liddon, 'these contrasts, while they enhance our sense of our
Lord's love and condescension, do not destroy our apprehension of
the Personal Unity of the Incarnate Christ'.[4] Liddon, that is, did
not see in the full two-natures doctrine any threat to the unity of
Christ's person. Gore did, and at this point begins to move away
from Chalcedonian orthodoxy. Something he has learnt from *Ecce
Homo* and from the gospels makes it impossible for him to see how
the incarnate Lord can be fully human and *both* omniscient *and*
ignorant. Quite clearly one thing that has happened is that whereas
Liddon understands 'personality' in the traditional metaphysical
sense, Gore is beginning to understand it in an historical, ethical
and psychological sense. He talks mainly about Jesus' human consciousness, and the upshot of what he says is that he does *not*
believe that the full panoply of divine attributes and all the attributes of humanity are co-present complete and entire, and where
appropriate displayed, during the earthly life of the one person of
the incarnate Lord. To save the unity of his person and the human
entirety of his life, some of the divine attributes must be dimmed or
veiled. The kenotic theory is the result.

I must emphasize that Gore did believe in the incarnation. A
count in reasonably closely-matched passages suggests to me that
Gore does not employ the term 'Jesus' any more than Liddon. Like
Liddon, he prefers more honorific expressions like 'our Lord',
'Christ', 'Jesus Christ', 'the incarnate Lord', 'the Son of God' and

so on. There is some linguistic shift, but it is not great; not as great as the same shift would be in a modern book. But he is moving away from the two-natures doctrine in its historic form. Thus he dislikes Pope Leo's Tome (of AD 449) which distributes to the Two Natures the words and deeds of Jesus, as if Jesus were at one moment merely Clark Kent and at the next Superman.[5] And if we object to Gore that he is 'psychologizing Jesus', he would surely have replied that Christian faith demands it, for it proposes a mutual sympathy between the believer and the Lord who condescended to share our sorrows.

Gore's kenotic theory is of merely historical interest now. He must describe an ethical, not a metaphysical, kenosis for the excellent reason that a metaphysical kenosis is incompatible with theism. Since the divine attributes belong to God not contingently but analytically it is logically impossible for the deity to doff one like a superfluous piece of clothing. But the ethical kenosis Gore describes (somewhat vaguely) is scarcely different from what may be found in Luther or Kierkegaard, or indeed Liddon himself. Besides which, the idea of kenosis in bourgeois Christian thought is clearly socially-conditioned. In a class society, where the Christian tradition was carried by people of very high status and privilege, there was a need for christological validation of the duty to 'condescend to men of low estate'. The change in the connotations of the word 'condescension' since those days gives us a revealing glimpse of theology's cultural relativity, and makes clear the hopeless inappropriateness of the idea of kenosis today.

But if Gore is remote from us, Liddon, the last defender of full orthodoxy, is a universe away. Liddon's Jesus is acutely aware of 'His rank in the scale of being', conscious of his own 'absolute sinlessness', speaks with 'intense authoritativeness' and 'increasing Self-assertion'. Indeed, for Liddon 'Self-assertion' is the dominant note in all Jesus' recorded teaching.[6] To read Liddon is to realize how far we have already travelled from full Chalcedonian orthodoxy. If Gore's Christ is that somewhat old-fashioned figure, a privileged person with an earnest social conscience, Liddon's Christ is a completely confident authoritarian monarch, the Christ of Christendom.

My suggestion is then that the themes of the present volume are not novel, even in a conservative country like Britain. Somewhere between Liddon and Gore a view of Christ which took shape in the fourth and fifth centuries began to collapse; and to collapse, not just in the minds of rationalist critics, but in the minds of the leading churchmen of the day. And if social and political changes at

least partly account for its breakdown, they were correspondingly
involved in its rise.

For if the 'orthodox' doctrine of Christ had an end, it also had a
beginning. We can gain some idea of the character of that beginning by considering one or two moments in the history of Christian
art.

The Bible contains (Ex. 20.4) a categorical prohibition, not
merely of any kind of image of God, but of any naturalistic or
representational art, a prohibition which has influenced Jews and
Muslims to this day. Nothing other than God can be an adequate
image of God, and God himself, being transcendent, cannot be
delineated. Early Christianity inherited and followed this rule. Old
Testament arguments against idolatry, pagan arguments and early
Christian arguments ran closely parallel.[7]

Preconstantinian Christian art was scarce, unofficial, of very
poor quality and often somewhat ambiguous. Many a pagan sculp-
tured frieze might incorporate the figures of a philosopher, holding
a codex, with his disciples; or of a youthful shepherd, or a vine.
There was just enough Christian art in the West for the Latin writer
Tertullian to take the trouble to denounce the practice of portray-
ing the Good Shepherd, but, Tertullian being what he was, that
does not amount to much.

Even in the fourth century Christian art as it began to emerge
met very sharp traditionalist opposition. The Emperor Constantine's
sister wrote to Bishop Eusebius of Caesarea, requesting a por-
trait of Christ. Few prelates have ever been more obsequious to
royalty than Eusebius, but he sharply refused her request, explaining the biblical and traditional grounds for the church's detestation
of idolatry. Christian art, he says, doesn't exist and cannot exist. In 343
Cyril, Bishop of Jerusalem, attacked the portrayal of the crucifixion
in his Easter Sermon; and later still (c. 380) Bishop Epiphanius of
Salamis, visiting Palestine, was so enraged to see a church hanging,
with a figure of Christ or a saint, that he tore it down and subsequently delivered himself of a fiercely polemical treatise against
icons, which he regarded as idols.

But the protests of these great churchmen were in vain: Christian
art was emerging as part of a complex process by which
Christianity was very extensively paganized in its faith, worship,
organization and social teaching. The period during which the classical doctrine of Christ was being framed was also the period in
which a largely pagan iconography of Christ was developed; and
these developments were both of them profoundly influenced by
political needs and pressures.

N. H. Baynes, in a brief article on 'Eusebius and the Christian Empire',[8] showed how very closely Eusebius' first sketch of the political theology of Byzantium followed the Hellenistic philosophy of kingship. As God is to the cosmos, so the king is to the state. The divine logos indwells the king, teaching him to mimic the divine virtue, to be a good shepherd of his people, to save them from sin and lead them by the path of salvation to the heavenly kingdom. The king was a kind of incarnate god, the one link between earth and heaven.

To 'Christianize' this scheme it was only necessary to declare Christ the universal cosmic Emperor, and make the earthly Emperor his servant and vicar. The entire imperial cult and ideology was refocused on Christ, while in return Christ crowned his earthly deputy and validated his rule. Eusebius took only the first step in this direction, but others soon followed.

In the new order, the church's chief ministers were granted secular dignity, privileges, dress and insignia, much of which they tenaciously maintain to this day, and the church's worship borrowed extensively from court ritual. And all this, says Theodore Klauser, 'served to transform permanently the way in which the person of Jesus Christ was represented . . . (He) began to be looked on as a ruler who as the "Pantocrator" governed the whole of creation . . . he assumed the outward marks of imperial rank; he was the ruler who sat on a throne adorned with jewels and purple cushions, who wore the royal halo, whose foot and hand were kissed, who was surrounded with a heavenly cortège of palace officials and much else besides'. Almost the only remaining trace of Jesus is his dark bearded semitic face, peering out with understandable sadness from its incongruous new setting. His associates were similarly exalted: 'Mary became the Mother and Empress, the apostles were turned into a senate, the angels now constituted the household of a heavenly court, and the saints were represented as guests seeking audience and bringing their offerings.'[9]

All this is familiar enough, and is exhibited more eloquently at Ravenna, or in a pontifical high mass, or in a coronation service, than ever it could be in words. Early Christianity had repudiated the Emperor-cult, but now conciliar Christianity came increasingly to be modelled on the Emperor-cult. It is scarcely surprising that the Emperors saw the correct definition of the dogma of Christ as a matter of high political importance; and when it was defined to their satisfaction they enforced it with all the power of the State, establishing a political order which in one form and another lingered on until the First World War.

Now it might be that in spite of the dubious political circumstances of its definition, the orthodox dogma of the incarnation might nonetheless be true. But in fact I believe that the way the dogma came to be defined had in the long run damaging effects upon belief in God, and upon the way man's relation to God was conceived. Four arguments will, I hope, make the point clear.

1. The assertion that deity itself and humanity are permanently united in the one person of the incarnate Lord suggests an ultimate synthesis, a conjunction and continuity between things divine and things of this world. As the popular maxim had it, Grace does not destroy but perfects Nature.

This idea distorts Jesus' message. Christianity's proper subtlety and freedom depended upon Jesus' ironical perception of *disjunction* between the things of God and the things of men, a disjunction particularly enforced in the parables, as distinct from similitudes, allegories and analogies.[10] Whether he is seen as an apocalyptic prophet or as a witty rabbi (or, as I think, both), what matters in Jesus' message is his sense of the abrupt juxtaposition of two opposed orders of things. The way things seem from one point of view is the opposite of the way they seem from the other. This emphasis on *contrasting* value-scales evokes the transcendent, and it underlies Jesus' paradoxes of righteousness and unrighteousness, loss and gain, death and life, poverty and riches, the manifest and the hidden, security and insecurity, prudence and folly, and justice and injustice. The essential thing is that the two contrasting orders must collide.

But the doctrine of the incarnation unified things which Jesus had kept in ironic contrast with each other, and so weakened the ability to appreciate his way of speaking, and the distinctive values he stood for. In a terminology I have used elsewhere, instead of a negative and indirect christology there was developed an icon-christology, the parables came to be seen as allegories, and disjunctions were turned into continuities. A world-view which expressed disjunction and free choice was exchanged for a world-view which stressed continuity, hierarchy and due obedience. For example, in biblical and early Christian thought Jesus' kingship is different in kind from, indeed the moral opposite of, gentile kingship. But in Christendom that distinction was lost. Christ crowned the Emperor, one a step higher in the scale of being merely stooping slightly to bestow authority upon one a step lower.[11] In the Christian iconography which ran from the late fourth century to the end of the Byzantine period Christ and the Emperor were virtually indistinguishable, and the theologians themselves declared the veneration of icons of the former to be precisely on a par with the veneration of tokens of the latter.[12] Christ's lordship was originally eschatological, and manifest in this age only indirectly and by ironic *contrast* with temporal lordship. But the dogma of the incarnation brought it forward into this present age. As the manifest Absolute in history, Christ became the basis of the Christian Empire and of political and ecclesiastical power in the present age. He was invoked to guarantee the very things Jesus had said were passing away. Delicate theological distinctions and contrasts such as are made in the Johannine dialogue between Christ and Pilate (John 18.33–19.16) and in Matthew 20.20–28, Luke 22.24–27, were as a result lost. Inevitably Christianity became, or rather was deliberately made, absolutist and authoritarian. The Jewishness of Jesus' teaching was lost, and has never since been allowed to influence christology. Almost the only human trait that was retained was the *philanthropia* which he shared with the ideal Hellenistic king.

A vivid illustration of this engrained habit of turning from the Jews to the Greeks is Rudolf Bultmann's explicit relegation of Jesus to the history of Judaism. Bultmann simply expels Jesus from Christianity as an irrelevance, and brazenly treats Christ as an ecclesiastical creation only tenuously linked with Jesus. This is all the more odd in that Bultmann's teaching about God is so impressive. Why cannot he see that the Jewish Jesus he rejects is a shrewder and more cunning witness to God than is his empty ecclesiastical Christ? Presumably he cannot see it because, as Hegel once put it, Judaea cannot and must not be the Teutons' fatherland; and because he is convinced that the heart of the gospel lies in Lutheran dogma rather than in the tradition of Jesus' own teaching. If that tradition were to be taken seriously, Chalcedon and later dogmatic systems derived from it would have to be abandoned in favour of a fresh start.

The point here is related to the old question of the infallibility of scripture. Fundamentalists regard scripture as the words of God and spend a great deal of time studying it, but totally fail to understand it. Their doctrinal view of scripture cuts them off from its reality. When scripture is regarded as the unitary expression of one absolute mind, its internal diversity and richness cannot be recognized. The same is true of Jesus. Just as a 'deabsolutized' scripture is of infinitely greater religious value than the flat oracle of fundamentalism, so a 'deabsolutized' Jesus can be recognized as revealing God to us in much more complex ways than the Christ of Chalcedon. If it was a religious gain to get rid of an absolutist view in the one case, it will be so also in the other. The transformation of our attitude in the one case must in the long run demand a corresponding transformation in the other. I believe the result will be a clearer grasp of the truth about God and Jesus, and of distinctively Christian values which have for long been obscured.

2. Orthodox doctrine asserts that the divine and the human are indissolubly united in the person of the divine Word, with effect from the moment of Christ's conception. This appears to assert that the union of God with man was miraculously accomplished by God independently of, because prior to, the struggles and suffering of Jesus' earthly life, which thus become peripheral. To this, two replies might be made, but neither is entirely satisfactory.

Orthodox dyotheletism claims that there is real and meritorious moral struggle in Jesus' life, because there are in him two wills, one human, the other divine. But the claim that in the incarnate Lord a divine will for which sin is a logical impossibility is hypostatically united with a human will for which it is a real and pressing temptation raises all the difficulties which Gore, as we saw above, felt so strongly.

In the second place, some early theologians appear to suggest[13] that the hypostatic union was dissolved upon the death of Jesus. His body was in the tomb, his soul in the underworld and the Logos reigned on in heaven. The hypostatic union was restored at the resurrection. But, though this theory certainly emphasizes the reality of Christ's passion, it clearly had to be rejected, for it suggests that death *can* after all put asunder what God has joined. In which case my question about whether the traditional dogma does justice to Jesus' human striving to bring men to God and God to men returns. In the traditional language, is the Chalcedonian doctrine compatible with a full recognition of Christ's priestly and mediatorial office?

3. If in Jesus the fullness of God himself is permanently incarnate, Jesus can be directly worshipped as God without risk of error or blasphemy. A cult of Christ as distinct from a cult of God thus becomes defensible, and did in fact develop. The practice of praying direct to Christ in the Liturgy, as distinct from praying to God through Christ, appears to have originated among the innovating 'orthodox' opponents of Arianism in the fourth century.[14] It slowly spread, against a good deal of opposition, eventually to produce Christocentric piety and theology. An example of the consequent paganization of Christianity was the agreement to constitute the World Council of Churches upon the doctrinal basis of 'acknowledgment of our Lord Jesus Christ as God and Saviour' – and nothing else.[15] Perhaps it was only when Christocentric religion

finally toppled over into the absurdity of 'Christian Atheism' that some Christians began to realize that Feuerbach might have been right after all; Chalcedonian christology could be a remote ancestor of modern unbelief, by beginning the process of shifting the focus of devotion from God to man. It could not put up any resistance to the focusing of piety upon the glory of the incarnate Lord rather than the glory of God, and then upon the humanity of Christ, and then upon humanity in general. On the contrary, it appeared to legitimate a cult of humanity. Similarly, it could not resist the giving of the title *Theotokos*, Mother of God, to Mary. The phrase 'Mother of God' is *prima facie* blasphemous, but it has had a very long run, and the orthodox have actively promoted its use, fatally attracted by its very provocativeness.

4. If it is the case that in the incarnation God himself has permanently assumed human nature, and can legitimately be depicted as God in human form, then eventually the ultimate mystery of deity will be conceived anthropomorphically, and the pagan notion of a deity as a superhuman person with gender will be restored. In due course this happened, aided by the traditional Father–Son imagery.

The Eastern Church was for long stricter in this matter than the Western. The nearest it came to permitting the Deity to be portrayed *in a human form different from the human form of Christ* was in the standard iconography of such a scene as the Baptism of Christ, where a hand, but no more than hand, emerges from the cloud to release the dove upon the Lord's head.[16] It was also permissible to portray the 'Old Testament Trinity' of Genesis 18.[17] There are some, highly exceptional, early representations of God: a miniature in the Smyrna Octateuch, a Paternity (depicting God the Father and God the Son as two men) in an eleventh-century Constantinopolitan codex; but such things are rare. Strictly, God remained unportrayable until, in the early sixteenth century, and under Western influence, images of him appeared in Moscow.[18] A layman, Djak Viskovaty, deserves to be remembered for having lodged a formal and well-documented protest in 1553/4. Unfortunately, the synod found against him, and though the decision went the other way in 1667, images of God the Father subsequently became common, especially in peasant icons.

The Western story is rather different. The whole religious style from early times emphasized instruction by narrative rather than the symbolic representation of timeless truth. But for centuries, in accordance with both orthodox theology and iconographical rules, the image of God the Son was used to represent the God of the Old

Testament when illustrating Genesis, or the visions of the prophets. It was clearly recognized (as at the time when the 'Caroline Books' were written, *c.* 790–2) that there are limits to Christian art. Just when these limits were transgressed is hard to discover exactly. Searching has persuaded me that one can only be quite certain, without the risk of misinterpretation, in the case of a single work of art unmistakably representing the Trinity, in which God the Father's human form is present alongside that of the Son, and is distinctly *different*. This rules out such images as the drawings in the Sherborne Pontifical described by Francis Wormald.[19] On my criterion, anthropomorphic images of God the Father become increasingly common after about 1100.[20]

It is not often realized what a theological monstrosity such images are; but if Deity itself has a human form already, prior to the incarnation, then the latter *must* be understood in a pagan way. Again, the absurdity comes out clearly in the common practice of using *two* men to portray Christ, one standing for his human nature and the other for his divine nature. The early work of art in which all these oddities are combined is the 'The Quinity of Winchester', now in Warsaw, which depicts three men, a woman and a bird – God the Father and his Eternal Son in a Paternity group, the Virgin and her child the incarnate Son in his human nature, and the dove nesting in her crown – all in one group.[21]

The emergence of God as an old man in the Western Christian imagination is, on the evidence of the history of art, a many-stranded process. One likely source of it is the Paternity group, modelled on the old theme of the Virgin and child, from which are derived the standard images of the Trinity at the baptism of Christ and the crucifixion. And it is my contention that the doctrine of Christ as God's divine Son has here humanized deity to an intolerable degree. The strangeness of it is seldom noticed even to this day. A sensitive theologian like Austin Farrer can dwell eloquently upon a medieval icon of the Trinity,[22] and a philosopher as gifted as Wittgenstein can discuss Michelangelo's painting of God in the Sistine Chapel,[23] and in neither case is it noticed that there *could* be people to whom such pagan anthropomorphism is abhorrent, because it signifies a 'decline of religion' in the only sense that really matters, namely, a serious corruption of faith in God.

In recent years Freudians and feminists (arguing very different cases) have assumed that the God of monotheistic faith is male. It sounds like a theological solecism on their part, but it is surely an excusable solecism, in view of the long tradition of extreme and barbarous anthropomorphism in Western art. The Council of Trent

(Sessio XXV, 3 and 4 December 1563) defended images of Christ and the saints on the old grounds laid down by Gregory I, but simply failed to comment on images of God the Father. Such images have never been officially defended in the West, it is true; but they were tolerated, and the old faith was forgotten.

From all this I conclude that the doctrine of the incarnation has had some harmful effects upon the understanding of Jesus' message, on the understanding of his relation to God and even upon faith in God. For Jesus' emphasis upon the divine transcendence, on the disjunction of things divine and human and the need for choice, it substituted a world-view which stressed continuity, authority and due obedience (1). It weakened appreciation of his human work (2). It tended to create a cult of the divine Christ which let Deity itself fade into the background (3), and when God the Father was reaffirmed, he was envisaged as an old man (4).

What we have been taught to call 'orthodoxy' was in fact merely the form of Christianity which happened to triumph over the others. In retrospect, the Christ of the Eastern Church looks all too like the Hellenistic king, exalted to heaven to become the ideological basis of the Christian Empire; and the Christ of the Western Church looks like one who died to seal the authority of the patriarchal family as a model for the organization of church and state. Neither Christ was Jesus, and neither reveals the one true God as Jesus did; and the political order with which conciliar orthodoxy was associated has now passed away for ever.

The discovery that the ecclesiastical Christ is not to be found in a critical reading of the records of Jesus led to scepticism about the historicity of the gospels. This scepticism served to protect the ecclesiastical Christ from historical refutation. But the figure behind the gospels is not quite unreachable. As enough remains of the Buddha to challenge the Mahayana so *a fortiori* enough remains of Jesus to challenge us to rethink our ideas of Christ. In doing so we will be furthering the theological task of the modern period, that of shifting Christianity from the dogmatic faith of the Christendom period to the critical faith which is to succeed it. Of course the shift from the dogmatic to the critical outlook is difficult, but it will not take us further from Jesus: it will bring us closer to him. It will enable us to *recover* truths which have been largely lost.

In this paper I have criticized the 'orthodox' view of Christ on various counts: that it 'realized' eschatology (i.e. brought forward ultimate things into the present age) so far as to validate this-worldly sovereignty and to politicize the transcendent, that it constantly tended towards anthropocentrism, and so on. But readers may still fear that the drift of the argument is such as to leave no room for a religiously-adequate christology – one, that is, which does full justice to the conviction that 'God was in Christ, reconciling the world to himself', committing himself in the midst of the human to redeem the human.

The objection is deeply felt, but I believe it is properly met by the insistence that the doctrine of Christ must be such as to strengthen and purify, not to compromise, men's understanding of the divine transcendence. For it is the divine *transcendence* which alone judges, delivers and restores, as Jesus, in his teaching and in his person, communicates the power of transcendence (the Holy Spirit) to his disciples. God is with man, in man, only in his transcendence. The criterion of religious adequacy, rightly understood, itself demands that christology be not any kind of man-cult: it must be theocentric, not christocentric.

APPENDIX

I relegate a bold hypothesis to an appendix. Iconographically, Christ is the Emperor, and the Father the Pope. God the Father emerges as a common theme in Christian art in the eleventh and twelfth centuries. His seniority is stressed: he is above and behind the Son, older, heavier in appearance. There may be a connection here with the Papacy's growing claims and confidence after Hildebrand. Certainly trinitarian images of the latter Middle Ages look like statements about papal authority.

Theologically, the representation of the Father and the Son as two different persons had important effects on the doctrine of the atonement from Anselm onwards. It became a transaction between an eternal Father and his eternal Son, a transaction which (envisaged as it was in anthropomorphic and indeed psychological terms) was bound in the end to occasion a moral revolt.

NOTES

1. In the Introduction to the Everyman edition of Renan's *Life of Jesus*, p. xvii.

2. Charles Gore, *The Incarnation of the Son of God*, Bampton Lectures, 1891, John Murray 1891, p. 143.

3. H. P. Liddon, *The Divinity of our Lord and Saviour Jesus Christ*, 1865, fourth edition 1890, pp. 153ff.

4. Ibid., p. 472.

5. Gore, *Dissertations on Subjects Connected with the Incarnation*, John Murray 1895, pp. 162ff.

6. Liddon, op. cit., pp. 164, 168, xxxvi, 175.

7. For what follows see N. H. Baynes, *Byzantine Studies*, Athlone Press 1955, especially VII, IX and XV.

8. Ibid., IX.

9. T. Klauser, *A Short History of the Western Liturgy*, Oxford University Press 1969, pp. 32–7.

10. See Eta Linnemann, *Parables of Jesus*, SPCK 1966.

11. E.g. John Beckwith, *Early Christian and Byzantine Art*, Penguin Books 1970, plates 176, 222, 256, 292.

12. E.g. Hans von Campenhausen, *Tradition and Life in the Church*, Collins 1968, p. 190. Notice too how in the late medieval West, God the Father was commonly portrayed as the Pope, wearing the Triple Crown, as in well-known works by Van Eyck and Boticelli.

13. A. Grillmeier has studied this question: e.g. *Der Logos am Kreuz*, Munchen 1956.

14. Klauser, op. cit., pp. 30ff. and notes. See especially A. Jungmann, *The Place of Christ in Liturgical Prayer*, Chapman 1965.

15. This original doctrinal basis agreed in 1938 was later, in 1961, exchanged for a trinitarian one.

16. F. Van der Meer and Christine Mohrmann, *Atlas of the Early Christian World*, Nelson 1966, illustration 321 (Palestine *c.* 600); Beckwith, op. cit., plate 118.

17. Images of the Trinity as three *similar* men go back as far as the 'Dogmatic Sarcophagus' in the Lateran Museum (*c.* 330).

18. Brief account in H. Skrobuche, *Icons*, Oliver & Boyd 1963, pp. 17f. In this section I acknowledge with grateful thanks the help of the Warburg Institute, and the courtesy of its librarian.

19. Francis Wormald, *English Drawings of the Tenth and Eleventh Centuries*, Faber & Faber 1952, plates 4(a), 4(b), 5(a). But see Pembroke College Cambridge, MS120, pl. 6, upper half, for what appears to be an early English Paternity.

20. A good example is the Father's head emerging from the cloud at Christ's baptism, on the font at S. Bartélemy, Liège, by Renier de Huy, 1111–18. And see F. E. Hulme, *Symbolism in Christian Art*, Blandford Press 1976 edition, pp. 43ff.; Margaret Rickett, *Painting in Britain: the Middle Ages*, Penguin Books 1954, plates 92, 102, 178; and W. Braunfels, *Die Heilige Dreifaltigkeit*, Dusseldorf 1954.

21. Studies of this work in the *Art Bulletin* by E. H. Kantorowicz, vol. 29, 1947, pp. 73ff.; and T. Dobrzeniecki, vol. 46, 1964, pp. 380ff. The latter has fascinating notes.

22. Austin Farrer, *Said or Sung*, Faith Press 1960, pp. 116ff.

23. Wittgenstein, *Lectures and Conversations*, Blackwell 1966, p. 63.

8

Myth in Theology [1]

MAURICE WILES

The word 'myth' occurs in the title we have given to this collection of essays. It has also figured in the argument of some of the earlier chapters. In his analysis of Christian origins Michael Goulder writes of 'the Galilean eschatological myth' and 'the Samaritan gnostical myth' as the two roots of the emerging Christian myth. [2] But the word has not figured only as a tool of historical analysis; it has been used also in giving expression to a confession of faith. Frances Young describes her own continuing belief in God as demanding 'a Calvary-centred religious myth'. [3] The loose and elusive character of the term cannot be denied. That fact does not require us to abandon its use altogether; it does require us to exercise careful discrimination in our use of it. In this chapter, therefore, I want to consider the meaning of the term and the appropriateness of using it in a christological context.

It is used in a wide range of disciplines; it plays an important role in the work of anthropologists and sociologists, of many psychologists, literary critics and historians. The ways in which it is used are very varied within as well as between disciplines. But there is also a long tradition of the use of the term within theology itself. It seems natural therefore to treat the way the term is already used in theology as the starting-point for any assessment of its possible significance in relation to incarnational christology. I propose, therefore, to approach my central concern gradually, through three preliminary stages – (1) the introduction of the term into theology in the nineteenth century; (2) its use in some more recent theological writing; (3) a critical discussion of its application to Christian doctrines other than the incarnation. An indirect approach of this kind should help to guard against a purely arbitrary and idiosyncratic handling of the term in relation to incarnation.

1. The Introduction of the Term 'myth' into Theology in the Nineteenth Century

Myth relates primarily to pre-history. But the English word 'myth' belongs to comparatively recent history. Mythology, mythological, mythical – all these go back many centuries, but 'myth' itself is less than 150 years old.

The opening words of the first edition of Keightley's *Mythology of Ancient Greece and Italy* (published in 1831) were these.

The mythology of a people consists of the various popular traditions and legendary tales which are to be found among them.

In the second edition (published in 1838) those opening words were changed to read:

Mythology is the science which treats of the *mythes*, or various popular traditions and legendary tales, current among a people and objects of general belief.

Keightley was well aware of the novelty of the word for we find him in 1846 complaining 'From the Greek μῦθος I have made the word *mȳthe*, in which however no one has followed me, the form generally adopted being *mÿth*'. He argues that no parallel derivation from a Greek or Latin root can be produced to justify the adoption of the form myth, but concludes sadly:

I am not simple enough to expect to alter the usual practice, I only want to show that analogy is on my side.[4]

The absence of any well-established English word 'myth' at the time is well illustrated by the earliest English reactions to Strauss' *Life of Jesus* which was published in 1835 – midway between the two editions of Keightley's *Mythology*. In both W. H. Mill's extended attack upon Strauss which appeared in various parts between 1840 and 1842 and in George Eliot's translation, published in 1846, the word regularly used is the transliterated *mythus* with its plural *mythi*, though strangely each author on one single occasion (as far as I have noted) uses, presumably through inadvertence, the Anglicized form 'myths'.[5] Undoubtedly the ensuing discussion of Strauss' thesis did much, not merely to establish the word more firmly in the English language, but also to place the concept at the heart of theological study and debate.

A number of issues about the nature of myth arise in those early discussions which continue to figure in contemporary debates about myth. Strauss himself, drawing upon the classification of earlier philologists and biblical scholars distinguishes three main kinds of myth – historical, philosophical and poetical. These he defines as follows:

Historical: 'narratives of real events coloured by the light of antiquity, which confounded the divine and the human, the natural and the supernatural'.

Philosophical: 'such as clothe in the garb of historical narrative a simple thought, a precept, or an idea of the time'.

Poetical: 'historical and philosophical mythi partly blended together, and partly embellished by the creations of the imagination, in which the original fact or idea is almost obscured by the veil which the fancy of the poet has woven around it'.[6]

Whatever qualifications one might want to make of the specific distinctions and definitions that he adopts, it seems to me reasonable to insist that myths may be basically historical in origin but that their historical basis may be either very slight or entirely non-existent.

A second distinction is between the conscious and unconscious origination of myths. In the first edition of his *Life of Jesus* Strauss had regarded the myths of the New Testament as having a gradual and unplanned origin in the life of the early Christian communities. 'It is', he wrote:

... by no means conceivable that the early Jewish Christians, gifted with the spirit, that is, animated with religious enthusiasm, as they were, and familiar with the Old Testament, should not have been in a condition to invent symbolical scenes such as the temptation and other New Testament mythi. It is not however to be imagined that any one individual seated himself at his table to invent them out of his head, and write them down, as he would a poem: on the contrary, these narratives like all other legends were fashioned by degrees, by steps which can no longer be traced; gradually acquired consistency, and at length received a fixed form in our written Gospels.[7]

But under pressure of criticism he came later to regard the process as a much more deliberate one. In acknowledging this change in his views in the introduction to his radically revised *New Life of Jesus* of 1864, he goes on to justify the retention of the word 'myth' to designate these more conscious creations.

In this new edition of the *Life of Jesus* I have conceded far more room than previously – mainly as a consequence of Baur's investigations – for the acceptance of conscious and intentional mythologizing; but I have seen no reason to change the term itself. On the contrary, to the question whether conscious fabrications of an individual are also properly to be called myths, I must – even after all the previous discussion on this point – still always reply: absolutely, as soon as they have been believed and have passed into the history of a people or a religious sect; at the same time, this also shows that they were formed by their author, not merely according to his own fancies, but in close association with the consciousness of a majority. Every unhistorical narrative – however it may have originated – in which a religious community recognises a constituent part of its sacred origins as an absolute expression of its fundamental sentiments and ideas is a myth; and if Greek mythology is desirous of distinguishing a more limited concept of the myth, which excludes conscious fabrication, from this wider concept, critical theology, conversely, is desirous – over against the so-called believers – of including all those Gospel narratives to which it ascribes only an ideal significance, under the general concept of myth.[8]

It is not my purpose here to discuss the relative plausibility or implausibility of the two versions of the mythologizing process as Strauss describes it in relation to the gospels. But I think he has a strong case in insisting that if something has the general character of myth and functions as a myth in the life of the community, the degree of intentionality in its origination ought not to be the decisive factor which prescribes whether or not it is to be regarded as a myth and also that the exact use of the term in any one discipline cannot be absolutely determinative of its use in all others.

A third issue that arose early on was the relation between myth and miracle. One of the attractions of the mythic approach to the gospels was that it provided a way out for those who were unable to accept the miracles as literally true accounts but who were also unhappy to have to choose 'between unmiraculous miracles and lying evangelists'.[9] Was then any story of a miracle that was not in fact true to be regarded as a myth? The point is brought out in another of the earliest English discussions of Strauss, which appears as an Appendix in Milman's *History of Christianity*, also published in 1840 but earlier than Mill's book. Milman, who treats Strauss' arguments with greater understanding than Mill, challenges the claim, essential to Strauss' position, that the age of Christ was a mythic age. The claim, he says, would be true if by a mythic age one meant simply 'any age, in which there was a general and even superstitious belief in wonders and prodigies'. 'But if the term mythic be more properly applied to that idealisation, that investing religious doctrines in allegory and symbol; above all, that elevating into a deity a man only distinguished for moral excellence . . . this appears to me to be repugnant to the genius of the time and of the country.'[10] Once again I am not now concerned with the relative merits of Strauss' case and that of Milman. But Milman

seems to me to have put his finger on a distinction that is important
for theology. The concept of myth impinges most vitally on
theology not in relation to particular miracle stories but rather in
relation to the whole structure of belief in divine action and divine
incarnation.

From the very beginning, then, the discussion of myth in
theology has recognized the imprecision of the term. It seems to me
important to be aware of this imprecision so as to avoid unneces-
sary misunderstanding, though impossible to eradicate it. Insistence
on a very precise definition of myth usually turns out to be part of a
Pyrrhic victory in which the author succeeds in proving the points
he wants to make about myth by the simple process of making
them true by definition. But even where confusion about the range
and meaning of the term has been safely avoided, the response to its
use in theology has from the very start been violently divided. The
sense of outrage which attended much English reaction to Strauss
was enhanced by the fact that the use of mythology in interpretation of the Old Testament was still comparatively little known in
this country. British scholarship was largely textual and
philological in character. An attempt to get the work of Eichorn,
the outstanding German Old Testament scholar in this field at the
turn of the century, translated into English was frustrated by lack
of support from church and university authorities.[11] So in England
the issue arose almost from the start in relation to the even more
contentious area of the gospels. Mill indeed comments that 'plausible as it might appear to carry' the concept of myth from the study
of heathen mythologies 'as several predecessors of Strauss have
ventured to carry them ... into the region of the earlier Old
Testament history, it required more hardihood than some of the
boldest of them possessed, to extend the application to the period
of the Gospel'.[12] For Mill to call something a myth was different
only in appearance but not in substance from calling it a deceit.
'The word *mythus*,' he wrote, 'is a milder as well as a less definite
term than *delusion* or *imposture*; and though the assertions are
perfectly equivalent, it shocks less to be told that Christianity
stands on the same footing of mental truth with heathen fables,
than to be told, as by the sceptics of a former age, that it is based
on falsehood like them.'[13]

The positive evaluation of myth found clearest expression in the
writings of Baden Powell, one of the contributors to *Essays and
Reviews*. In a work published the year before *Essays and Reviews*,
he cites with approval 'the remark, that parable and myth often
include more truth than history'. A myth he defines in his discus-

sion of Strauss as 'a doctrine expressed in a narrative form, an abstract moral or spiritual truth dramatised in action and personification; where the object is to enforce faith not in the *parable* but in the *moral*'. 'Thus,' he concludes, 'every dogma is more or less a myth, as it is necessarily conveyed in analogical language and anthropomorphic action.' [14]

2. The Use of 'myth' in More Recent Theological Writing

So the debate has continued. It flourished with particular intensity in the demythologizing controversy precipitated by Bultmann's famous essay in 1941.[15] But so much has been written about that particular controversy that it would be difficult to say anything at all fresh about it in the introductory section of a single chapter. My aim in this section is rather to give a general account of the use of the term in contemporary theology, very briefly in relation to biblical studies and somewhat more fully in relation to doctrine.

The Old Testament is clearly a collection of literature of a kind that includes a good deal of mythology and for whose interpretation an understanding of myth is essential. How mythological a person finds it will depend on two factors. It will depend in the first place, as with other forms of ancient literature, on the breadth or narrowness of the definition of myth with which the particular interpreter is working. But it will depend also on the prior expectations or the criterion of comparison with which he comes to it. If he feels, as so many nineteenth-century divines felt, that ideally scripture ought to consist of accurate historical writings, he will be likely to stress (if he is a careful observer) how mythological the Old Testament is. If on the other hand he has in mind by way of comparison the cosmogonies of other ancient societies, he is likely to be struck by the restrained character of, for example, the biblical creation stories and to emphasize their comparatively unmythological character.

The New Testament is not quite so straightforward. Strauss was concerned with the mythic character of the various discrete gospel stories. In the passage that I quoted he cited the temptation story as a prime example. When I look at the Lukan commentaries on my book shelves to see how they regard the incident, I find a wide range of judgment. 'We may be sure that, if the whole had been baseless invention, the temptations would have been of a more commonplace and probably a grosser kind. No Jewish or Christian legend is at all like this. It is from Christ Himself that the narrative comes; and He probably gave it to the disciples in much the same form as that in which we have it here.'[16] 'The picture,' whatever its origins, 'has been filled in by the imagination of the early Church.'[17] 'For many modern readers the mention of the devil invests the story with an air of unreality and even of superstition. Let us grant that the devil is a mythological figure. But myth is not to be confused with legend or fairy-tale. Myth is a pictorial way of expressing truths which cannot be expressed so readily or so forcefully in any other way.'[18] 'The testing of the hero is a favourite theme in Bible and fairy tales. . . . The presence of the devil as a character in the drama is a strong indication that we are in the region of fairy-tale.'[19] The fact that those four citations are arranged not merely in thematic but also in chronological sequence is due neither to chance nor to manipulation on my part, nor on the other hand should it be taken to imply that there is a steady evolution in the direction of more mythical interpretation of the New Testament narratives. For the most part commentators today are inclined to give the meaning of the story in the thought of the gospel writer and to leave on one side questions of its precise source and status as questions which we lack the evidence to answer with any confidence. To use the categorization of G. V. Jones in his book *Christology and Myth in the New Testament*, there is less interest in the legend-myths of particular narratives than there is in the broader metaphysical-myths of the word-made-flesh or the apocalyptic hope.[20] And at that point the work of the New Testament scholar relates much more closely to the work of the doctrinal theologian which is my primary concern.

In this broader sense one may speak of four basic Christian myths or of one myth with four principal moments – the creation, the fall, Christ's incarnation and work of atonement, the resurrection of the dead and final judgment. A contemporary consensus of critical opinion would, I suppose, speak quite readily of the first two and the last of those as 'myths' but feel some serious hesitation about the application of the term to the third. The sort of position that I have in mind is well set out by Norman Pittenger in his book *The Word Incarnate*, and I shall therefore quote his statement of it at some length.

However, the Incarnation of God in Christ and the Atonement wrought by him are in a different category. When we speak of these, we are not talking about things which like the creation and the consummation are 'before' or 'after' history. Nor are we talking about universal truths which are applicable to all men, as we are doing when we speak of the 'fall of man' into his present sinful situation. The stories of the Incarnation and the Atonement are tied up with a specific historical event; they have their grounding in something that actually happened in the course of human history; on the one hand they are not *outside* history, and on the other they are not true of *all* history. They are concerned with what Christians believe was done *in* history and through the factuality of *particular* historical happenings. Of course they are told to us, whether in the gospels or in the early Christian preaching, in language which has a metaphorical or 'mythological' quality. That is to say, they are told in the form which we must necessarily employ when we make God the subject of a verb and discuss in the only terms we possess our relationships to the realm of the divine, the infinite, and the eternal.

But it seems to me quite misleading to put the life of Christ in the same category as the 'myth' of creation, or to put the redeeming work of Christ in the same category as the 'myth' of man's sinfulness. I realize that some theologians would do this. But it is not only misleading; it is also dangerous to Christian faith because it is untrue to the real situation. By lumping all these materials together in one category, we may succeed in suggesting that the incarnate life of Christ and his redemptive work are nothing more than types or helpful representations of what is universally true of human experience in relationship with God. Hence we shall seem to deny the particularity of Christ – which is in fact the chief reason for the vividness of the faith; or we shall imply that what is ultimately true in Christianity is supra-historical.[21]

Pittenger's point is a fairly obvious and fairly traditional one – which should not be taken to mean that I regard it as lacking in force. The incarnation is related to datable events in a way that the others are not and that relation is integral to its traditional theological meaning. It is therefore perhaps worth giving another example of very much the same point from the pen of a theologian of a very different tradition. Wolfhart Pannenberg has written:

The idea of the incarnation of the Son of God, regarded as a myth, contains an extremely odd and disturbing element. For it does not merely state that God *appeared* in human form, but that he became *identical* with a human being who actually lived, a historical person, and even suffered and died as that person ... the idea of the incarnation linked the substance of the myth, the nature of deity itself, to a historical event, a historical person. It has rightly been stressed, time and again, that this amounts not just to an arbitrary variation of basically mythical conceptions, but to something which is contrary to the nature of myth itself. For what is historically unique is as far as anything possibly can be from myth, which expresses what is archetypal and valid for every age.[22]

Do we then simply have to acquiesce in this diversity of type within the central structure of Christian theology? It may be that in the end we should decide that that is what we ought to do. But there is an untidiness about such a solution that prompts the reflective mind to seek for some greater unity of structure. I want, therefore, to outline the approach of three scholars who have attempted to provide this greater unity, and then to comment on the implications of this whole debate.

In the first place we might choose to call into question the ready use of myth in relation to creation, fall and eschatology as too facile a categorization. I have already commented that the mythology of the Old Testament, when compared with the related mythology of other near-Eastern peoples, may appear more remarkable for the lack rather than for the profusion of its distinctively mythological features. Does this indicate that the characteristic direction of biblical thought, and derivatively of Christian theology, is to be seen in a move away from myth towards history? This approach is developed systematically by Gordon Kaufman in his book entitled *Systematic Theology, A Historicist Perspective*. He argues that there is a radical inconsistency in the position I have outlined with its central historical drama set within a framework of timeless myths. The biblical writers, he argues, in their determined attempt to provide a 'pre-historical' framework for the historical drama were 'more acute at this point than their modern critics'. 'An adequate reconciliation', he concludes, 'between the biblical and modern historical perspectives cannot be achieved by recourse in this way to the category of myth, which really goes counter to both. A thoroughly historical perspective must be maintained throughout.'[23] So he goes on to develop an understanding of creation not as 'a mythical expression for the relationship of finite being to the infinite' but as affirming a purpose of God in the actual emergence and development of the world as science and history depict it. The fall is a long drawn out historical event by which the natural struggle for survival attains 'the moral level of bitter hatred and jealous conflict and warfare'. The incarnation and atonement are that historical event which 'resulted in the successful establishment of a historical community of reconciliation among men'. And 'Christian hope is that the goal toward which history is moving is the transformation of this present world into God's perfect Kingdom.'[24]

Alternatively we may accept the word 'myth' as appropriate throughout. My second and third examples are both of scholars who do this, but who do it in radically different ways. Emil Brunner, in an appendix to his book *The Mediator*, entitled 'The Mythology of Christianity'[25] accepts the word 'myth' as applicable to all four moments of the one Christian myth (I took that particular phraseology which I used earlier from him) but gives to 'myth' a thoroughly idiosyncratic definition. 'The Christian "myth" is neither the abstract conceptual statement of the philosophy of

religion, nor is it "mythological" in the sense of pagan mythology
... It belongs to an entirely different category.'[26] He speaks of the
incarnation as an event but it is not a historical event, for then it
would be just one factor in the universal order of history; it belongs
to the same dimension to which the creation, the fall and the resurrection belong – the dimension of super-history. It is 'the crossing
of that frontier which separates all history from God', 'that event
which takes place between time and eternity'.[27]

My third example is the work of John Knox. Like Brunner he
argues in favour of using the term myth with reference to the incarnation but his actual position is very much closer to that of
Kaufman than to Brunner's. In his little book *Myth and Truth*,[28] he
takes issue directly with the position of Pittenger that I have
already outlined, and in his later book *The Humanity and Divinity
of Christ*,[29] he works out his approach in relation to the early
development of Christian belief about the person of Christ. The
three 'acts' of the Christian drama, to use his phraseology (three,
because he subsumes the fall under the heading of the creation) are
too interdependent for it to be at all satisfactory for us to categorize
them in such essentially disparate ways. Moreover, he insists, while
the creation and the consummation are outside 'history' they are
not outside 'time'. Thus all the acts of the drama are concerned
with happenings, and while the fact that only one of them is linked
with events for which we have documentary records makes a difference, it does not separate it in kind from the other two.[30]

Now, as I have already suggested, although Kaufman is the odd
man out as regards terminology, it is really Brunner who is the odd
man out in terms of theological substance. It is not very easy to give
precise meaning to Brunner's talk of 'super-history' and of 'that
event which takes place between time and eternity'. But it is not so
difficult to grasp his general intention. The basic thing that he is
seeking to do, as it seems to me, is to preserve for Christianity all
the benefits of its traditional links with history while at the same
time keeping it free from all the risks that appertain to normal
historical study. The special sense of Christian 'myth' that he postu-
lates is intended to have all the sense of reality that appertains to
the happenedness of historical events (indeed have it to an
enhanced degree since they are in fact super-historical) while being
unaffected by the acids of actual historical criticism. There are not
many today who would try to maintain Brunner's specific position,
and I do not propose to give it any more detailed discussion. But
we still need to be on our guard against an appeal to the category of
'myth' which seeks to use it as a way of meeting the challenge raised

by critical historical study without at the same time having to admit the need for any actual modification in traditional Christian doctrine.

Kaufman and Knox, as I have already indicated, do not seem to me to be very far apart in the actual substance of their positions. Both of them distinguish between the mythological and the historical, but both see an important relation between them; in both cases, for example, the actual historical establishment of a reconciling community is part of the meaning of the mythological accounts of the atonement. The Christian myth does not consist of superhistorical events; it is a way of conveying the meaning of historical events. The faith is thus less insulated from history and historical study than in the case of Brunner. If then their positions are rightly grouped together over against that of Brunner, what is the difference between them? I think it is mainly a matter of terminology and of emphasis. In his insistence on maintaining a historical perspective throughout, Kaufman says of the fall that 'to regard it as myth rather than in some genuine sense history shatters both the consistency and the meaning of the Christian faith'.[31] But the sense in which Kaufman claims it to be historical seems to me to be a tautological sense by which everything that is the case in an evolutionary world is historical, because it has come to be what it is gradually. I do not think that Knox would wish to deny the 'historicity' of the fall understood in Kaufman's sense. His contrasting insistence on the mythological character of Christian doctrine throughout derives from the greater value that he places on the creative and expressive power of the Christian message in its traditional narrative form.

3. *The Application of 'myth' to Christian Doctrines other than the Incarnation*

The vital problem facing anyone who approaches Christian theology in this way is what sort of link is there between the myth and the history? Is there a basic element of historical factuality that is necessary to warrant continued affirmation of the Christian myth? Does affirming the myth involve making truth claims for it? And if so what sort of truth claims?

Alasdair MacIntyre, writing primarily about Platonic myths but with a wider intended reference than Platonic myths only, denies the applicability of truth claims at all. He writes:

A myth is living or dead, not true or false. You cannot refute a myth, because as soon as you treat it as refutable, you do not treat it as a myth but as a hypothesis or history.[32]

That seems to me too sweeping a judgment. Clearly, a myth is not true or false in the way that straightforward empirical statements of 'the cat sat on the mat' variety or directly testable scientific hypotheses are true or false. For one thing myths, like poetry, can be interpreted at a variety of different levels and can have more than one legitimate interpretation even at the same level. Nevertheless, they are not indefinitely significant. In so far as they express certain fundamental aspects of the human condition, they may do so in a way which (apart from extremely far-fetched and implausible interpretations) turns out to be false. Thus while it is bound to be extremely difficult to apply the categories of truth and falsity with any confidence, I do not think it is a procedure which ought to be ruled out in principle in advance. Moreover, there are likely to be a good many midway cases, where we may judge that there are possible ways of understanding a myth that are true but that they are not the most obvious or natural interpretations of it. In such cases we may need to speak of certain myths as more or less appropriate.

I want therefore at this point to try to clarify some of the issues involved in raising questions of this kind about the various moments of the Christian myth other than the incarnation itself – leaving that central and most controversial instance until last.

If the universe as we know it is a wholly self-contained and self-evolving system, in no way dependent for its existence on anything other than itself, then the creation myth would seem to me to be religiously inappropriate or false. But if the world is in fact dependent on a transcendent, creative source, as the Christian theist claims, then the myth would be appropriate or true. The degree of correlation if any between the order in which the world is created in the story and the order of its evolution as a matter of historical fact is irrelevant to its truth or falsity as myth. But I acknowledge that if someone were to claim that he had a powerful (but in his judgment cognitively delusive) sense of a transcendent source of the world's existence and that the creation myth gave valuable expression to this inchoate but potent feeling, I could not in the strict sense of the word refute his interpretation of the myth. What I could and would say would be that if the world is in fact as he believes it to be then the creation myth seems to me to be a misleading and inappropriate one – and in that sense false.

The fall myth has frequently been treated as a form of theodicy, or myth of the origin of evil in a world of God's good creation. Understood in that way it seems to me clearly to be false. For even understood as myth – i.e. with no claim implied about the historical

existence of Adam and Eve or even more generally about monogen-
ism – it would have to be the case that the evil we experience were
wholly the result of wrong human choices. I am still prepared to
treat it as religiously appropriate or true, because I believe it is true
that men fall below the highest that they see and that they could
achieve. But I do so with misgiving, because there are very reasonable interpretations of the myth which I believe to be false. I have
already referred to its possible abuse as a complete theodicy.
Another equally reasonable interpretation which is also in my judgment equally false is one which sees in it the conviction that the
essence of man's moral failure lies in a refusal to accept and to obey
an externally imposed, deontological ethic.

The myth of the resurrection of the dead and the final judgment
poses even greater difficulties – not only for the obvious reason that
we are even less able to check up on the truth or falsity of our beliefs
on that topic but also because of the great variety of belief that is in
fact felt to be consistent with the affirmation of the myth. In my
judgment, for the myth to be religiously appropriate or true, it
would need to be true that in some sense man lives on beyond his
physical death. But other scholars deny that survival of bodily
death is necessary to a validation of the resurrection myth. This is
in fact Kaufman's position, but the point is made more explicitly by
Lloyd Geering in his well-argued book, *Resurrection – a Symbol of
Hope*. He writes:

> The term 'resurrection of the dead' should not be interpreted as a hope for
> the prolongation or restoration of our own conscious existence. It is a hope
> for the world in which we live, a hope for the meaning of human life, and a
> hope that when our conscious existence is ended, the historical life we have
> lived may be raised before the eternal Judge, and may be vindicated, as
> being of some value for that Kingdom which is eternal and for whose fuller
> manifestation on earth we pray.[33]

It would no doubt be possible to go even further than Lloyd
Geering and find some continuing meaning in the myth, even without the belief in God and in the Kingdom that he affirms. There
are those who wish to speak of the fundamental significance of a
sense of hope in human life, even though they believe such hope to
be ultimately delusive. If they were to claim that the myth of the
resurrection of the dead was valuably expressive of that sense of
hope, the position would be the same as in the parallel case of the
creation myth. I could not in any formal sense refute their use of
the myth, but I would regard it as a highly inappropriate myth for
their purpose.

In all these three cases, then, which I described as less controversial than the case of the incarnation, there are considerable difficulties in determining how the myth is to be understood. The criterion by which I have been trying to distinguish between true and false interpretations of them might be expressed something like this. There must be some ontological truth corresponding to the central characteristic of the structure of the myth. But such a criterion is not at all easy to apply. For one thing if the ontological truth were one that could be expressed with full clarity and precision there would be less need for the myth. In the case of creation I have spoken of the dependence of the world on a transcendent creative source other than itself. In the case of the fall I have spoken of men's falling below the highest that they see and could achieve. In the third case I have spoken of some kind of survival of human life beyond physical death. Thus while I would wish to allow room within Christianity for a wide range of interpretations of these central myths of the faith, I also want to claim that where interpretation of them abandons any ontological element of the kind I have tried to delineate, then the myths are being interpreted in what seems to me an inappropriate way and it would be better to abandon the use of them.

What then would be involved in a mythological understanding of the incarnation? I have been insisting that there will need to be some ontological reality corresponding to the central character of the structure of the myth. This, of course, is a fundamental characteristic of traditional interpretations with their insistence on an identity between the personhood of Jesus and the Second Person of the Godhead. But the difficulties inherent in this direct, metaphysical understanding of the incarnation are stressed in other papers in this collection. Could there be other, less direct interpretations which would still retain the kind of ontological correlation which seems to me to be required?

The incarnation has never been proclaimed simply as an account of something that happened at a point in past history. It has also been seen as that which makes possible a profound inner union of the divine and the human in the experience of grace in the life of the believer now and more broadly in the life of the church as a whole. So close are the links between the past event and present experience that the church has frequently been spoken of not only as 'the body of Christ' but even as 'the extension of the incarnation'. Now if this union of divine and human at the heart of the human personality is a reality, however hard to identify or to describe, may that not be the ontological truth corresponding to and justifying a mythological understanding of the incarnation?

The obvious difficulty about such an approach is that the incarnation is linked with the particular historical figure of Jesus in a way that is not characteristic of the other three moments of the Christian myth. Would it be reasonable to continue to link the incarnation so specially with the historical figure of Jesus while interpreting it as a mythological account of a potential union of the divine and the human in the life of every man? Any answer to that question must take account both of the character and mission of Jesus himself (in so far as those are accessible to us) and the historical relationship between Jesus and distinctively Christian experience in the subsequent life of the church.

In considering the first issue it needs to be remembered how flexible in practice have been the kinds of historical claim that have accompanied the traditional understanding of the incarnation. In the past those claims normally included such things as the absolute truth of all that Jesus said, his awareness of his divine status and the perfection of his moral life. Yet the form of these claims has changed considerably. The kenotic controversy at the end of the last century bears witness to the difficulty that very many people felt then in combining the idea of any kind of ignorance on the part of Jesus with traditional incarnational belief. Yet today such ignorance would be readily accepted by most upholders of the traditional doctrine, indeed many would regard ignorance of his own special divine status and the absence of any distinctive or privileged sources of knowledge as essential to the concept of incarnation. The empirical correlates of a traditional doctrine are therefore very variously understood and may not in practice be noticeably different from those assumed by a mythological interpretation. At the other end of the scale, if it were true that Jesus was an unscrupulous self-seeker or that his life and teachings were fundamentally misleading as indicative of the nature and purposes of God, then any kind of link between him as a historical person and the idea of incarnation however mythologically interpreted would be wholly inappropriate or false. Is it possible to delineate in any more precise way what would and what would not be compatible with affirming the incarnation myth in relation to Jesus? We would want, I suggest, to be able to affirm two things. First that his own life in its relation to God embodied that openness to God, that unity of human and divine to which the doctrine points. And secondly that his life depicted not only a profound human response to God, but that in his attitudes towards other men his life was a parable of the loving outreach of God to the world. Now both those things are firm features of the traditions about Jesus. And while we cannot be sure

how much of the detail of the accounts we have is later interpretation, it is most unlikely that the kind of historical knowledge about
Jesus available to us or that may become available to us in the
future could ever deform that picture to such a degree as to rule out
the appropriateness of linking the incarnation myth in this special
way with the person of Jesus.

But the appropriateness of that linking does not depend exclusively on the character of Jesus himself. It depends also on the
historical relationship between Jesus and the experience of grace in
the lives of believers. This can be affirmed in a weaker or a stronger
form. The weaker form would simply state as a matter of contingent historical fact that this truth about man's relation to God
came alive in our particular tradition through the figure of Jesus.
The stronger form would give to Jesus a more indispensable role.
While refraining from giving any distinctive metaphysical account
of Jesus' person, it might still claim that his life and all that has
stemmed from it are essential in practice to the full and effective
realization of this union of divine and human in the life of man.
The grounds for such a claim would have to be historical and
psychological reflection on the way in which man's spiritual life has
been and is formed within Christian faith. Its validity could only be
tested by the course of future history.

This historical dimension is an important element in any understanding of the incarnation as mythological. The tendency in most
theological discussions of myth is to think of myths as expressive of
timeless truths about God and his relation to the world. And as a
result many people whose attitude towards the category of myth is
not antagonistic in principle have none the less thought it a highly
inappropriate term to use of the incarnation. But, as Strauss
pointed out in the analysis I referred to at the beginning, there is
often a historical element in myth. Historical events may contribute
to the origin of a myth, and myths may fulfil a function in historical
and political life as well as in philosophical and psychological
reflection. The historical or political myth develops some event of
significance in the past, like the foundation of Rome, in a way
which enables a community to interpret its present and give direction to its future. Such myths provide a close parallel to one aspect
of the way in which the myth of the incarnation has functioned in
the life of the church. And since Christianity is concerned not
merely with declaring truths about God but with the historical
existence of a particular community, it is perfectly proper that it
should have myths of that kind. Perhaps we would make some
progress in unravelling the difficulties involved in the idea of the

incarnation linked to the historical figure of Jesus if we were more ready to recognize it as a mixed form of myth with both a more general function with regard to the relation of God and man and a more specifically historical function with regard to the Christian community.

But while wanting to claim that there are potential advantages in the approach I am suggesting, I recognize that there are a number of obvious objections that can very properly – and certainly will – be raised. In the first place the incarnation has frequently been seen as the primary doctrine that differentiates Christians from others and holds the faith together as a distinctive and coherent entity. Does not treating it as a myth, with the immensely wide range of admissible interpretation that that entails, undermine that coherence in an unacceptable and destructive way? Clearly it does lessen the nature of Christian cohesion, but I am not sure that the contrast is as great as might at first sight appear. In practice Christian belief, including incarnational belief, has been understood in very varied ways with very varied corollaries. And because it has been felt that there ought to be unity of belief, these variations have often been treated as evidence of unfaith and given rise to intolerance and persecution. If what held Christians together were seen as the use of the same myths rather than the holding of the same beliefs, it might be easier for Christians to accept the measure of variety that there both should and will be between them. There will, of course, still be grave problems, but at the very least I would want to claim that to treat the incarnation as myth does not simply destroy a coherent pattern of Christian belief and life that is at present functioning in a fully satisfactory way.

A second objection of a more general nature may be raised against any use of the concept of myth along the lines that I am suggesting. The popular understanding of a myth today is of something delusive, not only in the sense that it is not literally true but also that it is a kind of mirage, something that leads people astray. Those who spoke of the myth of the EEC were those who were opposed to it, not those who saw it as an important precursor of a united Europe of the future. This must be acknowledged, and the term may remain unusable in the general life of the church. I simply do not know. But the important role occupied by the concept in a great variety of other disciplines suggests that it may still be a valuable tool for theological analysis. If it does prove to be so, it will, I believe, be when theologians learn to recognize the mixed character of the Christian myths and to draw upon the insights of different disciplines in their use of the concept.

The third, and possibly most searching, difficulty of all is the question whether a myth can continue to function as a potent myth, once it is acknowledged that it is not literally true. Did Romans have to treat the stories of the foundation of Rome as literally true for those stories to convey the appropriate sense of the city's destiny? Obviously myths will always be understood at different levels by different people. I would want to express the conviction that where the myth has the kind of ontological correlate that I believe the Christian myth to have and where it has the degree of historical appropriateness that I believe there to have been in the life of Jesus, then the power of the myth will not be undermined by its being more widely recognized for what it is.

Simply to call something a myth does not of course in itself solve anything. I have earlier criticized Brunner for using the concept of myth in a way that provides only a specious solution to the real problems of theology. I hope I have not appeared to fall into the same trap myself. What I believe the approach to the incarnation that I am proposing can do is to provide a more creative perspective which may in the long run help us not only to see the intellectual problems more accurately but also to draw on the resources of faith more richly.

NOTES

1. The substance of this chapter was originally given as a John Rylands lecture in Manchester and a version of it appears in the *Bulletin of the John Rylands Library*, vol. 59, no. 1, 1976, pp. 226–46.

2. See p. 65 above.

3. See p. 34 above.

4. T. Keightley, *Notes on Virgil's Bucolics and Georgics* (1846), p. vii. The one earlier occurrence given by the Oxford English Dictionary is from an article on Buddhism in the Westminster Review for 1830 (XII, 44). The word is there in the English form *myths*, but is italicized. The form mythe was in fact used by some other writers of the period, such as Grote and Müller.

5. W. H. Mill, *Observations*, i.118; D. F. Strauss, *The Life of Jesus Critically Examined*, SCM Press 1973, p. 57.

6. Strauss, op. cit., p. 53.

7. Ibid., p. 58.

8. Strauss, *New Life of Jesus* (1865), vol. i, pp. 213–14; cited by H. Harris, *David Friedrich Strauss and his Theology*, Cambridge University Press 1973, p. 203.

9. W. O. Chadwick, *The Victorian Church*, A. & C. Black 1966, vol. i, p. 531.

10. H. H. Milman, *The History of Christianity* (1840), vol. i, p. 120.

11. See T. K. Cheyne, *Founders of Old Testament Criticism*, p. 22.

12. W. H. Mill, *Observations*, ii.10–11.

13. Ibid., ii.9.

14. Baden Powell, *The Order of Nature* (1889), pp. 275, 340, 341.

15. Originally given as a lecture under the title *Offenbarung und Heilsgeschehen* the

essay now appears as 'New Testament and Mythology', in *Kerygma and Myth*, ed., H.-W. Bartsch, SPCK 1953, vol. 1, pp. 1ff.

16. A. Plummer, *St Luke*, International Critical Commentary, T. & T. Clark 1910, p. 106.

17. J. M. Creed, *The Gospel According to St Luke*, Macmillan 1930, p. 62.

18. G. B. Caird, *St Luke*, Penguin Books 1963, p. 79.

19. J. Drury, *Luke*, J. B. Phillips' Commentary, Fontana 1973, p. 52.

20. G. V. Jones, *Christology and Myth in the New Testament*, Allen & Unwin 1956, p. 30.

21. Norman Pittenger, *The Word Incarnate*, Nisbet, and Harper & Row 1959, pp. 39–40.

22. W. Pannenberg, *Basic Questions in Theology*, vol. III, SCM Press 1973, 'Myth in Biblical and Christian Tradition', pp. 71–2.

23. G. Kaufman, *Systematic Theology*, Scribner's and Sons 1968, p. 271.

24. Ibid., pp. 274–87.

25. Emil Brunner, *The Mediator*, Lutterworth 1934, pp. 377–96.

26. Ibid., p. 378.

27. Ibid., p. 391.

28. John Knox, *Myth and Truth*, Carey Kingsgate Press 1964.

29. John Knox, *The Humanity and Divinity of Christ*, Cambridge University Press 1967.

30. *Myth and Truth*, pp. 56–8.

31. Kaufman, op. cit., p. 280.

32. Alasdair MacIntyre, 'Myth' in P. Edwards (ed.), *Encyclopedia of Philosophy*, Macmillan 1967, vol. 5, p. 435 (cited by I. Barbour in *Myths, Models and Paradigms*, SCM Press 1974, p. 24).

33. Lloyd Geering, *Resurrection – a Symbol of Hope*, Hodder & Stoughton 1971, p. 215.

9

Jesus and the World Religions

JOHN HICK

If we start from where we are, as Christians of our own day, we begin amidst the confusion and uncertainty which assail us when we try to speak about Jesus, the historical individual who lived in Galilee in the first third of the first century of the Christian era. For New Testament scholarship has shown how fragmentary and ambiguous are the data available to us as we try to look back across nineteen and a half centuries, and at the same time how large and how variable is the contribution of the imagination to our 'pictures' of Jesus. In one sense it is true to say that he has been worshipped by millions; and yet in another sense, in terms of subjective 'intentionality', a number of different beings, describable in partly similar and partly different ways, have been worshipped under the name of Jesus or under the title of Christ. Some have pictured him as a stern law-giver and implacable judge, and others as a figure of inexhaustible gracious tenderness; some as a divine psychologist probing and healing the recesses of the individual spirit, and others as a prophet demanding social righteousness and seeking justice for the poor and the oppressed; some as a supernatural being, all-powerful and all-knowing, haloed in glorious light, and others as an authentically human figure living within the cultural framework of his time; and he has been pictured both as a pacifist and as a Zealot, as a figure of serene majesty and as a 'man for others' who suffered human agonies, sharing the pains and sorrows of our mortal lot. . . . And each of these different 'pictures' can appeal to some element among the various strands of New Testament tradition. But in each case communal or individual imagination has projected its own ideal upon as much of the New Testament data as will sustain it, producing a Christ-figure who meets the spiritual needs of his devotees; while behind this gallery of ideal portraits lies the largely unknown man of Nazareth. Clearly, Feuerbach's account of the idea of God as a projection of human ideals has a certain application here. Jesus was a real man who really lived in first-century Palestine; but the mental images of him upon which Christian devotion has been focused in different ages and in different parts of the church are so widely various that they must in part reflect the variety of temperaments and ideals, and above all the varying spiritual needs, within the world of believers. Aspects of the traditions about Jesus have fused with men's hopes and desires to form these different 'pictures', so that like a great work of art the New Testament figure of Jesus has been able to become many things to many men.

To what extent is the exaltation in Christian faith of the man of Nazareth into the divine Christ, the only-begotten Son of God, Second Person of the Holy Trinity, a supreme example of this projection upon Jesus of ideals to answer our spiritual needs? At first sight the very possibility is alarming; for it questions the identification of the Galilean rabbi with the Christ-figure of developed Christian dogma. I shall argue, however, that the Nicene definition of God-the-Son-incarnate is only one way of conceptualizing the lordship of Jesus, the way taken by the Graeco-Roman world of which we are the heirs, and that in the new age of world ecumenism which we are entering it is proper for Christians to become conscious of both the optional and the mythological character of this traditional language.

It may be helpful to observe the exaltation of a human teacher into a divine figure of universal power in another religious tradition which we can survey from the outside. The founder of Buddhism, Gautama (or Sakyamuni) was a real historical individual who lived in north-east India from about 563 to about 483 BC. Born of a local princely family, he renounced his riches to seek spiritual truth. After finally attaining Enlightenment he travelled far and wide, teaching both individuals and groups. When he died at the age of about eighty he had founded a community of disciples, monks and nuns, which continues to this day and which has carried the Buddha's message throughout Asia, deeply influencing the lives of a considerable section of mankind. Gautama, the Buddha or Enlightened One, made no claim to be divine. He was a human being who had attained to *nirvāna* – complete transcendence of egoism, and oneness with eternal trans-personal Reality. But in the Mahāyāna Buddhism which began to develop at about the same time as Christianity the Buddha came to be revered as much more than an outstanding human individual who had lived and died some centuries earlier. In the distinctive mahāyānist doctrine of the Three Bodies (*Trikāya*) of the Buddha, the earthly or incarnate body (*Nirmānakāya*) is a human being who has become a Buddha and who teaches the way to others. Gautama was the most recent of these and the one in the period of whose spiritual influence the world still is; but there have been others before him and there will be yet others in the future. The *Sambhogakāya*, sometimes translated as the Body of Bliss, is a transcendent or heavenly Buddha, a divine being to whom prayer is addressed. The earthly Buddhas are incarnations of the heavenly Buddhas, projections of their life into the stream of this world. But these transcendent Buddhas are ultimately all one in the Dharma Body (*Dharmakāya*), which is Absolute Reality.

Thus Buddhology and christology developed in comparable ways. The human Gautama came to be thought of as the incarnation of a transcendent, pre-existent Buddha as the human Jesus came to be thought of as the incarnation of the pre-existent Logos or divine Son. And in the Mahāyāna the transcendent Buddha is one with the Absolute as in Christianity the eternal Son is one with God the Father. Thus Gautama was the *Dharma* (Truth) made flesh, as Jesus was the Word made flesh: indeed the Burmese translation of the New Testament treats Dharma as the equivalent of Logos, so that the opening sentence of St John's gospel reads (in Burmese) 'In the beginning was the Dharma . . .')[1] However, I am not concerned here to explore more fully the very interesting analogies between Christian and Mahāyānist themes. The fact to which I am drawing attention is that in Mahāyāna Buddhism – the situation differs in Theravāda or southern Buddhism – the human Gautama has been exalted into an eternal figure of universal significance, one with his human brethren through the incarnate life lived two and a half thousand years ago and one with Ultimate Reality in the *Dharmakāya* or Cosmic Buddha. This exaltation has presumably been powered by the hunger of the human spirit for a personal Saviour and has been supported intellectually by the sophisticated metaphysical doctrine of the Three Bodies. Mahāyāna Buddhists of course claim that this entire development was implicit in the work of the historical Gautama and that later thought has only brought out the fuller meaning of his teaching. Thus B. H. Streeter has aptly remarked that 'Mahayana stands to primitive Buddhism in a relation not unlike that of the gospel according to St John to that according to St Matthew'.[2]

In noting this Mahāyānist development of Buddhism one is not implying that the later interpretation of the human Gautama as cosmic Saviour and object of devotion is right or that it is wrong. But we are seeing at work a tendency of the religious mind which is also to be seen within the history of Christianity. The exaltation of the founder has of course taken characteristically different forms in the two religions. But in each case it led the developing tradition to speak of him in terms which he himself did not use, and to understand him by means of a complex of beliefs which was only gradually formed by later generations of his followers.

But, it will be said, there is at least one all-important difference between Jesus and Gautama which justifies the ascription of divine attributes to the one and not to the other – namely that Jesus rose from the dead. Does not his resurrection set him apart from all other men and show him to be God incarnate? Such an argument inevitably suggests itself; and yet it proves difficult to sustain. That there was some kind of experience of seeing Jesus after his death, an appearance or appearances which came to be known as his resurrection, seems virtually certain in view of the survival and growth of the tiny original Jesus movement. But we cannot ascertain today in what this resurrection-event consisted. The possibilities range from the resuscitation of Jesus' corpse to visions of the Lord in resplendent glory. But it must be doubted whether the resurrection-event – whatever its nature – was seen by Jesus' contemporaries as guaranteeing his divinity. For the raising of the dead to life, understood in the most literal sense, did not at that time and in those circles seem so utterly earth-shaking and well nigh incredible as it does to the modern mind. This is evident from the numerous raisings of the dead referred to in the New Testament and the patristic writings. Jesus is said to have raised Lazarus (John 11.1–44), a widow's son (Luke 7.11–17), and Jairus' daughter (Mark 5.35–43 and Luke 8.49–56) and to have told John the Baptist's messengers to report that they had seen not only that the blind receive their sight and the lame walk but also that the dead are being raised up (Matt. 11.5); and Matthew records that at the time of Jesus' crucifixion 'the tombs also were opened, and many bodies of the saints who had fallen asleep were raised, and coming out of the tombs after his resurrection they went into the holy city and appeared to many' (Matt. 27.52–3). Again, the writer of the Epistle to the Hebrews claims as a sign of faith in olden times that 'Women received their dead by resurrection' (Heb. 11.35. Cf. I Kings 17.17–24). And Irenaeus, writing in the last quarter of the second century, refers to raisings of the dead both by the apostles and, frequently, within the later fellowship of the church.³ Thus the claim that Jesus had been raised from the dead did not automatically put him in a quite unique category. It indicated that he had a special place within God's providence; but this was not equivalent to seeing him as literally divine. For Jesus is not said to have risen in virtue of a divine nature which he himself possessed but to have been raised by God. Accordingly the first Christian preachers did not draw the conclusion that he was himself God but that he was a man chosen by God for a special role and declared by his resurrection to be Messiah and Lord (Acts 2.22 and 36).

From our point of view today it is less easy to accept stories of a physical resurrection, particularly when they refer to an event nearly twenty centuries ago and when the written evidence is in detail so conflicting and so hard to interpret. But nevertheless if we imagine a physical resurrection taking place today it is still far from evident that we should necessarily regard it as a proof of divinity. George Caird has put the point well:

Let us suppose that tomorrow you were confronted with irrefutable evidence that an acquaintance whom you had good reason to believe dead had been seen alive by reliable witnesses. You would certainly feel compelled to revise some of your ideas about science, but I doubt whether you would feel compelled to revise your ideas about God. I doubt whether you would conclude that your acquaintance was divine, or that a stamp of authenticity had been placed on all he ever said or did. . . .⁴

Returning, then, to the theme of the exaltation of a human being to divine status, the understanding of Jesus which eventually became orthodox Christian dogma sees him as God the Son incarnate, the Second Person of the Trinity living a human life. As such he was, in the words of the 'Nicene' creed, 'the only-begotten Son of God, Begotten of the Father before all the ages, Light of Light, true God of true God, begotten not made, of one substance with the Father'. But this is as far from anything that the historical Jesus can reasonably be supposed to have thought or taught as is the doctrine of the Three Bodies from anything that the historical Gautama can reasonably be supposed to have thought or taught. If we accept, with the bulk of modern New Testament scholarship, that the Fourth Gospel is a profound theological meditation in dramatic form, expressing a Christian interpretation of Jesus which had formed (probably in Ephesus) fairly late in the first century, we cannot properly attribute its great christological sayings – 'I and the Father are one', 'No one comes to the Father but by me', 'He who has seen me has seen the Father' – to Jesus himself. But we do nevertheless receive, mainly from the synoptic gospels, an impres-

sion of a real person with a real message, lying behind the often
conflicting indications preserved in the traditions. These documents
give us three sets of communal 'memories' of Jesus, variously
influenced by the needs, interests and circumstances of the
Christian circles within which they were produced. In offering my
own impression I am of course doing what I have already suggested
that everyone else does who depicts the Jesus whom he calls Lord:
one finds amidst the New Testament evidences indications of one
who answers one's own spiritual needs. I see the Nazarene, then, as
intensely and overwhelmingly conscious of the reality of God. He
was a man of God, living in the unseen presence of God, and
addressing God as *abba*, father. His spirit was open to God and his
life a continuous response to the divine love as both utterly
gracious and utterly demanding. He was so powerfully God-
conscious that his life vibrated, as it were, to the divine life; and as a
result his hands could heal the sick, and the 'poor in spirit' were
kindled to new life in his presence. If you or I had met him in first-
century Palestine we would – we may hope – have felt deeply disturbed and challenged by his presence. We would have felt the
absolute claim of God confronting us, summoning us to give ourselves wholly to him and to be born again as his children and as
agents of his purposes on earth. To respond with our whole being
might have involved danger, poverty, ridicule. And such is the
interaction of body and mind that in deciding to give ourselves to
God, in response to his claim mediated through Jesus, we might
have found ourselves trembling or in tears or uttering the strange
sounds that are called speaking with tongues.

But as well as challenge, the New Testament shows that we might
also have been conscious, as the other side of the same coin, of a
dynamic joy, a break-through into a new and better quality of
existence, in harmony with the divine life and resting securely upon
the divine reality. Thus in Jesus' presence, we should have felt that
we are in the presence of God – not in the sense that the man Jesus
literally *is* God, but in the sense that he was so totally conscious
of God that we could catch something of that consciousness by
spiritual contagion. At least this was what *might* happen. But there
was also the possibility of turning away from this challenging
presence, being unable or unwilling to recognize God's call as coming to us through a wholly unpretentious working-class young man,
and so of closing ourselves to him and at the same time to God.
Therefore to encounter Jesus, whether in the flesh or through the
New Testament pictures of him, has always been liable to be a
turning point in anyone's life, a crisis of salvation or judgment.

If this interpretation is at all on the right lines, Jesus cannot have failed to be aware that he was himself far more intensely conscious of God, and that he was far more faithfully obedient to God, than could be said of any contemporaries whom he had met or of whom he had heard. He must have been aware that whereas ordinary men and women had, most of the time, only a faint and second-hand sense of the divine presence, and while the scribes and pharisees were often using religion to support their own privileged position, he was himself directly and overwhelmingly conscious of the heavenly Father, so that he could speak about him with authority, could summon men and women to live as his children, could declare his judgment and his forgiveness, and could heal the sick by his power. Jesus must thus have been conscious of a unique position among his contemporaries, which he may have expressed by accepting the title of Messiah or, alternatively, by applying to himself the image of the heavenly Son of Man – two categories each connoting a human being called to be God's special servant and agent on earth.

Jesus' specially intimate awareness of God, his consequent spiritual authority and his efficacy as Lord and as giver of new life, required in his disciples an adequate language in which to speak about their master. He had to be thought of in a way that was commensurate with the total discipleship which he evoked. And so his Jewish followers hailed him as their Messiah, and this somewhat mysterious title developed in its significance within the mixed Jewish–Gentile church ultimately to the point of deification.

But how did Jews come, with their Gentile fellow-Christians, to worship a human being, thus breaking their unitarian monotheism in a way which eventually required the sophisticated metaphysics of the Trinity? For whereas in the earliest Christian preaching, as we have echoes of it in Acts, Jesus was proclaimed as 'a man attested to you by God with mighty works and wonders and signs' (Acts 2.22), some thirty years later the gospel of Mark could open with the words, 'The beginning of the gospel of Jesus Christ, the Son of God . . .' And in John's gospel, written after another thirty or so years' development, this Christian language is attributed to Jesus himself and he is depicted as walking the earth as a consciously divine being.

Why and how did this deification take place? It is obvious, from the effects of his impact upon mankind, that Jesus was a figure of tremendous spiritual power. Those who became his disciples were 'born again', living henceforth consciously in God's presence and gladly serving the divine purposes on earth; and their experience was transmitted scarcely diminished for several generations, Christian faith perhaps even being toughened in the fires of persecution. This vital and transforming stream of religious experience was focused on Jesus as Messiah and Lord. No doubt for the ordinary believer, living within the tightly-knit Christian fellowship, it was sufficient to think and speak of him simply as the Lord. But before long pressures must have developed to use titles which would more explicitly present the challenge of Jesus' saving power, first within the Jewish community and then within the Gentile world of the Roman empire. And these could only be the highest titles available. Once men and women had been transformed by their encounter with Jesus, he was for them the religious centre of their existence, the object of their devotion and loyalty, the Lord in following whom they were both giving their lives to God and receiving their lives renewed from God. And so it was natural that they should express this lordship in the most exalted terms which their culture offered. Accordingly we find within the New Testament itself a variety of terms being tried out. Some of them failed to catch on: for example, Jesus' self-designation as the eschatological Son of Man who was to come on the clouds of heaven is not used outside the reports of his own teaching; and St Paul's distinctive designation of him as the second Adam, although it has persisted down to today, has never been very widely or centrally used. St John's use of the idea of the Logos has remained important, though mainly as a theologian's title. But the central development is that which began with Jesus as the Messiah of the Jews and culminated in the Nicene identification of him as God the Son, Second Person of the Trinity, incarnate. Michael Goulder and Frances Young show in chapters 4 and 5 how widespread in the ancient world were ideas of divinity embodied in human life, so that there is nothing in the least surprising in the deification of Jesus in that cultural environment. Within Judaism itself the notion of a man being called son of God already had a long tradition behind it. The Messiah was to be an earthly king of the line of David, and the ancient kings of David's line had been adopted as son of God in being anointed to their office: the words of Psalm 2.7, 'He said to me, You are my son, today I have begotten you', were probably originally spoken at the coronation ceremony. Another key text is II Sam. 7.14, 'I will be his father, and he shall be my son', again originally said of the earthly king. Thus the exalted language which the early church came to apply to Jesus was already a part of the Jewish heritage. Of the splendid poetry, for example, of the annunciation story, 'He will be great, and will be called the Son of the

Most High; and the Lord God will give to him the throne of his father David, and he will reign over the house of Jacob for ever; and of his kingdom there will be no end' (Luke 1.32–3), R. H. Fuller says, 'There is nothing specifically Christian about this passage, except for the context in which Luke has inserted it, and it may well be a pre-Christian Jewish fragment.'[5] Such language, so far from being newly created by the impact of Jesus, was already present in the Jewish cultural tradition and was readily applied to Jesus by those who saw him as the Messiah.

How are we to understand this ancient language of divine sonship? Was the king thought of as literally or as metaphorically the son of God? The question is probably too sharply posed; for the early cultures did not draw our modern distinction. But, in our term, the title seems to have been metaphorical and honorific. To quote Mowinckel, 'The king stands in a closer relation to Yahweh than anyone else. He is His "son" (Ps. ii, 7). In mythological language it is said that Yahweh has "begotten" him, or that he was born of the dawn goddess on the holy mountain (Ps. cx, 3).'[6] But 'in spite of all the mythological metaphors about the birth of a king, we never find in Israel any expression of a "metaphysical" conception of the king's divinity and his relation to Yahweh. It is clear that the king is regarded as Yahweh's son by *adoption*.'[7] (Indeed it is probably only with the stories of the virgin birth of Jesus in Matthew's and Luke's gospels that the Lord's anointed is thought of within Israel as being physically God's son. However, this physical meaning of divine sonship is contradicted in the account of Jesus' baptism, at which one of the ancient adoption formulae used at the coronation of the king, 'Thou art my son' (Ps. 2.7), is spoken from the sky).[8] This, then, seems to have been the point of entry of the notion of divine sonship into the Hebrew tradition; and the belief that Jesus was of the royal line of David, and the application to him of the title of Messiah, revived around him the image of divine sonship. Hence the phrase, with which Mark begins his gospel, 'Jesus, Messiah, son of God'. And as Christian theology grew through the centuries it made the very significant transition from 'Son of God' to 'God the Son', the Second Person of the Trinity. The transposition of the poetic image, son of God, into the trinitarian concept, God the Son, is already present in the Fourth Gospel and has ever since been authorized within the church by a pre-critical acceptance of the Fourth Gospel reports of Jesus' teaching as historical. For it is characteristic of the Fourth Gospel that in it Jesus' message centres upon himself as Son of God in a unique sense which is virtually equivalent to his being God incarnate. In this gospel Jesus is the subject of his own preaching; and the church's theology has largely followed the Johannine re-writing of his teaching. It *is* a re-writing, however, for it is striking that in the earlier, synoptic gospels Jesus' teaching centres, not upon himself, but upon the kingdom of God.

There can I think be no doubt that this deification of Jesus came about partly – perhaps mainly – as a result of the Christian experience of reconciliation with God. The new life into which Jesus had brought his disciples, and into which they had drawn others, was pervaded by a glorious sense of the divine forgiveness and love. The early Christian community lived and rejoiced in the knowledge of God's accepting grace. And it was axiomatic to them, as Jews influenced by a long tradition of priestly sacrifice, that 'without the shedding of blood there is no forgiveness of sins' (Heb. 9.22). There was thus a natural transition in their minds from the experience of reconciliation with God as Jesus' disciples, to the thought of his death as an atoning sacrifice, and from this to the conclusion that in order for Jesus' death to have been a sufficient atonement for human sin he must himself have been divine.

Thus it was natural and intelligible both that Jesus, through whom men had found a decisive encounter with God and a new and better life, should come to be hailed as son of God, and that later this poetry should have hardened into prose and escalated from a metaphorical son of God to a metaphysical God the Son, of the same substance as the Father within the triune Godhead. This was an effective way, within that cultural milieu, of expressing Jesus' significance as the one through whom men had transformingly encountered God. They had experienced new life, new power, new purpose. They were saved – brought out of the darkness of worldy self-concern into the light of God's presence. And because of the inherent conservatism of religion, the way in which the significance of Jesus was expressed in the mythology and philosophy of Europe in the first three centuries has remained the normative Christian language which we inherit today. But we should never forget that if the Christian gospel had moved east, into India, instead of west, into the Roman empire, Jesus' religious significance would probably have been expressed by hailing him within Hindu culture as a divine Avatar and within the Mahāyāna Buddhism which was then developing in India as a Bodhisattva, one who has attained to oneness with Ultimate Reality but remains in the human world out of compassion for mankind and to show others the way of life. These would have been the appropriate expressions, within those cultures, of the same spiritual reality.

In the past Christians have generally accepted the established language about Jesus as part of their devotional practice without raising the question of its logical character. They have not asked what kind of language-use one is engaging in when one says that 'Jesus was God the Son incarnate'. Is it a factual statement (a combined statement, presumably, about empirical and metaphysical facts), or does it express a commitment, or make a value-judgment; and is its meaning literal, or metaphorical, or symbolic, or mythological, or poetic . . .? Such questions, although often grappled with indirectly, have only been posed directly in the recent period in which philosophical attention has been directed systematically upon the uses of language, including religious language; and as inhabitants of our own cultural world we properly, and indeed inevitably, ask them.

We have to direct these questions particularly to the two-natures christology of Nicea and Chalcedon, which eventually emerged as the orthodox Christian doctrine. This is partly metaphysical and partly empirical: empirical in asserting that Jesus was a human being and metaphysical in asserting that he was God. If we distinguish between, on the one hand, a literal statement (whether it be empirical or metaphysical), and on the other hand metaphorical, poetic, symbolic and mythological statements, the Nicene formula was undoubtedly intended to be understood literally. It asserts that Jesus was literally (not merely metaphorically) divine and also literally (and not merely metaphorically) human. As divine he was not analogous to God, or poetically-speaking God, or as-if God; he was, actually and literally, God – incarnate. And again, as human he was really, truly and literally a man.

The big question today concerning this doctrine is whether it has any non-metaphorical meaning. It is clearly literally meaningful to say that Jesus was a man, part of the genetic stream of human life; finite in intelligence, information and energy; and conditioned by a particular cultural and geographical milieu. But what does it mean to say that this man was the Second Person of the Holy Trinity? Prolonged efforts were made in the patristic period to give it a meaning, but they all proved unacceptable (i.e. heretical). To say with the Adoptionists that Jesus was a man adopted because of his special spiritual fitness into divine sonship, although (as we have seen) in agreement with the original Jewish notion of the king as adopted son of God, did not allow Jesus to be 'of the same substance as the Father'. Neither did the suggeston that Jesus was a man uniquely indwelt by the Holy Spirit or, in a modern version, the supreme instance of the 'paradox of grace'. Nor again was it

thought sufficient to say that Jesus was a man completely responsive to God's will; for this did not acknowledge his divine status as
pre-existent Logos and Second Person of the Trinity. Again, the
suggestion (of Apollinaris) that in Jesus the eternal Logos took
the place of the rational soul, whilst his 'animal soul' and body were
human, affirmed Jesus' divinity at the cost of his humanity; for on
this view his essential self was not human but divine. Against all
these theories – which were well-meant attempts to give meaning to
the God–Man formula – orthodoxy insisted upon the two natures,
human and divine, coinhering in the one historical Jesus Christ. But
orthodoxy has never been able to give this idea any content. It
remains a form of words without assignable meaning. For to say,
without explanation, that the historical Jesus of Nazareth was also
God is as devoid of meaning as to say that this circle drawn with a
pencil on paper is also a square. Such a locution has to be given
semantic content: and in the case of the language of incarnation
every content thus far suggested has had to be repudiated. The
Chalcedonian formula, in which the attempt rested, merely
reiterated that Jesus was both God and man, but made no attempt
to interpret the formula. It therefore seems reasonable to conclude
that the real point and value of the incarnational doctrine is not
indicative but expressive, not to assert a metaphysical fact but to
express a valuation and evoke an attitude. The doctrine of the
incarnation is not a theory which ought to be able to be spelled out
but – in a term widely used throughout Christian history – a
mystery. I suggest that its character is best expressed by saying that
the idea of divine incarnation is a mythological idea. And I am
using the term 'myth' in the following sense: a myth is a story which
is told but which is not literally true, or an idea or image which is
applied to someone or something but which does not literally
apply, but which invites a particular attitude in its hearers. Thus the
truth of a myth is a kind of practical truth consisting in the appropriateness of the attitude to its object. That Jesus was God the Son
incarnate is not literally true, since it has no literal meaning, but it
is an application to Jesus of a mythical concept whose function is
analogous to that of the notion of divine sonship ascribed in the
ancient world to a king. In the case of Jesus it gives definitive expression to his efficacy as saviour from sin and ignorance and as giver
of new life; it offers a way of declaring his significance to the world;
and it expresses a disciple's commitment to Jesus as his personal
Lord. He is the one in following whom we have found ourselves in
God's presence and have found God's meaning for our lives. He is
our sufficient model of true humanity in a perfect relationship to

God. And he is so far above us in the 'direction' of God that he stands between ourselves and the Ultimate as a mediator of salvation. And all this is summed up and given vivid concrete expression in the mythological language about Jesus as the Son of God 'who for us men and for our salvation came down from the heavens, and was made flesh of the Holy Spirit and the Virgin Mary, and became man, and was crucified for us under Pontius Pilate, and suffered and was buried, and rose again on the third day according to the Scriptures, and ascended into the heavens and sitteth on the right hand of the Father, and cometh again with glory to judge living and dead, of whose kingdom there shall be no end' (The 'Nicene' Creed).

For more than a thousand years the symbols of Jesus as Son of God, God the Son, God incarnate, Logos made flesh, served their purpose well. Within the life of the church they have been for countless people effective expressions of devotion to Jesus as Lord. It did not matter very much that they had quickly come to be understood by the Christian mind not as symbols but as components in literal statements. This was probably inevitable, and was of a piece with the literal interpretation of the Bible in the same period. From a twentieth-century point of view this use of the Bible was always mistaken; but nevertheless it probably did comparatively little harm so long as it was not in conflict with growing human knowledge. However, beginning in the seventeenth and culminating in the nineteenth century such conflicts did develop, and the literalistic interpreters of the scriptures were led into the false position of denying first what astronomy and then what palaeontology and evolutionary biology were revealing. Today as we look back we see the inability of churchmen in the past to accept scientific knowledge as ultimately God-given, and their refusal to be prompted by it to a larger and more adequate understanding of the Bible, as deeply damaging to the Christian cause. Something rather similar, many of us are now beginning to realize, applies to the literalistic interpretation of the essentially poetic and symbolic language of our devotion to Jesus. For understood literally the Son of God, God the Son, God-incarnate language implies that God can be adequately known and responded to *only* through Jesus; and the whole religious life of mankind, beyond the stream of Judaic-Christian faith is thus by implication excluded as lying outside the sphere of salvation. This implication did little positive harm so long as Christendom was a largely autonomous civilization with only relatively marginal interaction with the rest of mankind. But with the clash between the Christian and Muslim worlds, and then on an

ever broadening front with European colonization throughout the
earth, the literal understanding of the mythological language of
Christian discipleship has had a divisive effect upon the relations
between that minority of human beings who live within the borders
of the Christian tradition and that majority who live outside it and
within other streams of religious life.

Transposed into theological terms, the problem which has come
to the surface in the encounter of Christianity with the other world
religions is this: If Jesus was literally God incarnate, and if it is by
his death alone that men can be saved, and by their response to him
alone that they can appropriate that salvation, then the only door-
way to eternal life is Christian faith. It would follow from this that
the large majority of the human race so far have not been saved.
But is it credible that the loving God and Father of all men has
decreed that only those born within one particular thread of human
history shall be saved? Is not such an idea excessively parochial,
presenting God in effect as the tribal deity of the predominantly
Christian West? And so theologians have recently been developing
a mass of small print to the old theology, providing that devout
men of other faiths may be Christians without knowing it, or may
be anonymous Christians, or may belong to the invisible church, or
may have implicit faith and receive baptism by desire, and so on.
These rather artificial theories are all attempts to square an
inadequate theology with the facts of God's world. They are
thoroughly well-intentioned and are to be welcomed as such. But in
the end they are an anachronistic clinging to the husk of the old
doctrine after its substance has crumbled.

It seems clear that we are being called today to attain a global
religious vision which is aware of the unity of all mankind before
God and which at the same time makes sense of the diversity of
God's ways within the various streams of human life. On the one
hand, we must affirm God's equal love for all men and not only for
Christians and their Old Testament spiritual ancestors. And on the
other hand we must acknowledge that a single revelation to the
whole earth has never in the past been possible, given the facts of
geography and technology, and that the self-disclosure of the
divine, working through human freedom within the actual conditions of world history, was bound to take varying forms. We must
thus be willing to see God at work within the total religious life of
mankind, challenging men in their state of 'natural religion', with
all its crudities and cruelties, by the tremendous revelatory
moments which lie at the basis of the great world faiths; and we
must come to see Christianity within this pluralistic setting. There is

no space here to develop a theology of religions along these lines, taking account of the many problems which arise for such an approach; but I have attempted to do this in *God and the Universe of Faiths*[9] and can refer the reader to that attempt. I suggest that we have in the end to say something like this: All salvation – that is, all creating of human animals into children of God – is the work of God. The different religions have their different names for God acting savingly towards mankind. Christianity has several overlapping names for this – the eternal Logos, the cosmic Christ, the Second Person of the Trinity, God the Son, the Spirit. If, selecting from our Christian language, we call God-acting-towards-mankind the Logos, then we must say that *all* salvation, within all religions, is the work of the Logos and that under their various images and symbols men in different cultures and faiths may encounter the Logos and find salvation. But what we cannot say is that all who are saved are saved by Jesus of Nazareth. The life of Jesus was one point at which the Logos – that is, God-in-relation-to-man – has acted; and it is the only point that savingly concerns the Christian; but we are not called upon nor are we entitled to make the negative assertion that the Logos has not acted and is not acting anywhere else in human life. On the contrary, we should gladly acknowledge that Ultimate Reality has affected human consciousness for its liberation or 'salvation' in various ways within the Indian, the semitic, the Chinese, the African . . . forms of life.

Finally, should *our* revelation of the Logos, namely in the life of Jesus, be made available to all mankind? Yes, of course; and so also should other particular revelations of the Logos at work in human life – in the Hebrew prophets, in the Buddha, in the *Upanishads* and the *Bhagavad Gīta*, in the *Koran*, and so on. The specifically Christian gift to the world is that men should come to know Jesus and take him into their religious life – not to displace but to deepen and enlarge the relationship with God to which they have already come within their own tradition. And we too, in turn, can be spiritually enriched by God's gifts mediated through other faiths. For we must not think of the religions as monolithic entities each with its own unchanging character. They are complex streams of human life, continuously changing, though in some periods so slowly that the change is barely perceptible and in other periods so fast that recognizable continuity is endangered. Thus Christianity seemed virtually static through the long medieval centuries but today seems to be in bewildering flux; and the oriental religions are now emerging from the tranquil flow of their own 'medieval' periods to enter the turbulent rapids of scientific, technological and cultural revolution. Further, the religions are now meeting one another in a new way as parts of the one world of our common humanity. They are for the first time encountering each other peacefully, as variations within the global human consciousness which is emerging through the increasingly complex network of modern communications. In this novel situation they will inevitably exert a growing influence upon one another, both by the attraction of elements which each finds to be good in the others and by a centripetal tendency to draw together in face of increasing secularization throughout the world. We may therefore expect a cumulative sharing of religious insights and ideals, such as has already occurred in the influence of the Christian 'social gospel' within Hinduism and in the influence on the West of the Hindu and Buddhist traditions of spiritual meditation. This interpermeation of positive values has now, for all practical purposes, replaced the attempt at the mass conversion of the adherents of one world religion to another. In the case of Christianity the older missionary policy of the conversion of the world, proceeding largely along the highways opened up by Western arms and commerce, can now be seen to have failed; and any hope of renewing it has been ruled out by the ending of the era of Western political and religious imperialism. From now onwards the Christian mission in lands dominated by any of the other world religions must rest upon the positive attraction of the person and teaching of Jesus and of the life lived in discipleship to him, and not upon the power of an alien culture seeking to impose itself upon politically vulnerable or economically less developed peoples. Further, we have to present Jesus and the Christian life in a way compatible with our new recognition of the validity of the other great world faiths as being also, at their best, ways of salvation. We must therefore not insist upon Jesus being always portrayed within the interpretative framework built around him by centuries of Western thought. The Christian gift to the world is Jesus, the 'largely unknown man of Nazareth' whose impact has nevertheless created such powerful images in men's minds that he is for millions the way, the truth and the life. Within the varying cultures and changing circumstances of history he can still create fresh images and can become men's Lord and liberator in yet further ways. For in the different streams of human life a faith-response to Jesus can express itself in a wide variety of religious myths; and our own Western mythology of the incarnation of the Son of God must not be allowed to function as an iron mask from within which alone Jesus is allowed to speak to mankind. The Jesus who is for the world is not the property of the human organization called the

Christian church, nor is he to be confined within its theoretical constructions.

We see in the life and thought of Gandhi, the father of modern India, a paradigm of the immense impact which Jesus and his teaching can have upon the adherents of another faith. Gandhi has been widely recognized as one of the great saints of the twentieth century; and he freely acknowledged the deep influence of Jesus upon him. A devoted life-time missionary in India, E. Stanley Jones, said of Gandhi that 'a little man, who fought a system in the framework of which I stand, has taught me more of the Spirit of Christ than perhaps any other man in East or West', and described him as 'more christianised than most Christians'.[10] The New Testament, Gandhi said, gave him 'comfort and boundless joy'.[11] Again, 'Though I cannot claim to be a Christian in the sectarian sense, the example of Jesus' suffering is a factor in the composition of my undying faith in non-violence which rules all my actions.'[12] Nevertheless he remained a Hindu. He could never accept the orthodox Christian theology: 'It was more than I could believe,' he said, 'that Jesus was the only incarnate son of God and that only he who believed in him would have everlasting life. If God could have sons, all of us were His sons.'[13] Thus Gandhi was influenced by Jesus, not as he appears on the stained-glass window of the Nicene theology, but as he presents himself through the New Testament and above all in the Sermon on the Mount:

What, then, does Jesus mean to me? To me, He was one of the greatest teachers humanity has ever had. To His believers, He was God's only begotten son. Could the fact that I do or do not accept this belief make Jesus have any more or less influence in my life? Is all the grandeur of His teaching and of His doctrine to be forbidden to me? I cannot believe so. To me it implies a spiritual birth. My interpretation, in other words, is that in Jesus' own life is the key to His nearness to God; that He expressed, as no other could, the spirit and will of God. It is in this sense that I see Him and recognise Him as the son of God.[14]

The further influence of Jesus, then, as we may hopefully foresee it, will be both inside and outside the church. Within, the traditional liturgical language will no doubt continue to be used, Jesus being spoken of as the Son of God, God the Son, the Logos incarnate, the God–Man. But there will be a growing awareness of the mythological character of this language, as the hyperbole of the heart, most naturally at home in hymns and anthems and oratorios and other artistic expressions of the poetry of devotion. Christianity will – we may hope – outgrow its theological fundamentalism, its literal interpretation of the idea of incarnation, as it has largely outgrown its biblical fundamentalism. As the stories (for example) of the six day creation of the world and the fall of Adam and Eve after their temptation by the serpent in the Garden of Eden are now seen as profound religious myths, illuminating our human situation, so the story of the Son of God coming down from heaven and being born as a human baby will be seen as a mythological expression of the immense significance of our encounter with one in whose presence we have found ourselves to be at the same time in the presence of God. The outgrowing of biblical fundamentalism was a slow and painful process which has unhappily left the church scarred and divided, and we are still living amidst the tension between a liberal and a continuing and today resurgent fundamentalist Christianity. The church has not yet found a way to unite the indispensable intellectual and moral insights of the one with the emotional fervour and commitment of the other. Will the outgrowing of theological fundamentalism be any easier and less divisive? If not, the future influence of Jesus may well lie more outside the church than within it, as a 'man of universal destiny' whose teaching and example will become the common property of the world, entering variously into all its major religious and also secular traditions. I can claim no prophetic insight into the ways in which God is going to enter our human future. But all who believe in the reality of God must believe that he will in his own ways be with mankind in the centuries to come; and all who have been deeply impressed and changed by the life and words of Jesus will confidently expect this central figure of the gospels to continue to play his part in God's dealings with us.

NOTES

1. Trevor Ling, *A History of Religion East and West*, Macmillan 1968, p. 87.

2. B. H. Streeter, *The Buddha and the Christ*, Macmillan 1932, p. 83.

3. Irenaeus, *Against Heresies*, bk. II, ch. 31, para. 2.

4. G. B. Caird, 'The Christological Basis of Christian Hope', *The Christian Hope*, SPCK 1970, p. 10.

5. R. H. Fuller, *The Foundations of New Testament Christology*, Fontana 1969, p. 34.

6. S. Mowinckel, *He That Cometh*, trans., G. W. Anderson, Blackwell 1959, p. 67.

7. Ibid., p. 78.

8. Mark, 1.11. The quotation from Psalm 2.7 continues: 'You are my son, today I have begotten you,' this completion also occurring in some manuscripts of the account of the baptism in Luke 3.22.

9. John Hick, *God and the Universe of Faiths*, Macmillan, London 1973, and St Martin's Press, New York 1974. Fontana edition 1977.

10. E. Stanley Jones, *Mahatma Gandhi: An Interpretation*, Hodder & Stoughton 1948, pp. 12 and 76.

11. M. K. Gandhi, *What Jesus Means to Me*, compiled by R. K. Prabhu, Navajivan Publishing House, Ahmedabad 1959, p. 4.

12. Ibid., p. 6.

13. M. K. Gandhi, *An Autobiography: The Story of my Experiments with Truth*, 1940, Beacon Press, Boston 1957, p. 136.

14. *What Jesus Means to Me*, pp. 9–10.

10

Epilogue

DENNIS NINEHAM

When I was originally invited to contribute to this book, I felt
bound to refuse because of other writing commitments; but I will-
ingly agreed to take part in the discussions in the course of which
the various essays have been hammered into their present shape.
From these discussions I have learned a great deal, but I found
myself repeatedly voicing a concern which, though in a sense
obvious enough, seemed to the others sufficiently important to
deserve to be put in writing, even if it had to be done in a rather
hurried way.

My concern relates to a tendency which I observed in some of the
essays, at any rate in their original form, and which I have observed
in a good deal of other modern theological writing, namely a tendency to argue in the following sort of way: although some of the
imagery or models by means of which traditional theology has
sought to express the uniqueness of Christ may no longer be possible
or suitable for us, we can be sure about the reality and character of
some at least of the unique facts to which the traditional models
were intended to do justice, and so do justice to them in ways
appropriate to our situation.

Descriptions of the unique facts in question vary a good deal but,
whatever precise wording may be used, the view I have in mind
usually boils down to something like this: whereas before the time
of Christ all men had, in varying ways and degrees, put themselves,
rather than God, in the centre of their lives and so turned out 'self-
centred' in the usual sense of the term, Jesus' life was at every stage
and at every level centred entirely upon the being, grace and
demands of God, and so introduced into history a new humanity, a

new way and possibility of being human. Jesus, it is said, was 'the bearer of the new being', 'the man for others' – that is, the (only) one whose entire concern, so far as the life of this world is concerned, has been for the well-being of others – or as Bishop Montefiore prefers to put it, 'the man for God', the one, that is, whose entire life was dominated by a passion for God. His was 'the new humanity'. Thus Professor Hick in the first draft of his essay for this book spoke of Jesus as 'intensely, *totally*, and overwhelmingly conscious of the reality of God' and of his spirit as '*wholly* open to God'. The fact that he wrote in such terms is significant, and the absoluteness of the claim expressed can be illustrated from the work of many other writers. For example Dr John Robinson wrote in *Honest to God*:

It is in Jesus, and Jesus *alone*, that there is *nothing* of self to be seen, but *solely* the ultimate, unconditional love of God. It is as he emptied himself *utterly* of himself that he became the carrier of the 'name which is above every name'.[1]

A similar position is advanced at length by Dr Arthur Peacocke in his book *Science and the Christian Experiment*,[2] although he, in reliance on the thought of D. E. Jenkins, uses it not so much as the basis for an *alternative* symbolization to that of incarnation, as in support of the incarnation model itself. The humanity of Jesus, he writes, 'is potentially what all men have it in their nature to be. His life is a perfect life in the society of other men.' And it 'thereby opens up for the individual and society a way forward to realize all that they have it in them to be according to the divine purpose'. He writes of 'the realization of all that men might be, all that God intended men should be, in the person of Jesus of Nazareth', and speaks of the willingness of the man Jesus 'to go on being the vehicle of expression of the divine will even when it meant turning his face back towards Jerusalem and the bitter death which awaited him there'. Again he speaks of affirming that 'in Christ a "transmutation" . . . of human life was effected at a new depth of the personality and that men who participate in, or acquire, this new depth of life in Christ are becoming a new sort of human being (dare we say "species"?)'.[3]

These passages are typical of a large number of others that could be quoted, and undoubtedly represent a widespread tendency in contemporary English theology, and indeed theology in general, as witness, for example, Dr L. E. Keck's summary of the view of Professor Joachim Jeremias:

What kind of Jesus does Jeremias find? He is a Jesus who makes the same claim for faith as the kerygma. This historical Jesus, reached by sophisticated methods, he finds to be completely without parallel with respect to his demeanor, his message, his audacity in calling God Father.[4]

My question about the tendency to which I am drawing attention concerns the *status* of the claims which tend to be made. So long as the doctrine of the incarnation was taken as a statement of an objective metaphysical fact, that Jesus was literally divine, then the unique perfection of his humanity was a legitimate deduction from the fact of its hypostatic conjunction with divinity, even if the connotation of perfect humanity in this context could not be precisely specified. In the passages we have quoted, however, the perfection of Jesus is being used as a support for the doctrine of the incarnation (Peacocke and ?Jeremias) or as a starting-point for an alternative conceptualization or symbolization (Robinson). In that case, it is difficult, at any rate at first sight, to see how the claim for the perfection of Jesus' humanity could be supported except on historical grounds; and the words of the authors concerned suggest that that is what they have in mind. Dr Peacocke speaks in this context of 'the historical fact which is Jesus Christ', and he writes that 'the "things concerning Jesus" [i.e. presumably, the events of his life] led their witnesses and successors inexorably to the conclusion that, in that Person, man was transformed so that he was "a new creation" drawn up into the very life of God himself'.[5] In the same vein Professor Wiles quotes Pannenberg as referring in this connection to 'the historically unique', and Dr Keck speaks of Jeremias' 'historical Jesus, reached by sophisticated methods'.

Is it, however, possible to validate claims of the kind in question on the basis of historical evidence? To prove an historical negative, such as the sinlessness of Jesus, is notoriously difficult to the point of impossibility. How, for example, could even the most constant companion of Jesus have been sure that he remained unbrokenly true to his own principles and never, for example, 'looked on a woman to lust after her' in the sense of Matthew 5.28? Such a question is not for a moment asked with any intention of casting doubt on the sexual purity of Jesus; it is meant simply as an example designed to show that the sort of claims for Jesus we are discussing could not be justified to the hilt by *any* historical records, however full or intimate or contemporary they might be, and even if their primary concern was with the quality and development of Jesus' inner life and character.

In fact, as everyone knows, the gospels are not at all documents of that kind. They are extremely brief – B. H. Streeter once calculated that, apart from the forty days and nights in the wilderness (of which we are told virtually nothing) everything reported to have been said and done by Jesus in all four gospels would have occupied only some three weeks, which leaves the overwhelmingly greater part of his life and deeds unrecorded. On the other hand, it may be replied that what *is* recorded leaves a strong impression of consistency both in character and outlook, which will very probably have carried over into the unrecorded periods and deeds. That is perfectly true, but against it must be set the fact that those who transmitted the gospel material were primarily concerned to vindicate certain supernatural claims for Jesus, to make clear their meaning as applied to him, and to record some of the teaching he gave and the demands he made with the authority of this supernatural status. No doubt they took his moral perfection for granted, and expected others to do the same, but that very fact means that they retailed very little information relevant to the establishing of it now. The judgment of the American scholar H. J. Cadbury is, as usual, judicious. 'The gospel narratives,' he writes, 'do not often disclose the motives of Jesus, nor were they written by persons sensitive to the criterion of moral originality.' Accordingly, 'we must admit that we have not evidence enough to guarantee the self-consistency of Jesus'.[6]

Certainly one cannot dissociate a man from his teaching, and if Jesus' distinctive teachings were reinforced by his own practice the total impression would be enhanced. Christians assume that this was the case, but apart from his teachings unambiguous evidence on the character of Jesus is somewhat scanty. The teachings themselves have a certain unity of suggestion, but they are not point by point confirmed by examples of Jesus' own conformity to them.[7]

The Jewish scholar C. G. Montefiore went further and wrote in connection with Jesus' teaching about the duty of loving one's enemies:

Jesus is to be regarded as the first great Jewish teacher to frame such a sentence. . . . Yet how much more telling his injunction would have been if we had *a single story* about his doing good to and praying for a single Rabbi or Pharisee! Luke xxiii, 34 is of doubtful range and of doubtful authenticity.[8]

Perhaps the matter can be put succinctly like this: in his book *Caesar and Christ*[9] the secular scholar Dr W. Durant offers on the whole a very sensitive appreciation and high evaluation of the person and activity of Jesus. Nevertheless, his reading of the evidence compels him to mingle with his generous appreciation these two judgments relative to the originality and moral perfection of Jesus.

Our own moral heritage and ideals are so closely bound up with him and formed on his example that we feel injured at finding any flaw in his character. His religious sensitivity was so keen that he condemned severely those who would not share his vision. . . . He had the puritan zeal of the

Hebrew prophet rather than the broad calm of the Greek sage. His convictions consumed him; righteous indignation now and then blurred his profound humanity; his faults were the price he paid for that passionate faith which enabled him to move the world. For the rest he was the most lovable of men.

The parable form that he used was customary in the East, and some of his fetching analogies had come down to him, perhaps unconsciously, from the prophets, the psalmists and the rabbis; nevertheless, the directness of his speech, the vivid colours of his imagery, the warm sincerity of his nature lifted his utterances to the most inspired poetry. Some of his sayings are obscure, some seem at first sight unjust, some are sharp with sarcasm and bitterness; nearly all of them are models of brevity, clarity and force.[10]

It is not being suggested here that Dr Durant's strictures, very mild though they will be seen to be if read in their full context, are necessarily justified. The question is rather whether his interpretation of the texts – the only relevant texts we have – is so self-evidently wrong, as contrasted with that which lies behind the judgments quoted earlier, as to render the latter self-evidently right. Must we not admit that, *qua* historical interpretations of evidence, Dr Durant's judgment, and even perhaps others more severe, are at least plausible. If so, the certainty about the moral character of Jesus and his relation to God evinced by the authors quoted earlier cannot rest, or rest solely at any rate, on historical grounds. Cadbury writes:

... of course Jesus differed from his contemporaries in some undefinable degree. But uniqueness, whether as God or as man is a very different matter, and in the case of Jesus appears to be a modern inference from theological presuppositions or perhaps a human substitute for divine attributes, rather than a deduction from a careful comparison of the historical evidence ...[11]

It may be objected, however, that I have unduly limited the scope of the historical evidence available. 'Where there is smoke,' it may be said, 'there is a fire.' No one would have brought crucifixion upon himself as Jesus did, unless his behaviour and teaching had offered a novel and almost total affront to the wickedness of those who crucified him.[12] By the same token no one could have attracted men and women to such passionate devotion and discipleship as Jesus did, or could have produced the results he did, 'a new community whose keynote was *agape*',[13] unless he had himself exemplified *agape* and been a good man through and through, one whom men felt able to admire to the point of worship. Once again, a perfectly fair and very important point is being made: no one doubts that a figure very remarkable, morally and in many other ways, is required to explain the appearance of the early Christian church and the writings it produced. To concede that fully, however, falls far short of providing justification for the absolute claims made in such quotations as those from which we began.

Let H. J. Cadbury be heard again. First on the implications of the fact that Jesus incurred crucifixion.

Independence, originality, uniqueness – if I may use an ascending scale of terms – is sometimes assumed for Jesus on the basis of general considerations. That he was put to death out of Jewish hostility seems an unquestioned fact. That a new and revolutionary religious movement grew out of his career is another datum of history. But neither the crucifixion nor the Christian church is testimony to any extreme novelty in Jesus.[14]

I have often wondered just how different a man must be to be hanged for it. We are increasingly aware in modern times of the Jewishness of Jesus. He moved within the field of thought current in First Century Judaism. If he had been a total alien he might have been less suspected and feared. The bitterest controversy is often over the narrowest margin. There must be some difference between enemies, rivalry of conflicting self-interest if nothing more; but it need not be great or significant. The differentia of Jesus that would estrange the Jews might be quite different from what would 'found' the church, and in neither case need his position have been very different from the position of other Jews, either quantitatively or qualitatively.[15]

Then about what can be deduced from the emergence of Christianity:

The ultimate success of early Christianity in winning a wide and devoted adherence rests not exclusively on the life and teaching of Jesus. How far success was due to this influence, personally, directly and accurately transmitted to the first and succeeding generations of his followers, and how far to a religious propaganda in which there was an idealized Jesus who was the future Messiah, or the present Lord, or the actual deity of an attractive cult, we find it at this late day extremely difficult to tell. In such circumstances the proverb is usually cited, that there can be no smoke without fire. But the ratio of smoke and fire varies enormously and the smoke often is misleading as to the exact location of the fire. I am not disposed to join those who deny ... the historicity of Jesus, but one must be prepared to admit that the religion which became the Christianity of the Roman Empire may have had but slight relation to the historical actuality of its founder. In any case the things preached about Jesus which, whether historically accurate or not, appealed to the mentality of the ancient world (like the guarantee of immortality, or protection from the power of demons) are not the things which we moderns find so significant in our restoration of him (like moral originality, or perfect spiritual or mystical harmony with God). ... Even if we should regard Jesus as entirely freed from the limitations of his environment, we can hardly extend the miracle to the whole medley which constituted his early followers. *They were not moderns and if Jesus was modern it would have been in spite of, not because of, his modernness that they believed in him.*[16]

The last sentence has been italicized because it brings us to a vitally important issue in connection with the question we are considering, namely the great cultural gap which separates Jesus and his contemporaries from all things 'modern'. In the light of modern understandings of history and historical change, it is almost meaningless to talk, as one modern theologian has done, in an unpublished lecture, about what would happen 'if as a twentieth-century man Jesus were to walk into the room now and talk to us'. Anyone who walked into a room now as a twentieth-century man would not be the historical Jesus, and if Jesus walked into the room now, it could not be as a twentieth-century man. We may well hope that, as this scholar says, if by some miracle we could meet the genuine historical Jesus, we should feel 'deeply disturbed and challenged by his presence', but the challenge could not be direct. It would have to reach us across the great cultural gulf which is fixed between his day and ours. Albert Schweitzer wrote:

As a water-plant is beautiful so long as it is growing in the water, but once torn from its roots, withers and becomes unrecognisable, so it is with the historical Jesus when He is wrenched loose from the soil of eschatology and the attempt is made to conceive Him 'historically' as a Being not subject to temporal conditions.[17]

Dr J. T. Sanders, who quotes those well-known words, adds:

Specifically regarding Jesus' ethical teachings, this means that Jesus' ethical outlook was conditioned by his eschatological outlook. That is true even for the oft quoted Sermon on the Mount[18]

Modern historical methods have rendered obsolete any talk of 'assured results' in relation to the figure of Jesus; but if we take the majority of competent modern New Testament scholars as our guides, we can expect that if we were indeed to meet the historical Jesus we should find that what essentially made him tick, so to speak, was his conviction that with the emergence of John the Baptist and his own appearance as John's successor, the process of the arrival of the kingdom of God had begun to occur. He will have expected that within his lifetime, or at latest that of some of his contemporaries, the course of history would be brought to a close and the Son of Man would appear in the glory of his father with his holy angels to judge and wind up the universe; there is no reason to think that the general way in which he envisaged the process differed significantly from the ways in which it was conceived in some of the Jewish apocalyptic writings which have survived from the period.

It followed that the basic demand he had to make on himself and his hearers was that they should be ready for God when he appeared. If we could ask him in what he took such readiness to consist, we might well be surprised by parts of his answer. For one thing, his understanding of man's relationship to God might strike us as in some aspects rather servile and juridical[19] – to describe God as 'father' meant something very different in his situation from what it does in ours. So far as he defined the requisite readiness in moral terms, for example in terms of love, we might perhaps be surprised at the extent to which he accepted the meanings those terms bore in the Old Testament and the later Jewish writings with which he was familiar, and at his lack of concern with some of the moral considerations which weigh very strongly with us – with altruism, for example, or with the rights or needs of the other party, to say nothing of the interests of society in general.[20] According to Wellhausen, at any rate:

Jesus was not a Christian; he was a Jew. He did not preach a new faith, but taught men to do the will of God; and in his opinion, as also in that of the Jews, the will of God was to be found in the Law and in the other books of scripture.[21]

It was also to be found in the post-canonical writings, writings which should by no means be underrated. Montefiore, for example, describes Jesus' teaching about the fatherhood of God as 'an old familiar doctrine of the rabbis', though he confesses to finding it expressed by Jesus with 'a high degree of purity, warmth and concentration'.[22]

As that implies, Jesus may often have been original in the new light or emphasis he brought to bear on old familiar truths; and there is no reason to doubt – and certainly no thought of doubting here – that he also introduced profound new moral insights of his own. We have already seen that Montefiore accepts the originality of Jesus' teaching about the duty of loving our enemies, and he and many other Jewish scholars find equal originality, for example, in Jesus' stress on seeking out the lost.[23]

Cadbury, however, echoes E. F. Scott in wondering whether a high valuation of originality as almost a virtue in itself[24] is not mainly a characteristic of the modern, Western scientific world. 'There is a grave confusion in most people's minds,' writes Scott, 'as to what constitutes originality in the sphere of morals and religion.'[25] Cadbury comments,

We may well enquire whether in the field of religion and morals novelty has any inherent value. . . . We shall do well not to seek with great desire for the originality of Jesus or to exaggerate what we find. It will provide no criterion of his greatness or his contribution to history. .... In Jesus we shall look for what was distinguished if not distinctive, what was characteristic and *sui generis*, rather than for something that would seem to us or his contemporaries original or novel. Fidelity to the best of the past, moral maturity, good balance and sensible judgment are rare enough at all times and may well have elicited in the First Century, as in our own, surprise and deserved praise.[26]

He goes on 'Perhaps more nearly accurate than the words novel, original, unique, for describing any differentia of Jesus would be such adjectives as radical, intense, extreme'; and he is surely right. If there is any truth at all in the gospel picture, Jesus' demand was that his followers should go to the limit and beyond in their response to the coming God. They were to turn not one cheek but both; they were to go not one mile but two; they were to forgive not seven times but seventy times seven. In fact they were to be perfect as perfection was then understood; they were to give their whole livelihood (cf. Mark 12.44, effectively the last verse before the passion narrative), if need be their life itself, as their response to the situation. While none of that must be minimized, it must be remembered that, given Jesus' near expectation of the end, the situation in question was not one in which 'thought for the morrow' made any sense. Questions such as we rightly ask about our responsibilities for the future, the future of ourselves, our families, our institutions, our country, our environment, simply did not arise.

What is the relevance of all this to the subject under discussion in this book? Briefly this: the *metaphysical* uniqueness of Jesus, as traditionally taught, has always been taken to have carried with it a unique *moral* perfection. The considerations which lead some theologians today to question the claim for Jesus' metaphysical uniqueness, at least as traditionally conceived, do not seem to apply in the same way to his moral uniqueness, and it is natural to want to hold on to belief in the latter for a number of reasons. If Jesus alone among men was morally perfect, that virtually proves that God must have been uniquely at work in him (however such unique divine intervention is to be conceptualized in current cultural circumstances), and the claim of Christianity to be based on a unique divine intervention remains unimpaired. What is more, if such perfection was possible in *his* humanity the belief can remain that it is possible in ours, given the appropriate relation to, or dependence on, his.[27]

The chief concern of this paper is to ensure as far as possible that those who continue to make such a claim for the uniqueness of

Jesus and speak, for example, of 'the new humanity', 'the man wholly for others', or 'the man wholly for God', are fully aware of the problems involved in making and justifying any such claims.

Two things at any rate seem clear. First, it is impossible to justify any such claim on purely historical grounds, however wide the net for evidence is cast. So far as the gospels are concerned, the material in them is too scanty, and too largely selected and organized with reference to other considerations, to provide the necessary evidence.[28] As for the rise of the early church, Jesus must of course have been all that he needed to be to account for the rise of Christianity; and on any sober assessment that certainly suffices to guarantee his basic historicity and his possession of many outstanding qualities. It does not, however, suffice to justify the sort of absolute claims we have in mind; for, as we have seen, first-century Jews, given their assumptions and perspectives, are quite likely to have accepted someone as Messiah (which means, it must be remembered, the inaugurator of the end), and to have formed a community in his name, on the basis of things – supposed fulfilments of prophecy, for instance, or apparent success in overcoming demons – which have very little to do with what we understand by moral perfection or such phrases as 'the man for others'.

That links with the second point, which is that because of the cultural gulf which separates us from Jesus and his times, what moral perfection, or being 'the man for others', would have meant to him and his contemporaries might well be significantly different from what such phrases imply for us. We must therefore recognize that if the historical Jesus were to walk into the room in the way suggested above, the first disturbing impression might be not so much of his greatness as of his strangeness. To say that of course is simply to state a fact about cultural change; it is not in the least to derogate from Jesus' moral greatness or moral authority in his time.

It will scarcely surprise any reader to be told that New Testament scholars have been well aware of these issues for a long time; indeed this matter has been one of the main preoccupations of one important school of German theologians for at least the last thirty-five years. In the course of a very interesting discussion of the views and debates of this school Dr Norman Perrin distinguishes three different kinds of knowledge about Jesus. The first, which he calls 'descriptive historical knowledge (or 'hard' or 'empirical' or 'post-Enlightenment historical knowledge') of Jesus of Nazareth', is the sort of historical knowledge about which we have been speaking in

this paper so far.[29] Dr Perrin stresses that knowledge of this kind
'is difficult to achieve' about any historical person, and in the case
of Jesus he emphasizes particularly 'the difficulty of determining the
meaning of first-century categories to first-century man and the
natural tendency of a twentieth-century man to read them in terms
of his own understanding, literalistic, existentialistic or whatever'
(p. 52). Dr Perrin is more optimistic than many of the scholars he
discusses about the possibility of finding historical methods which
will enable us to achieve this sort of knowledge about Jesus, at any
rate so far as the general thrust of his activity and teaching is
concerned. He would, however, have been the first to agree that we
can never hope to achieve such knowledge to anything like the
extent required to justify the absolute claims quoted at the beginning of this essay; and what is more, he is emphatic that such
knowledge is always 'subject to correction and change on the basis
of further research or discovery'. To show how seriously he takes
this, he adds that 'it is theoretically possible, however practically
doubtful, that we may one day have to concede that Jesus was
carried to the cross, railing against God and his fate'; or, for that
matter, 'that Socrates had to have his jaws forced open to drink the
hemlock' (p. 236).

Nothing in Dr Perrin's account of modern work on the subject
gives reason to think that he would have disagreed with the drift of
the present essay so far. He goes on to point out, however, that
'historical knowledge can . . . under certain circumstances become
"historic knowledge", i.e. it can assume a direct significance for the
present' (p. 236). The word 'historic' in this context is his equivalent
for the German word *geschichtlich* when used in contrast to *his-
torisch*. In the sense of the word *geschichtlich*, knowledge is 'historic'
when it makes an impact on its recipient, causing him to change his
mind or outlook or self-understanding or way of life. Just as an
occasion can be historic if it has important practical consequences
for those who come after, so can any event or person, if knowing
about them produces a significant change of mind or attitude in
some later person or group. That knowledge of Jesus has been
historic in this sense for many groups and innumerable individuals
is simply a fact, and a fact for which we cannot be too thankful.
Indeed some theologians see the heart of the Christian matter in the
possibility of such historic knowledge of Jesus. A scholar such as Dr
Schubert Ogden, for example, would say that it is the possession of
such historic knowledge of Jesus which is decisive for the Christian.

Without attempting any comprehensive assessment of such a
view, we must make two points about historic knowledge. First,

being a possible object of it is not peculiar to Jesus. Socrates or John Wesley, for example, have been objects of historic knowledge; and men have had their lives and outlooks changed decisively through knowledge of St Francis of Assisi or Mother Teresa. Secondly, 'historic knowledge can be affected by the vicissitudes of historical factuality' (Perrin, p. 237), in the sense that, for example, a Jesus railing against God and his fate, or a Socrates being forced to drink the hemlock would have historic significance very different from what they have had on the basis of the usual empirical-historical picture of their deaths. Historic knowledge is dependent on historical knowledge.

Now, as everyone knows, 'vicissitudes of historical factuality' have occurred frequently and on a large scale where the history of Jesus is concerned, and there is no reason to suppose that the situation will change significantly in this respect. Which suggests that historic knowledge of him, for all its undoubted importance, will hardly provide an underpinning for the absolute claims contained in the quotations from which we began.

It is rather with Dr Perrin's third kind of knowledge of Jesus that absolute claims must be connected. He calls it 'faith-knowledge', that is, 'knowledge of Jesus of Nazareth which is significant only in the context of specifically Christian faith, i.e. knowledge of him of a kind dependent upon the acknowledgement of him as Lord and Christ' (p. 234). His account of this faith-knowledge deserves to be given in his own words. He writes:

'Faith-knowledge' depends upon special worth being attributed to the person concerned, so that knowledge of that person assumes a significance beyond the historic. Historic significance can be attributed to almost any number of people from the past ... but 'faith-knowledge' could be attributed only to the one figure who comes to be of special significance in terms of revelation, religious experience, religious belief. Also, the use of these categories necessarily introduces a reference to a transhistorical reality – strictly speaking, a non-historical reality – in that it introduces the idea of God and his activity. So, for the Christian, it is possible to say: 'Christ died for my sins in accordance with the scriptures'. This, however, is a statement of faith, not of history in the normal sense. It is faith-knowledge, not historical knowledge. It depends upon recognition of Jesus as the 'Christ, the Son of the living God'; it necessitates a recognition of his death as having significance in terms of the religious concept 'my sins'; and it requires that the cross be recognized as being in accordance with the 'definite plan and foreknowledge of God'. .... None of this is history in the post-Enlightenment sense of that word; nor is it dependent upon the manner or mode of the death of Jesus, only on the fact that it happened. The value here ascribed to that death is not ascribed to it because of what Jesus did, but because of what God is regarded as having done. The death of

Jesus is not efficacious for 'my sins' because he died nobly, or because he showed confidence in God, but because the cross is believed to have fulfilled the purpose of God. That Jesus died nobly or showed confidence in God are historical statements, subject to the vicissitudes of historical research, but that his death fulfilled the purpose of God in regard to 'my sins' is certainly not such a statement, and it lies beyond the power of the historian, even to consider it, even though, as a Christian, he might believe it (pp. 237–8).

The third kind of knowledge becomes significant to us at the level of religious faith, belief or commitment. It is distinct from the second [*sc.* historic knowledge] in that it is particular, i.e. for the individual concerned it has a value beyond that to be ascribed to any other historical knowledge, or to knowledge of any other historical individual. Also, it is particular in the sense that it has this value only to certain individuals or groups, those who share the particular faith, belief or commitment. It is also distinct from both the first and the second in that it is not necessarily historical knowledge. Historical knowledge can come to have this significance, but then so can myth, legend, saga – and any combination of these! (pp. 235–6).

No one is likely to read the last two quotations without being led to ask in what sense the phenomenon they describe can be called 'knowledge', even 'faith-knowledge'. The object of such faith-knowledge according to Perrin is a 'faith-image of Jesus' (p. 243) and he describes how his own faith-image of Jesus was built up in the context of an Anglo-Saxon liberal Baptist tradition:

... all the various forms of proclamation to which we have been subject have served to produce for us what we would call a 'faith-image' of this Jesus. Part of this faith-image is certainly made up of traits of the liberal historical Jesus, but then the writings of the liberal 'questers' were in their own way kerygmatic; the mistake is to claim them as historical. Again, part of the faith-image could be the result of the existential impact of knowledge of Jesus mediated by a modern historiography, historic knowledge, for to a believer brought up in this tradition almost anything that talks about Jesus can become kerygma, that is, it can contribute to the faith-image. This faith-image is, so far as the individual believer is concerned, the kerygmatic Christ, since it is an image mediated to him by the multiple forms of Christian proclamation, and it has to be distinguished from the historical Jesus, even though historical knowledge of Jesus may have been a constituent factor in its creation. It has to be distinguished from the historical Jesus because its ultimate origin is not historical research, but Christian proclamation, even if it may have been historical research which has unwittingly become proclamation, as in the case of much liberal life of Christ research. It also has to be distinguished from the historical Jesus because the results of historical research are not a *determining* factor in the constituence of this figure; like the Christ of the gospels, the Jesus of one's faith-image is a mixture of historical reminiscence, at a somewhat distant remove, and myth, legend and idealism (pp. 243–4).

As Dr Perrin says, 'our faith-knowledge of Jesus ... arises in response to the challenge of the proclamation of the Church; ... its ultimate origin is not historical research, but Christian proclamation' (p. 243), and some of the implications of that are explicated in these two further quotations:

What gives this faith-image validity is the fact that it grows out of religious experience and is capable of mediating religious experience; that it develops in the context of the particular mixture of needs, etc., which originally created, and continues to create, an openness towards the kerygma; and that it can continue to develop to meet those needs (p. 244).

And if we ask to what tests the validity of alleged faith-knowledge should be subject the answer is:

Religious or 'faith' knowledge ... should be subject to quite different tests [sc. from those applicable to historical knowledge]: the understanding of ultimate reality it mediates, the kind of religious experience it inspires, the quality of personal and communal life it makes possible, and so on. It may also be subjected to the test of determining whether or not the knowledge is also factual or true in an empirical historical sense, so far as any such test is possible in connection with it, but it must always be recognized that although historical knowledge can have this kind of significance this kind of significance is not limited to knowledge that is also historical (p. 241).

Such a position is intelligible enough; indeed it will already be familiar to those who know Kähler's and Bultmann's distinction between the 'historical Jesus' and the 'preached Christ'. The relation between these two phrases can be formulated in various ways. Perhaps we may put it like this: the career of the historical Jesus occurred at such a time and in such circumstances that it was like a lighted match applied to a powder-keg. The powder represents the religious expectations and aspirations of the period, which were many and varied, including, according to Bultmann, the apocalyptic expectations of the Jews, the diverse Jewish and Gentile beliefs and speculations known to us as Gnosticism, and the mystery-religions of the Gentile world, with their notions of sacramental union with a divine hero-figure (often a dying-and-rising god) and consequent sharing in his divinity and eternity. The impact of Jesus, and particularly of his crucifixion, on his contemporaries was such that they were driven – always, be it remembered, under the providence of God – to use these and other similar categories to understand and interpret him. What the New Testament offers us is thus a number of accounts of Jesus differing according as one or other of these backgrounds predominated in the writer's mind. Bultmann insists that there is no one consistent picture in the New Testament, no *one* New Testament theology or christology. Yet the categories employed by the early Christians were sufficiently similar to be capable of synthesis, and in the course of time they were fused together round the figure of Jesus to form the incarnate Son of Nicene and later orthodoxy.

It is only comparatively recently, with the rise of modern historiography, that Christians have become aware that the preached Christ is not identical with the historical Jesus. If it is asked why, now that they are aware of the distinction, they continue to believe in the preached Christ, the answer is in essence: 'God help them, they can no other.' Their experience is that if this Christ is truly preached and they truly listen to, and hear, the preaching, he does something to them, he faces them with an inescapable choice. He shows them just what their previous way of living has been worth and puts before them an alternative possibility, the possibility of living entirely out of God's power and grace. In other words, he is the lens through which all the demands and promises of God to them are focused. He can only fulfil that function, however, if he is an ever-changing figure. Just as he changed greatly between apostolic and Nicene times, so he has changed down the generations and must continue to change if, as cultural change accelerates, he is to continue to mediate the nature, grace and demands of God to succeeding generations. Unless, with Bultmann and some of his followers, we are to posit 'an unchangeable fundamental structure of the human spirit as such' [30] – a very doubtful thing to do – a preached Christ must surely be a changing figure – no impossibility, it will be noted, if the tests of his validity are those quoted from Dr Perrin above.

Yet, although Dr Perrin's position is intelligible enough, it is undoubtedly highly sophisticated. It must be confessed that it would be difficult to define, let alone make clear to an ordinary congregation, the precise status of the 'preached Christ', or of Dr Perrin's 'faith-image' of Jesus, the object of what he calls 'faith-knowledge'. It is small wonder that many preachers fall back on the implicit assumption that the preached Christ and the historical Jesus are identical; or that the sort of writers who were quoted at the beginning of this essay seek some empirical anchorage of the one figure in the other. However, as we have seen, even the degree of anchorage they seek is incapable of historical validation, and Professor Wiles seems nearer the truth about this aspect of the matter when in his second essay he confines himself to the demand that the historical Jesus, so far as we can recover him, should not constitute any signal contradiction of the preached Christ in his relationship either with God or with his fellows. The basis of that demand lies in our doctrine of God. For what conceivable reason should God choose to proclaim salvation through a series of false statements about the life of a man who never lived or was in fact *toto caelo* different from the statements about him? It would surely be impossible to ask anyone to believe that God acted in such a way. Fortunately, however, the considerations brought forward in this essay serve, if anything, to strengthen Professor Wiles's claim that 'while we cannot be sure how much of the detail of the accounts we have is later interpretation, it is most unlikely that the kind of historical knowledge about Jesus available to us, or that may become available to us in the future, could ever deform that picture to such a degree as to rule out the appropriateness of linking the . . . myth in this special way with the person of Jesus' (p. 163).

The question is, as Professor Wiles goes on to suggest, what *sort* of linking this should be. The contributors to this book have given reasons for doubting whether it can any longer be by way of the idea that Jesus was God incarnate, as that idea has traditionally been understood. The aim of the present postscript has been to put a 'No thoroughfare' against any alternative routes which may be suggested by way of claiming uniqueness of some sort for Jesus on historical grounds; and the argument could easily be extended to meet claims that Jesus was historically unique in the sense of having been the only person ever to have experienced literal resurrection.

If the positions adopted in this book have any validity, the question obviously arises how the link between Jesus and contemporary Christianity is to be conceived and imagined. Professor Wiles suggests that it 'can be affirmed in a weaker or a stronger form. The weaker form would simply state as a matter of contingent historical fact that this truth about man's relation to God came alive in our particular tradition through the figure of Jesus. The stronger form would give to Jesus a more indispensable role' (p. 163). Further explication would be needed to make this distinction entirely clear: what, for example, is meant by 'a matter of contingent historical fact' in the context of an understanding of history as providentially governed? That said, this paper may conclude with a plea that the former of Professor Wiles' alternatives should not be dismissed too lightly.

No one, I think, will deny that it is at the level of the *imagination* that contemporary Christianity is most weak. Men find it hard to believe in God because they do not have available to them any lively imaginative picture of the way a God and the world as they know it are related. What they need most is a story, a picture, a myth, that will capture their imagination, while meshing in with the rest of their sensibility in the way that messianic terms linked with the sensibility of first-century Jews, or Nicene symbolism with the sensibility of philosophically-minded fourth-century Greeks. No doubt, as Lord Hailsham has suggested,[31] we shall not get such a picture until some *doctor angelicus* – or should we rather say some prophet? – is raised up to give it to us; but that in no way exonerates us from doing all we can meanwhile to prepare his way before him.

In that context one of the things we shall surely have to take seriously is the question posed by Professor Wiles, which I take to be the question: shall the Christian myth or story of the future be a story primarily about God or shall it, if I may put it so without irreverence, be a story which co-stars Jesus and God? Shall it be a story in which Jesus shares the leading role and has a unique or perfect status of some sort assigned to him? Or shall it be a story in which the protagonist's role belongs undividedly to God, though of course the story would tell how once he worked in a vitally important way – though not a way *necessarily* in principle unique – through the man Jesus to bring the Christian people into a relationship of reconciliation and oneness with himself?

Simply in order to stimulate discussion, perhaps we may conclude by posing three questions:

(*i*) In a situation of galloping cultural change, which has brought the doctrine of the literal divinity of Jesus into question, is it any longer worthwhile to attempt to trace the Christian's ever-changing understanding of his relationship with God directly back to some identifiable element in the life, character and activity of Jesus of Nazareth?

(*ii*) If, in the circumstances described, such an attempt is made, will it lead inevitably to a degree of sophistication which is unintelligible to the majority of Christians and brings the so-called christological thinking involved into disrepute?[32] Significantly, Dr Perrin more than once points out that his doctrine of the three types of knowledge of Jesus presupposes as its context 'a tradition which "believes in Jesus" ' (p. 244; cp. p. 243). Is it necessary to 'believe in Jesus' in a sense which requires sophistication of this sort?

(*iii*) Is it possible that the right course in this connection is to accept our own limitations and gladly 'leave God's secret to himself'? Is it necessary to 'believe in Jesus' in any sense beyond that which sees him as the main figure through whom God launched men into a relationship with himself so full and rich that, under various understandings and formulations of it, it has been, and continues to be, the salvation of a large proportion of the human race? Professor John Knox has written that 'the divinity of Jesus was the purpose and activity of God which made the events which happened round him, but also in and through him, the saving even it was'.[33] He himself appears to believe that this necessitates some claim for empirical uniqueness in the case of Jesus, but would it not be possible to content ourselves with another formulation in connection with the Christ-event which he himself offers in the same book?

That this event had the particular result it had – a new community in which are found a new forgiveness, victory, and hope – is a matter of empirical knowledge in the Church; but why this particular event had this particular result is a matter altogether beyond our knowing. God's thoughts are not our thoughts, and his ways are not our ways. The event was a whole event, and its effect was a whole effect. We cannot break the event into parts and attribute the whole effect to one part, nor can we ascribe any particular part of the effect to any particular part of the event. Both event and effect are one and indivisible; and moreover, they belong indissolubly together. Of this whole the remembered death of Jesus is the poignant centre.[34]

NOTES

1. J. A. T. Robinson, *Honest to God*, SCM Press 1963, p. 74; my italics.
2. A. R. Peacocke, *Science and the Christian Experiment*, Oxford University Press 1971.
3. Ibid., pp. 175, 173, 170, 171 and 165.
4. L. E. Keck, *A Future for the Historical Jesus*, SCM Press 1971, p. 59.
5. Peacocke, op. cit., pp. 167 and 165; cp. also p. 161.
6. H. J. Cadbury, *Jesus, What Manner of Man?*, SPCK 1962, p. 64.
7. Ibid., p. 81.
8. C. G. Montefiore, *Rabbinic Literature and Gospel Teachings*, Macmillan 1930, p. 103.
9. W. Durant, *Caesar and Christ*, Simon & Schuster 1944.
10. Ibid., pp. 561 and 564.
11. H. J. Cadbury, *The Peril of Modernizing Jesus*, SPCK 1962, p. 68.
12. Cp, for example, Dr Goulder on p. 53 above.
13. See Dr Goulder on p. 59.
14. *The Peril of Modernizing Jesus*, p. 69.
15. *Jesus, What Manner of Man?*, p. 57.
16. *The Peril of Modernizing Jesus*, pp. 40–1; italics mine.
17. Albert Schweitzer, *The Quest of the Historical Jesus*, A. & C. Black 1910, third edition 1954, p. 399
18. J. T. Sanders, *Ethics in the New Testament*, SCM Press 1975, p. 3.
19. For a discussion of the sort of point involved, see my book *The Use and Abuse of the Bible*, Macmillan 1976, e.g. pp. 110–11, 190, 203–4.
20. Cp. e.g. *The Peril of Modernizing Jesus*, ch. V, 'Limitations of Jesus' Social Teaching'.
21. J. Wellhausen, *Einleitung in die Drei Ersten Evangelien*, Reimer 1905, p. 113.

22. Montefiore, *Some Elements of the Religious Teaching of Jesus*, Macmillan 1910, p. 93.

23. Cp. e.g. Mark 2.13–17, and my comments on it in *St Mark*, Penguin Books 1963, pp. 95ff., including the quotations from Montefiore and Harnack.

24. Dr Goulder is perhaps guilty here; cp. his phrase: Jesus' 'totally original interpretation of the kingdom', p. 53 above.

25. *Journal of Biblical Literature*, vol. 48, 1929, pp. 111–12.

26. Cadbury, *Jesus, What Manner of Man?*, pp. 66–7; cp. G. B. Shaw, *Androcles and the Lion*, Constable, standard edition 1931, preface, p. 5.

27. On the last point cp. the view of Cato Forbes, the budding priest, in Iris Murdoch's novel *Henry and Cato*, p. 26: 'Christ himself was . . . untouchably pure and had never put a foot wrong . . . no vulgarity there, no vanity, not a shadow of trickery or falsehood, but what this showed was how vastly perfectible human beings were after all.'

28. Cp. the article by J. M. Robinson in *Journal of Bible and Religion*, 1962, pp. 198ff.

29. Norman Perrin, *Rediscovering the Teaching of Jesus*, SCM Press 1967, pp. 234–5.

30. Hans Jonas, *Augustin und das paulinische Freiheitsproblem*, 2 Auflage (1965), p. 82.

31. See his article in *The Times* for 21 February 1976, p. 28.

32. In that connection it is perhaps worth noting that so friendly a critic as Philip Toynbee who describes the word 'Christology' as 'the most-favoured jargon-term in the whole vocabulary of modern theology', also characterizes it roundly as 'arid'. See *Towards the Holy Spirit*, SCM Press 1973, p. 67.

33. John Knox, *The Death of Christ*, Collins 1959, p. 125.

34. Ibid., p. 159.

A Final Comment

DON CUPITT

May I comment on Dennis Nineham's warning in the last chapter?
I acknowledge the limitations of our critical–historical knowledge
of Jesus. However, the core of a religion does not lie in the biography or personality of the founder, but in the specifically religious
values to which, according to tradition, he bore witness. By these
values I mean possible determinations of the human spirit whereby
it relates itself to the ultimate goal of existence, such as are embodied in the injunction to 'Repent, for the kingdom of God is at
hand'.

This cluster of 'principles of Spirit' is at the centre of the tradition, and I believe it to be contingently the case that Jesus proclaimed them, though it is not strictly necessary to prove it by the
critical method. Precisely because they command us to die to the
self, to the world which is passing away and so on, they assert the
possibility of transcending relativity. As principles of transcendence
they are the only non-relativistic criterion of the subsequent
development of the tradition.

In history, a man proclaimed the possibility of transcending history; and we, in history also, can verify his claim in practice. How
can we depend upon the uncertainties of historical tradition for our
knowledge of, and our power to attain, a history-transcending
truth? Here the doctrine of Christ and the doctrine of man coincide;
for this is not just *a* problem, but the human condition itself.

INDEX